Let Justice Be Done

Nevada Studies in History and Political Science

Eleanore Bushnell and Don W. Driggs,
The Nevada Constitution: Origin and Growth (6th ed., 1984)

Ralph J. Roske,
His Own Counsel: The Life and Times of Lyman Trumbull (1979)

Mary Ellen Glass,
Nevada's Turbulent '50s: Decade of Political and Economic Change (1981)

Joseph A. Fry,
Henry S. Sanford: Diplomacy and Business in Nineteenth-century America (1982)

Jerome E. Edwards,
Pat McCarran: Political Boss of Nevada (1982)

Russell R. Elliott,
Servant of Power: A Political Biography of Senator William M. Stewart (1983)

Donald R. Abbe,
Austin and the Reese River Mining District: Nevada's Forgotten Frontier (1985)

Anne B. Howard,
The Long Campaign: A Biography of Anne Martin (1985)

Sally Zanjani and Guy Louis Rocha,
The Ignoble Conspiracy: Radicalism on Trial in Nevada (1986)

James W. Hulse,
Forty Years in the Wilderness: Impressions of Nevada, 1940–1980 (1986)

Jacqueline Baker Barnhart,
The Fair But Frail: Prostitution in San Francisco, 1849–1900 (1986)

Marion Merriman and Warren Lerude,
American Commander in Spain: Robert Hale Merriman and the Abraham Lincoln Brigade (1986)

A. Costandina Titus,
Bombs in the Backyard: Atomic Testing and American Politics (1986)

Wilbur S. Shepperson, ed.,
East of Eden, West of Zion: Essays on Nevada (1989)

John Dombrink and William N. Thompson,
The Last Resort: Success and Failure in Campaigns for Casinos (1989)

Kevin J. Mullen,
Let Justice Be Done: Crime and Politics in Early San Francisco (1989)

Nevada Studies in History and Political Science

LET JUSTICE BE DONE

Crime and Politics in Early San Francisco

Kevin J. Mullen

UNIVERSITY OF NEVADA PRESS

RENO AND LAS VEGAS

Nevada Studies in History and Political Science No. 28

Studies Editor
Wilbur S. Shepperson

Library of Congress Cataloging-in-Publication Data

Mullen, Kevin J., 1935–
    Let justice be done : crime and politics in early San Francisco /
Kevin J. Mullen.
        p.   cm. — (Nevada studies in history and political science ;
no. 28)
    Bibliography: p.
    Includes index.
    ISBN 0-87417-146-6 (alk. paper)
    1. Criminal justice, Administration of—California—San
Francisco—History—19th century.   2. San Francisco Committee
of Vigilance of 1851.   3. Criminal justice, Administration of—
Political aspects—California—San Francisco.   I. Title.
II. Series.
HV9956.S28M85   1989
364'.979461—dc 19   89-4750
                                                                    CIP

The paper used in this book meets the requirements of American National
Standard for Information Sciences—Permanence of Paper for Printed Library
Materials, ANSIZ39.48-1984. The binding is sewn for strength and durability.
University of Nevada Press, Reno, Nevada 89557 USA
Copyright © 1989 Kevin J. Mullen
Design by Dave Comstock
Printed in the United States of America

1 2 3 4 5 6 7 8 9

In memory of my father, James Mullen,
an Achill man and a *shanachie* who, as such,
didn't write it down.

Contents

Fiat Justitia Ruat Coelum

"Let justice be done, though the heavens fall"
—motto inscribed on the emblem of the
San Francisco Vigilance Committee

Introduction

THE DEFINITIVE EXPERIENCE in the early history of American San Francisco was the California Gold Rush: within a year of the great gold strike on the American River in 1848, the previously undistinguished trading hamlet on Yerba Buena Cove exploded into the roiling port of entry for men and goods headed for the California goldfields.[1] The central criminal justice reality of that Gold Rush migration was that on two occasions, in 1851 and 1856, the city's leading citizens—confronted with what they considered intolerable conditions of crime and disorder—formed themselves into committees of vigilance, shoved aside the regular institutions of justice, and summarily punished the criminal predators they found in their midst. By the time their work was done, each of the San Francisco committees of vigilance had hanged four men and banished a number more from the state under the threat of immediate execution should they return.

The seizure of the reins of government of an American city by an illegally constituted body of citizens was an unprecedented event in the history of the republic. In the short, turbulent history of the young nation, there had been a long tradition, true enough, of the administration of summary justice by groups of outraged citizens; but always before the rising of the first Vigilance Committee in San Francisco in 1851, vigilante activities had grown out of a governmental vacuum.

In the westward march of American civilization in advance of the arrival of formal institutions of law, the desire for justice had often expressed itself in the exaction of summary penalties following informal "trials" that did not always observe all the niceties of the law. In the early decades of the nineteenth century before the establishment of municipal police departments, settled communities with organized civil governments had also had their share of problems with public disorders and criminal rowdies, often resolved only by the intervention of private citizens organized into some kind of committee of public safety or voluntary military organization. But in settled communities such citizen groups had always been organized under the auspices of the regularly established authorities.

In the middle years of the century, the nation's large cities were beset by decades of criminal violence and disorders that gave rise to the institutions of municipal policing with which we are now familiar. But as bad as conditions became in the cities of the eastern seaboard, none of them resorted to vigilantism as a means of maintaining order.

It was truly extraordinary then, when in 1851, in a city with a fully articulated criminal justice system, the "best" citizens took it upon themselves to bypass the established institutions of government, to assume the functions of the regular criminal justice system, and to exercise all the prerogatives of that system on their own account.

The Vigilance Committee of San Francisco in 1851 was to provide a model for the later and larger committee formed in San Francisco in 1856 and for many other urban committees of vigilance in the latter half of the nineteenth century, which came to be looked upon as the legitimate alternative to unsatisfactory municipal governmental systems. Continuing interest over the years in the extraordinary events of the Gold Rush era has spawned a vast literature exploring every facet of the argonauts' experience. Many of the books have dealt with the issues of crime and criminal justice, expressing all shades of opinion about whether or not the actions of the Vigilance Committee were justified by the conditions it faced.

Yet in all the accounts that touch on matters of crime and punishment in the turbulent youth of the city, the full story of the criminal justice history of early-day San Francisco has never been told. "The extraordinary emphasis on vigilantism has meant that the sensational and atypical aspects of law enforcement have nearly crowded out the ordinary," according to Roger Lotchin, able chronicler of San Francisco's transformation from hamlet to city. "The committees that usurped part of this duty . . . have received endless attention at the expense of the police who held the job most of the time."[2] The same thing can be said about the other institutions of justice.

Much of what we know of the justice system in San Francisco in the years following the American conquest can be found in a few sentences usually trotted out to explain or justify the establishment of the Committee of Vigilance. By all accounts, the underpaid and understaffed police were inefficient and corrupt. Albert Benard de Russailh reported: "Policemen here are quite as much to be feared as the robbers; if they know you have money, they will be the first to knock you in the head."[3] The courts were not any better. According to the *Annals of San Francisco*, "At the period of which we write, the tribunals of justice were considered altogether insufficient for those dangerous times, and many of the individuals connected with them as both incapable and corrupt."[4] Those few criminals who did somehow find themselves in jail, by some odd chance, had no problem bribing or breaking their way out.

The men who formed the committee in 1851 were clear enough in the introduction to their constitution that the inadequacies of the justice system were in the forefront of their concerns:

> Whereas it has become apparent to the citizens of San Francisco that there is no security for life and property, either under the regulations of society as it at present exists or under the laws as now administered, the citizens whose names are hereunto attached do unite themselves into an association for the maintenance of the peace and good order . . . and to sustain the laws when faithfully and properly administered but *we are determined that no thief, burglar incendiary [sic] assassin shall escape punishment either by the quibbles of the law, the insecurity of prisons, the carelessness or corruption of the police or a laxity of those who pretend to administer justice.* (emphasis added)[5]

One of the "facts" underpinning the argument favoring the establishment of the Committee of Vigilance is that violent crime ran rampant in the permissive boomtown society. "Midnight assaults ending in murder were common," recounted the contemporary *Annals*. "Not one criminal had yet been executed, yet it was notorious that, at this period [before the establishment of the Vigilance Committee of 1851], at least one hundred murders had been committed, within the space of a few months."[6] Other accounts of murder in Gold Rush San Francisco put the number at 1,000, 1,200, or 1,400 in the years leading up to the establishment of the second Committee of Vigilance.

In a recent article in *California Living* magazine titled "The Bad
Old Days," Paul Drexler joins a host of others in reminding us of what
the time was like:

> In 1984, 75 murders were committed in San Francisco. That's ten
> fewer homicides than in the previous year, but it's still a chilling statis-
> tic, evidence of the climate of violence that surrounds us.
>
> Yet between 1850 and 1856, when the population of San Francisco
> was well under 100,000, the city averaged an estimated 230 murders
> a year, a rate more than twenty times the current one. This was more
> than a climate of violence; it was a monsoon of carnage.[7]

The common belief held for many years following the reign of the
committees of vigilance was that it was this unchecked crime that called
the committees into existence. Recent scholarship has shown, however, at least as it relates to the second Vigilance Committee in 1856,
that predatory crime did not play a large part in bringing about its formation. Rather, it was a businessmen's revolution, the roots of which
lay in the desire of members of the merchant community, or emerging
"frontier elite," to take the governance of the city out of the hands of
professional politicians and institute what they saw as needed fiscal and
political reforms. Allegations of unchecked crime were used as one of
the excuses for overthrowing the existing government.[8]

As to the Vigilance Committee of 1851, however, the record to
date is less clear. Perhaps the revisionists stand in awe of Mary Floyd
Williams, who, it would seem—in her monumental *Papers of the San
Francisco Vigilance Committee of 1851* and its accompanying *History
of the San Francisco Committee of Vigilance of 1851*—had the final
word on the committee, its purposes, and the outcome of its endeavors.
Some say that murder and other crime was rampant; others say no.
Even Richard Maxwell Brown, whose scholarship has demonstrated
the true nature of the 1856 committee, as noted above, treats the 1851
committee as a straightforward assault on criminal predators.[9]

It would seem that investigating how much predatory crime there
really was in the period preceding the adoption of such extraordinary
crime control measures would be fundamental to an understanding of a
period about which so much else has been written. But no one has yet
made a successful attempt to do so. This book analyzes the incidence of
crime, particularly criminal homicide, robbery, and burglary, for the
same period, to get some idea about how much crime there actually
was in the early days of American San Francisco. It is only with such
information in hand that one can fully understand the extraordinary
events of the summer of 1851.

By all accounts, the figures are unavailable. According to Robert M. Senkewicz, most recent biographer of the vigilante era:

> It is difficult to determine accurately the specifics of crime in gold rush San Francisco. . . . Court records are incomplete. . . . There are some available fragmentary figures. For instance, the *Alta* published on May 2, 1850, what it called a complete list of arrests from September 4, 1849, to March 26, 1850. The total the paper gave was 741, mostly for larceny and assault and battery. These statistics led Mary Floyd Williams to assert, concerning the period preceding that during which the need for a vigilance committee was recognized, "Order was preserved in the city with fair success . . . violence in the city was not of the alarming proportions sometimes attributed to it." If such statistics had been continued throughout the period, there might be a basis for further generalization. But, alas, the figures are not there.[10]

In fact, there are, as we shall see, still extant tabulations not mentioned by Senkewicz that carry arrest figures into a later period that can be used as a cross-check on figures obtained elsewhere.

This book also describes the development of the institutions of criminal justice in San Francisco—the courts, the police, and the jails—from the American conquest in 1846, through the tenure of the first Committee of Vigilance in 1851, to the end of 1852. There are no really new sources of information (no smoking gun, as it were), for the field has been examined so many times before, but it is possible to look at the existing material in a fresh light. For example, the Affair of the Hounds in 1849, in which the first quasi-committee was formed, has been written of repeatedly. The accounts usually consist of a rehash of the account given in the *Annals of San Francisco*.[11] But in looking to secondary sources, historians neglect one of the best accounts of the affair, the abstract of testimony given in the trial contained in the August 2, 1849, edition of the *Alta California*, which has much enlightening detail not found elsewhere. Similarly, this book takes a fresh look at existing sources to draw a picture of the justice system, other than that provided by the Vigilance Committee, and how it worked.

In looking for the amount of crime that occurred in Gold Rush San Francisco, we shall look to an as yet untapped but readily available resource, the daily issues of the *Alta California*, the one newspaper that, in some form or another, was published continuously from almost the beginning of the American conquest of California through and beyond the period being examined.[12] Mary Williams, unquestionably the most comprehensive biographer of the 1851 Committee of Vigilance, believed, it must be admitted, that accounts of crime carried in the newspapers of the time, "at best, are incomplete and inadequate."[13] More recent commentators, remarking on the apparent absence of crime news in the contemporary press, have concluded that perhaps there was not as much crime in Gold Rush San Francisco as is generally believed, but those conclusions have not yet been put to the test.

In fact, the news columns of contemporary newspapers are an excellent source of information about the incidence of crime in Gold Rush San Francisco, but that is an issue to be dealt with in the chapters that follow. As the story of crime and criminal justice in the early days of San Francisco unfolds, the reader will have ample opportunity to judge the completeness and accuracy of the sources.

While we shall find that the legends about the amount of violent crime in Gold Rush San Francisco are incorrect, and that the institutions of justice were perhaps not as black as painted, there certainly was something unusual going on. Crime did in fact increase (up from almost nothing) in the year before the formation of the Vigilance Committee, and it is true enough that established justice agencies were far from free of the taint of corruption. However, those circumstances in themselves, common enough in the mid-nineteenth-century urban experience, are not sufficient to explain what happened in San Francisco.

Part of what created the impression of general lawlessness in San Francisco was that for a long period, beginning almost with the conquest, prominent citizens—at odds first with the military-backed government and later with officials who did not suit their taste—inflated the figures of crime to further their political purposes. The victors write the history—and as things turned out, the victors were those who opposed the established government.

Richard Maxwell Brown and others have shown that, in 1856, the "frontier elite" in San Francisco, the leading merchant and landowning class, incorrectly claimed that the town was beset by rampant predatory crime, to justify seizure of the government from the regularly established authorities. Those same forces were already at work in San Francisco even before the discovery of gold and played a significant part even in the establishment of the first Committee of Vigilance in 1851.

In a larger sense, though, what was going on was part of a phenomenon affecting nineteenth-century American cities generally and was not unique to San Francisco. The tumult in San Francisco is usually treated strictly as an outgrowth of the frontier or Gold Rush experience. Actually, much of what happened in San Francisco in the 1850s can be traced to the urban experience of nineteenth-century America. The nation was going through a major social upheaval as the great internal migration proceeded from farm to city, just as a flood of European refugees poured into the eastern seaboard of the United States. Disparate groups with alien value systems came together in the teeming American cities. In the clash of cultures that ensued, conflicts arose and violent crime increased. Institutions of government, designed for an earlier, simpler time, were often found wanting. As new governmental forms were developed and tested in the crucible of experience of the nation's cities, America in the middle decades of the nineteenth century went through a period of great social disruption.

In San Francisco, all the forces at work in other American cities came together with the flood of gold seekers from around the world; in the hothouse Gold Rush environment, all the problems of older established American cities were magnified. If young males commit most violent crime (and they do), San Francisco was a city almost entirely populated by young males. If cultural differences can lead to misunderstandings that contribute to violent crime (and they do), Gold Rush San Francisco was a polyglot mélange of the nations of the world. If population mobility, creating an anonymous city of strangers, contributes to the incidence of violent crime (and it does), Gold Rush San Francisco—with people constantly going to and from the mines and back to the "states" again—provided the perfect breeding ground for crime and disorder.

Eventually, the unique confluence of emerging urban social forces, frontier customs, and the objects of special interests that came together in San Francisco would result in the establishment of the first Committee of Vigilance formed in an American city with a functioning criminal justice establishment.

This book, then, is not intended as just another account of the events surrounding the establishment and activities of the Vigilance Committee of 1851. Rather, it takes a fresh look at the conditions preceding, surrounding, and even following the tenure of the committee and examines some heretofore unexplored areas and undiscussed issues, all in an attempt to gain a better understanding of the extraordinary events of the summer of 1851. To do that, we shall sometimes consider events far from San Francisco and start even before the beginning.

Part I **GENESIS**

CHAPTER 1

Hispanic Arcadia

TRYING TO FIGURE OUT how much crime there actually was in any past age is at best an uncertain business. First of all, we must define what we mean by crime. The term does not mean the same thing to everyone. Crime can be defined generally as any act or omission contrary to a statute prohibiting or commanding it. A wide array of behaviors come under that definition, from universally recognized offenses like murder "by lying in wait" to less conventionally agreed upon offenses like employee theft and, much in the news these days, obstruction of justice. For some crimes like armed robbery and burglary, there is usually a clear distinction between the roles of the perpetrator and the victim. For others—vice and drug violations, for instance, and even some mutual combat assaults in which the victim is a willing participant —the distinction is less clear.

This analysis looks at predatory crime of the sort that is condemned in just about all societies and that, we are assured, led the residents of San Francisco to take the law into their own hands in 1851: burglary and robbery, both classic crimes of predation, and arson and criminal homicide, which, while not always strictly predatory crimes, were much in the minds of our Gold Rush predecessors. This task is difficult, because records of crime in the early days are sketchy and often inconsistent. It has only been in the last fifty years that any systematic, uniform method of reporting the incidence of crime according to categories lending themselves to comparative analysis has been employed in the United States.[1] Before that, classification of crime by types was more or less up to the person doing the counting, with the result that comparisons of statistics, particularly between different times and places, are a chancy affair. Also, some critics would say that much of what we know about the incidence of predatory crime in both the past and present depends to some extent on the self-serving reports of politicians of one persuasion or another.

The record of crime in Hispanic California before the American conquest is mixed. On the one hand, there are those, like Hubert H. Bancroft, the exhaustive chronicler of life in the "Pacific States," who characterize pastoral California as an idyllic paradise. "There were then no jails, no juries, no sheriff, law processes or courts," he writes; "conscience and public opinion were law and justice held an evenly balanced rule."[2] Others, however, speaking of the same era, point to the criminal depredations of *cholo* soldiers sent by Mexican authorities to Alta California as one of the reasons for the many revolts by *californio* settlers during the Mexican era.[3] One thing is for sure. Perceptions about the amount of crime and the efficiency of official efforts to keep it under control vary widely, depending on point of view.

Alta California had been settled in the 1770s according to the time-tested Spanish plan of colonization: agricultural missions run by Franciscan padres to christianize the native Indians; military presidios (institutional descendants of frontier Roman outposts) to protect Europeans from attacks by hostile Indians and incursion by foreign powers; and pueblos (civil towns) to produce foodstuffs for the presidios. The province was ruled directly by military authority until members of the native population were educated to take their place as citizens of a secular society, at which time, it was expected, the missions and presidios would evolve into civil pueblos.

Growth was slow in Spanish California, particularly in San Francisco, situated at the very end of the imperial reach. Spanish authorities lost interest in the enterprise when the colony failed to turn a profit; it became increasingly difficult to find settlers from the sunny south willing to go to the godforsaken fog-swept outpost on San Francisco

Bay. The Spanish authorities finally resorted to recruiting from Mexican prisons and foundling homes to make up settlement parties and military escorts for Alta California.

Late in 1776, the Presidio was established on the southern entrance of the Golden Gate to repel foreign intruders entering the bay; a bit later, the Mission, familiarly called Mission Dolores, was located a few miles inland where the right combination of arable land and fresh water made an agricultural settlement possible. Civil pueblos were established at San Jose and Los Angeles during the Spanish era, and later at the site of the future city of Santa Cruz.

Recognizing the military weakness of its far-flung colony on the upper coast of California, and aware of the attraction of the magnificent San Francisco Bay for foreign adventurers, Spanish authorities prohibited any foreign immigration or trade between colonists and foreign shipmasters. Despite the imperial prohibition, an occasional foreign ship did visit Alta California during Spanish times, and a few foreign seamen did jump ship, remaining ashore when their mates departed. For the most part, though, the colony of Alta California remained in the backwash of history during the Spanish era, a mystery to most of the rest of the world. After 1821, when Mexico won its independence from Spain and long-delayed plans to secularize the missions were finally put into effect, the economic base of California shifted from clerically run agricultural settlements to great secular ranchos, presided over by paternalistic dons who harvested the hides and tallow of the enormous herds of cattle inherited from the padres. The settlements at San Francisco still did not prosper.

The first celebrated crime in San Francisco is remembered chiefly for the political furor that surrounded it. In August 1828, even before the settlement on Yerba Buena Cove that would one day grow into the American city of San Francisco was founded, Ignacio Olivas, a soldier at the Presidio, went with his wife to a fandango, leaving their five-year-old daughter and infant son in the nearby family residence. When the parents returned later that night, they found their children murdered. Both had been strangled. The little girl had been raped.[4] Francisco (El Coyote) Rubio, a fellow soldier at the Presidio with a record of bad conduct, was immediately suspected of the crime. There was circumstantial evidence pointing to his guilt; when accosted, he made self-incriminating statements. In the following weeks, he was tried by a military tribunal and found guilty of the murders; but, for the next several years, under the easygoing administration of the military governor, he remained in a judicial limbo under loose house arrest at the Presidio.

At the beginning of 1831, Manuel Victoria, a man of sterner stuff, was appointed military governor of California by a newly installed conservative regime in Mexico. Victoria's appointment caused consternation among the *californios*, who had begun to question why they should be governed from Mexico at all. Furthermore, the appointment of the conservative Victoria promised to delay the secularization of the missions, from which a number of the *hijos del país* (children of the country) expected to profit mightily.[5] In the end, they did. Victoria was a strict law and order man who thought crime had gotten out of hand. Soon after his arrival, he shocked the *californios* by ordering the execution of an Indian convicted of burglary in Monterey. The governor also ordered a rehearing in the Olivas murder; after a second tribunal found Rubio guilty in July 1831, he was taken behind the Olivas residence at the Presidio and executed by a military firing squad.[6]

The story was circulated by Victoria's political enemies that the Indian at Monterey had been executed for stealing a few buttons. This was not true—the buttons were merely evidence that he committed the burglary, which according to the law in force at the time was a capital crime.[7] Victoria's enemies also spread the story around that the murders of the Olivas children had actually been committed by someone other than Rubio.[8] By the end of 1831, *californio* opposition to Victoria had crystallized into a revolutionary force that in the end drove the governor from California and replaced him with a regime controlled by his political enemies. Whether Victoria got what he deserved and whether Rubio was actually guilty are matters for historical debate. Suffice it to say for our purposes that crime and the governor's management of the justice system—issues sure to stir up public emotions in any age—were seized upon by his political opponents to attack him. The versions of the stories they spread were distorted to serve their political ends. We shall see that sort of thing again.

In truth, there was probably about as much predatory crime in Hispanic California as one would expect in such a society: more than envisioned by Bancroft in his panegyric but less than would afflict later American settlers. Violent crime, especially crimes of passion like that of Rubio, seem to be part of the human condition; but the predatory crime of the sort that would later cause Bancroft and others to look back with nostalgic longing to pastoral California was really an urban phenomenon that grew out of the heterogeneous social maelstrom of the California Gold Rush. By the time Americans became genuinely concerned about crime in San Francisco, the city's population was twice that of the whole of Hispanic California at its high point.

It is not that the inhabitants of Hispanic California were morally superior to those who came later—it could be dangerous for a stranger to be alone and unarmed in the remote regions of California in either era. It is just that there was less opportunity to commit crimes successfully in the small homogeneous settlements that predominated at the time. Field anthropologists have long noticed the absence of locks in "underdeveloped" societies. In the words of an old African tribal aphorism about simple societies, "the problem is not how to steal the king's bugle but where to play it." (In the time of the Ohlone, who peopled the San Francisco Bay area before the coming of white settlers, there was almost none of the behavior we would characterize as in-group crime. In their stone age communities, which had no metals, domesticated animals, or cultivated foodstuffs, there were not even the beginnings of governmental institutions. Neither was there any concept of formal law or crime. Errant behavior was greeted with community disapproval. If the behavior persisted, the malefactor was ostracized from the group, a most effective deterrent in a society made up of a number of exclusive tribelets, hostile to strangers, even those from a neighboring group. There was no place else for an exile to go.)

Aside from the Rubio case, there was an occasional Indian murder and from time to time a theft in Hispanic San Francisco, but the settlements at the end of the peninsula before the coming of the Americans never did advance too far toward a "higher civilization," with regard to predatory crime or anything else.

After the successful Mexican Revolution, although some restrictions on trade with foreigners remained in effect, large numbers of New England and European ship captains made their way around Cape Horn, bringing manufactured goods to trade for California hides and tallow. They settled representatives in the coastal settlements to manage their affairs ashore, many of whom married the daughters of leading *californio* families and were absorbed into California society.

At San Francisco, in the early years of the Mexican period, foreign shipmasters, finding the old Spanish anchorage in front of the Presidio unsuitable during winter storms and perhaps too close to nosy customs officials, took to anchoring in a small cove in the shelter of a hill called Loma Alta (Telegraph Hill) on the northeastern point of the peninsula. From that location on Yerba Buena Cove under Telegraph Hill the future city of San Francisco would grow. From its very beginning, the little settlement of Yerba Buena was stamped with a character different from other California settlements, a factor that would figure prominently in later events.

Previous California settlements had been established by Spanish or Mexican authorities as missions, presidios, or pueblos for other than strictly commercial reasons. In 1835, an English immigrant, William Richardson—who had come to California a decade before as the mate of a British ship—erected the first crude dwelling on Yerba Buena Cove (near the present intersection of Grant Avenue and Clay Street). There he established a trading post where he gathered the hides and tallow from ranchos around the bay to trade with foreign merchant ship captains. Richardson was soon joined by Jacob Leese, an American, and other foreign traders; as Yerba Buena grew in size and prosperity, the other two settlements on the peninsula declined still further. The Presidio garrison was moved to the frontier at Sonoma the year Yerba Buena was founded; after the Mission was secularized, most of the christianized Indians followed the *californios* to their ranchos around the bay.

From its very start, then, unlike other California settlements, the village that would grow into the city of San Francisco was founded as a commercial settlement, dominated culturally, socially, and economically by non-Hispanic merchant traders. In the years to come, even after the disruption of the great California Gold Rush, this mercantile/ maritime establishment, in place from the start, would form the dominant faction in public affairs—its views would shape public perceptions about the amount of crime in early San Francisco and what should be done about it.[9]

CHAPTER 2

Conquest

THE UNITED STATES had long lusted after San Francisco Bay; when the Americans went to war with Mexico in 1846, the seizure of the great estuary was one of their principal objects. But while farseeing geopoliticians might have predicted the commercial potential of the great landlocked harbor, the sailors and marines of the United States sloop of war *Portsmouth* who marched ashore one July morning that year to the accompaniment of fife and drum found little to suggest that in a few short years the sleepy little settlement on Yerba Buena Cove would be the setting of wild excitement and claims of widespread criminal disorders. By the time of the American conquest, the Presidio had been all but abandoned and the Mission was in a state of irretrievable decline. So it was to Yerba Buena, the principal commercial settlement on the bay, that the invading Americans came, and it was in front of the Mexican Customhouse on the plaza (soon to be renamed Portsmouth Square) that they raised the American flag claiming San Francisco for the United States.

In 1846, the town did not amount to much. The settled portion was bounded roughly by the future lines of Pacific, California, and Dupont (Grant) streets and the waterfront a few feet to the east of Montgomery Street—in all, a few thousand square yards. There were perhaps two hundred permanent residents in the settlement at the time and some fifty buildings scattered about the slope of sandy beach that ran between the shoreline and the wilderness of scrub oak to the rear of Dupont Street. At the center of the town and its affairs was the adobe Customhouse on the plaza. The southern limit of the town was marked by a ravine near California Street where the trail to the Mission began. In the north, the settled portion of the little hamlet straggled off through the *puertosuelo* (little gate), the cleft between Telegraph Hill and Russian Hill, to the start of the trail to the Presidio. Down by the beach at Montgomery Street were the commercial warehouses and grogshops for sailors on shore leave to slake their thirst. There were more saloons and a boardinghouse over by the deep-water landing place (embarcadero) at Broadway and Battery streets, forming the embryo of what would one day be the notorious Barbary Coast.

At the approach of the invading Americans, Mexican officials of Yerba Buena, in keeping with long-standing invasion plans, buried the town cannon, turned over the municipal documents and the Mexican flag to a friendly foreigner, and fled inland. A few days later, after it became evident that the Americans meant them no harm, the officials returned to town. In the meantime, in his proclamation announcing the seizure of California for the United States, Commodore John Sloat, commander of the Pacific Naval Squadron, invited Mexican officials to retain their positions in local government. Some *californios* in the more heavily populated regions of southern California agreed to do so; but, for the most part, Hispanic residents in the north declined to serve. They were replaced by American appointees of the victorious military forces.

The government found in place by the invading Americans had been established by Mexican law in the late 1830s after years of governmental experimentation during the revolutionary turbulence of that era. The Department of California, headed by a governor and legislative body (*junta departamental*) had been divided into two geographic districts headed by executive officials called prefects. The districts were further subdivided into *partidos* headed by subprefects located in their main towns (*cabeceras*). Larger settlements (San Francisco did not qualify) were governed by alcaldes (mayor/judges) who were voting members of *ayuntamientos* (town councils). In smaller settlements,

like San Francisco, the *cabecera* of the northernmost *partido*, local
government was provided by a *junta municipal* comprised of a *juez de
paz* (justice of the peace) and one or more prominent private citizens
who answered to the subprefect.

According to Sloat's proclamation (and the law of nations), Mexican
governmental forms were to be observed until the military issues of
the war were resolved. Americans of a later period, trying to figure
out the reasons for the governmental disorganization of their own era,
would conclude that they had inherited a land with no governmental
traditions. In fact, much of the political discord that afflicted the new
American possession during the interregnum would stem in large part
from a misunderstanding of the nature of Mexican governmental forms
and the powers of government officials.

Bancroft, as we have already seen, remarked on the absence of
juries, sheriffs, and courts in pastoral California. He was technically
correct. The Mexican system of law found by the Americans on their
arrival was based on the Roman legal system, modified by the Code
Napoleon, not the common law system with which Americans were
familiar. There was no exact equivalent in the Mexican law of sheriffs
to carry out the orders of judicial officials or the jury system found
in English and American law.[1] The system of trial courts provided
for by law had never been established in the revolutionary upheavals
that afflicted California during the Mexican era. (Hispanic Californians
were not particularly litigious. The object of the civil law was con-
ciliatory, not adversarial—its main thrust was to maintain community
harmony, not to protect individual rights.) Under the laws of Mexico,
however, executive officials from top to bottom were empowered with
judicial authority to try criminal matters in certain clearly limited circumstances.

The invading American commanders did not (or did not want to)
understand the Mexican system and tried to get by at first by appoint-
ing alcaldes answerable only to the military commanders as the sole
civil administration of California towns. According to Walter Colton,
appointed alcalde of the Monterey district, "My jurisdiction extends
over an immense extent of territory. . . . It devolves on me duties similar to those of a mayor of one of our cities, without any of those judicial
aids which he enjoys. . . . Such an absolute disposal of questions affecting property and personal liberty never ought to be confided to one
man."[2] Colton was more properly describing the duties of a prefect
under the Mexican system, but his error is understandable, for, in

the first years after the conquest, the Americans failed to provide all the supporting governmental offices called for by the law. It was to be alcaldes, answerable at first to local military commanders and later only to the military governor of California (with offices adapted from the American system of municipal government tacked on from time to time), who represented the only civil government establishment during the interregnum.

In August 1846, the local military commander appointed Washington A. Bartlett, a bilingual naval lieutenant assigned to the *Portsmouth*, as alcalde for the District of San Francisco. George Hyde, an attorney from Philadelphia who had come to California as the secretary to Sloat's replacement, Commodore Robert Stockton, was appointed second (assistant) alcalde, but shortly thereafter he resigned from office. In September, in an election called by Commodore Stockton, who favored the idea of elected rather than appointed officials, Bartlett was returned as alcalde by the voters of San Francisco.

Neither had there been any police officers in Hispanic California. In that, as discussed in a later chapter, pueblos in Mexican California were much like similarly situated settlements in preindustrial America. Mexican law provided for the establishment of a civil police by prefects in districts, and in smaller settlements justices of the peace "were entrusted with police in such numbers as may be desired by the Departmental Junta in concert with the Governor."[3] But no real police department had ever been organized in California, even in the more densely populated sections of the south. Labor-intensive as they are, police departments are an expensive proposition in any society—there was neither the tax base nor the inclination in Hispanic California to establish any.

It was expected that the people would obey the edicts of magistrates; failing that, the army was there to back up the local officials. In 1844, two residents of the town of Yerba Buena were listed in the records as *agentes de policía*, but they do not seem to have performed any law enforcement duties. The same year, when trouble threatened in the town, the governor ordered the few remaining troops at the Presidio to march to Yerba Buena to suppress disturbances. In 1845, there was some sort of a volunteer police patrol in Yerba Buena, but its members seem to have caused more trouble than they prevented.[4]

After the American conquest, Lieutenant Henry B. Watson was assigned to the Customhouse with a detachment of twenty-four of his marines from the *Portsmouth* as a garrison to defend against a feared Mexican counterattack and to serve as town police. After the American flag was raised, the previously somnolent little settlement on Yerba Buena Cove took on new life almost at once. Within a month of the conquest, two hotels opened where there had been none before to serve the needs of the increased shipping expected now that the Americans were in control.

A few weeks after the conquest, the population of the town more than doubled at a stroke with the arrival of the ship *Brooklyn*, carrying more than two hundred immigrant settlers, most of them Latter-day Saints, looking for a new life far from the troubles they had encountered in the United States. While Elder Brigham Young led an overland contingent of Mormons in search of a new home, which resulted in the founding of Salt Lake City, Elder Samuel Brannan led a seaborne contingent around Cape Horn to California. When they set out on the long voyage, California was a province of Mexico, and it was under that rule that they intended to settle. By the time they arrived in late summer, the Americans had taken control. The Mormons set about with their characteristic industry to remake the town.

Brannan was born in Maine in 1819, the son of an Irish immigrant who had settled there; after traveling the United States in his young manhood as a tramp printer, he joined the Mormon church in 1842. For several years, until he led the party to California, Brannan published the Mormon church's official house newspaper. He was soon to divorce himself acrimoniously from his Mormon brethren; in the turbulent years that followed, the former elder was to become one of the wealthiest men in California from land speculation and business ventures. With his excitable nature, he figures large in our story of crime and disorder, for he was to play a leading role (usually favoring the summary hanging of someone) in the forefront of opposition to every social disruption that afflicted the young country. The *Brooklyn* colonists came to found a new society and brought with them a flour mill, plows and other farm implements, a printing press, type, and paper stock with which to spread the word. Brannan would use that press to start the first newspaper in San Francisco.

The town changed fast. The *Brooklyn*, on its arrival at the end of July, found "four or five battered hulks in the harbor." Less than two months later, a more recent arrival observed that the harbor was occupied by "thirty large vessels, consisting of whalemen, merchantmen,

Sam Brannan. (*California State Library*)

and the U.S. Sloop of War *Portsmouth*," along with other smaller craft, "giving the harbor a commercial air, of which some of the large cities on the Atlantic coast would feel vain."[5]

For all its rapid growth and uncertain governmental status in the months immediately following the American conquest, the cultural ethos of the settlement remained that of small-town America. Already, the population of frontier merchants, Mormon settlers, and native *californios* lent the flavor of diversity, but still the old social values of self-help and neighborliness obtained. However, lounging around the grogshops near the shore, a few beached sailors (a group our prede cessors would correctly blame for much of the predatory crime that followed) had begun to appear. But in a town the size of Yerba Buena in 1846, where all can watch each other, there was little opportunity for predation.

As soon as the town began to thrive, its new prosperity was postponed by events in the south. In the autumn of 1846, outraged at the high-handed practices of the American garrison commander at Los Angeles, the *californios* there revolted against their conquerors and drove them from the town. A call for help was raised, and all able-bodied Americans in the north (from Yerba Buena, Sonoma, and Sacramento) were mobilized into a volunteer battalion sent south to assist in the reconquest.

Regardless of the times, it is among young adult males that most criminal predators are found. With all the young men away from Yerba Buena, there was little chance for criminal predation, and the records of the time report none. Before the year of conquest drew to a close in the settlement whose name would soon be synonymous the world over for crime and disorder, "the peace and quiet of the town was undisturbed by anything more serious than the arrest of a few of the *Portsmouth*'s men for disorderly conduct and one or two causeless alarms."[6]

CHAPTER 3

The Politics of Crime

LINCOLN STEFFENS EXPLAINS in his autobiography how he and another turn-of-the-century New York news reporter created a nineteenth-century crime wave even though there had been no actual increase in crime.[1] It all started when Steffens wrote a news story for his paper about the burglary of the house of a prominent citizen, and the crime reporter for a competing paper was hailed before his editor to explain why he had not known of the crime. To set things right, Steffens's competitor wrote up a crime story that otherwise would not have received any coverage, and the war was on. Other reporters, goaded by their editors, joined in, creating in the minds of New Yorkers the belief that they were in the midst of an unprecedented crime wave. Before the press war was ended by the intervention of police commissioner Teddy Roosevelt, it appeared that the top brass of the New York Police Department would be shaken out of office for not being able to do anything about runaway crime. During the period of the "crime wave," according to Steffens, crime had actually decreased in New York City.

Steffens's "crime wave" was caused by inadvertence. Others have not been so accidental. Politicians and the politically ambitious know that one of the best ways to bring an enemy down is to blame intolerable crime conditions or dramatic single crimes on an opponent's wrongheaded policies. The actual number of crimes that occur is not as important as public perceptions about the amount of predation—and sometimes that is a very different thing. Such claims about an adversary, if they make their way into the records of the time and get passed on by undiscriminating commentators, have a way of turning into received historical wisdom. Contemporary press reports, the rough draft of history, do much to shape our view of times that have gone before. Governor Victoria's detractors had to spread their gossip against him by word of mouth; but after the American conquest, the establishment of a newspaper press multiplied the ability of the politically ambitious to publicize the putative failings of their enemies.

By early 1847, American forces had crushed the California insurgents in the south and, with the signing of the Treaty of Cahuenga in January, hostilities between Mexican and American forces ended in California. After the end of hostilities, the volunteers recruited in northern California returned home to a different town. One returning volunteer, who had arrived the year before on the *Brooklyn*, was struck by the change: "It was early evening as we entered the town by the old Mission Road—a three mile stretch of deep sand. Lights gleamed on shore and shipboard, fifty for one that we had been accustomed to see when martial law was first proclaimed in the quiet little pueblo of the Summer before."[2]

Much of the change (and increased population and prosperity) was caused by the arrival of Colonel Jonathan Stevenson's regiment of New York volunteers at the end of March. The regiment had been formed in 1846 and sent to California to assist in the Mexican War. It was a condition of enlistment that, at the end of the war, the volunteers agreed to accept their discharges there and to become settlers in the newly acquired territory. By the time the regiment made its way around the Horn in plodding transport ships, hostilities had ended in California; after landing in San Francisco, the various companies were distributed on garrison duty around California. Two companies were assigned to the Presidio at San Francisco and a detachment under Lieutenant Edward Gilbert was assigned to the Customhouse at Yerba Buena, replacing Watson's marines as the town police. First on the ground, as they were, the officers and men of the volunteer regiment and their commander, Colonel Stevenson, were to play major roles in the social disruptions that accompanied the first great growth of San Francisco.

As Commodore Stockton had made his way south in late 1846 to engage the rebellious *californios,* General Steven Watts Kearny and a force of army dragoons were making their way overland from Kansas with orders to seize California and establish a civil government there. As Kearny approached San Diego, his force was engaged by a party of California lancers at San Pasquale who gave his men a sound drubbing. A number of Americans were killed, and the general himself was wounded. They were forced to hold a defensive position for a few days until rescued by a relief party sent by Stockton from San Diego. For some reason (perhaps because of his wounds and the ignominy of his recent defeat), Kearny did not immediately assert his authority as the senior military commander in California. On the march to Los Angeles in the brief campaign that ended the war in California, he subordinated himself to Stockton's command. With hostilities at an end, however, Kearny presented his credentials and claimed his right to superior authority in the conquered province.

Stockton, in the meantime, had appointed a territorial government according to his earlier announced plan of governmental organization; for a time, there was confusion in the minds of American settlers about whom they should obey. The ambiguities were put to rest with the arrival of orders that clearly gave precedence to Kearny. Kearny's ideas about how the conquered province should be governed differed from those of Stockton. California was to be held and governed by direct military rule until the war with Mexico was ended and the final ownership of the territory was decided. Instead of elected public officials as envisioned by Stockton, Kearny and his successor as military governor appointed alcaldes who were to report directly to them.

Having had a taste of self-rule during Stockton's brief administration, the leading civilian settlers of San Francisco bridled at the imposition of military controls. For the next few years, until the end of the period of military rule, members of the merchant and landowning establishment in San Francisco would oppose military domination— and that of those appointed by military officers to local offices.

In February 1847, the military commander in San Francisco sent Lieutenant Bartlett back to his ship, and shortly thereafter General Kearny appointed Edwin Bryant to replace him as alcalde. Soon afterward, Bryant resigned his office to accompany the general back to the "states." One faction in San Francisco wanted John Townsend, a settler from before the American conquest, to be appointed to the vacancy, but the military governor appointed George Hyde instead. A public meeting was called for May 30 at which the citizens intended to elect their own alcalde. The military commander of the Presidio put a stop to that idea. Not surprisingly, perhaps, Hyde's tenure in office was marked by controversy. One of the accusations made against him was that he did nothing about rampant crime.

In January, using the press brought on the *Brooklyn*, Sam Brannan began publishing the first newspaper in San Francisco, the *California Star*. From its start, the *Star* was an organ of protest against what its publisher considered the tyranny of the military government.[3] Before the American conquest, Monterey had been the capital of northern California and it was there that the first newspaper in California, the *Californian*, was published in 1846. By early 1847, it had become evident, however, that the commercial future of California lay on San Francisco Bay; in May, the publishers of the *Californian* moved their press north, making San Francisco a two-newspaper town. The *Californian* tended to be more friendly toward the military government and its appointees.

Hyde's opponents would coalesce around Brannan and the *Star*. Aside from his opposition to the military appointment, Brannan had personal reasons for opposing Hyde. Attorney Hyde had appeared for the plaintiff in a lawsuit against the publisher in 1846 in the first jury trial in San Francisco and had been on the opposite side in an altercation that erupted at a public meeting in February 1847. The first salvo in the attack on Hyde was fired in June 1847 by Brannan's *Star* not long after Hyde took office. It took the form of an accusation that the alcalde was not doing anything about crime. In June, the paper editorialized that "our town is fast relapsing into a state of lawlessness and becoming a Sunday resort of noisy drunken and profane Indians and Kanakas." "Had we an alcalde devoted to the interests of the place and people," the editor continued, "the holiday sports of the sort of character alluded to would be discontinued in the streets of San Francisco at least. . . ." He added that "while the outskirts of our town are infested with drunken Indians, who parade the main roads brandishing drawn knives and insulting unprotected females, life and property are not altogether safe. . . ."[4]

Whatever the true crime situation was, Governor Richard B. Mason saw the need for a town government in San Francisco "more than is in the power of the alcalde to put in force."[5] So he wrote Hyde

Swasey's view of San Francisco in 1846–47. This depiction is close to the settlement's actual appearance shortly after the American conquest. (*California State Library*)

in mid-July directing him to hold a town meeting to elect a council. Before the letter reached him, Hyde had already appointed a council, but in September he conducted an election anyway, at which the first popularly elected council in American San Francisco was chosen.

By midsummer, according the census taken by Lieutenant Gilbert of the volunteer regiment, the town had a population of 459, not counting military personnel and residents of the Mission. Men, most of them under forty years of age, outnumbered women by two to one. About 20% of the population was identified as Indians, blacks, and Sandwich Islanders (Hawaiians). As described by Gilbert, the boundaries of the town extended for three-quarters of a mile from north to south and two miles from east to west. More than thirty new structures had been erected in the first year of American occupation, and another forty-eight were under construction.

Right after the council election, the *Californian* reminded the new council that one of the objects of its election was to appoint a "good and efficient police for the protection of the residents on shore and vessels in the harbor."[6] What was wanted, according to Mason's directive establishing the town government, was "an efficient town police, proper town laws, town officers, for the enforcement of laws, for the preservation of order, and for the proper protection of persons and property."[7] At its meeting of September 27, the council passed an ordinance establishing a town police in San Francisco.

Sec. 1. Be it ordained by the Town Council of the Town of San Francisco, that there shall be elected two constables who shall constitute the chief police of the town.

Sec. 2. Be it further ordained, that the constables shall perform all the duties required of other ministerial officers within the town—shall faithfully execute all process directed to them in accordance with the law and make due return thereof—shall strictly enforce and obey every law, ordinance and resolution passed by the council.

Sec. 3. Be it further ordained, that the Constables shall receive for the service of any writ or other process, one dollar, to be paid out of the fines imposed upon cases, one dollar for the service of any writ or other process to be paid by the defeated party, also ten cents per mile for every mile which they may travel to serve any writ or other process beyond the limits of the town.[8]

The town police formed in San Francisco in 1847 was established according to forms then prevalent in American settlements. The constables were not municipal police officers such as modern city dwellers would recognize. The largely homogeneous settlements in preindustrial America, like Bancroft's ideal of pastoral California, were to a large extent governed by custom and common agreement about how things should be done, and the idea of large bodies of police officers to enforce the law or keep the peace was alien to them. There was some predatory crime, of course, and the usual crimes of passion that afflict all societies, but violence on a scale that would lead to the formation of urban police departments was still not a fact of everyday life.[9]

American institutions of urban law enforcement, dating from colonial times (and adapted from still earlier English models), usually consisted of a "watch" of citizens to patrol the town between dusk and dawn and one or more constables to provide law enforcement and peacekeeping services, such as they were, during the day. Watchmen were to patrol at night (an activity often observed in the breach) to suppress disorders and to guard against fires. Constables, few in number, were charged with arresting drunks and criminals and enforcing a wide array of local ordinances during the daylight hours.[10] With growing concern about crime in the comparatively densely populated settlements of the East since the turn of the nineteenth century, some constables had evolved into a detective force, hired on a fee basis by private citizens to restore stolen property.[11]

The constables appointed in San Francisco in 1847, however, were looked upon principally as agents of the courts to carry out judicial orders according to a set schedule of fees; despite language contained in the authorizing ordinances, they were not expected to carry out general law enforcement duties. It was an age, for the most part, when a man was expected to "kill his own snakes." (Changing conditions, however, not just in San Francisco but in urban America generally, would call into being a different type of police officer.)

At its meeting of October 11, 1847, the town council appointed W. S. Thorp and Henry Smith as constables, to be "the chief police of the town." Two months later, the police ordinance was amended to provide a monthly salary of $50 in addition to the usual fees and reduced the number of constables from two to one. The sole constable was to devote his full time to his official duties and was "empowered to arrest anyone guilty of any crime, misdemeanor," and, with a provision sure to stir the heart of a constitutional lawyer, "other improper conduct."[12] Thomas Kittleman, who had arrived in San Francisco with Brannan on the *Brooklyn* and was brother-in-law to Councilman Elbert P. Jones, one of Hyde's principal adversaries, was named as the sole constable to replace both Smith and Thorp. The council also began enacting a set of laws to govern the town affairs. One of the reasons offered by Mason for the need for a town government was that "there may soon be expected a larger number of whalers in your bay, and a large increase in your population."[13] The first ordinance enacted by the town council was designed to further the interests of the mercantile/maritime establishment by making it a criminal offense for a sailor to jump ship.

Many of the first non-Hispanic settlers in California had been runaway sailors; indeed, the founder of the settlement at Yerba Buena had arrived that way. It is not surprising that seamen jumped ship, considering the way nineteenth-century sailors were often pressed into service for lengthy voyages under bucko mates. While nineteenth-century workmen ashore began to organize to improve their lot, seamen, isolated from others in a like condition, remained at the mercy of shipmasters who were a law unto themselves once sight of the land was lost. It was a common practice for seamen to jump ship at the first opportunity and forsake the pay coming to them.

As early as 1840, the existence of a group of beached sailors lounging around the waterfront grogshops in Yerba Buena was remarked upon. And in 1846, the captain of the USS *Portsmouth* commented on the hundreds of defectors from the whaling and merchant fleet as well as the naval squadron. It is one thing to jump ship in a busy seaport where a captain can pick up a replacement, but in San Francisco, then the end of the world, there was little chance to replace runaway crewmen. Whaling captains informed the town officials that unless they did something about runaway sailors, the fleet would winter—and reprovision—in the Sandwich (Hawaiian) Islands. The first legislative enactment was thereupon passed by the San Francisco council, prohibiting seamen from jumping ship and the residents of San Francisco from harboring them if they did so.[14]

There were other enactments by the 1847 town council. One ordinance prohibited the discharge of firearms within one mile of Portsmouth Square. Another prohibited the killing of carrion fowl—the town's first garbage collection service. Still another prohibited disorderly conduct; after a drunken sailor fell down an uncovered well near the embarcadero on Halloween, an ordinance was passed, with the usual legislative hindsight, requiring that all wells be covered.[15] Under other business, members of the council, joined by Sam Brannan and prominent citizens of the town, went after Alcalde Hyde's scalp.

Then as now, the real movers and shakers in a community usually do not serve in public office themselves. Members of the establishment want the freedom to pursue their own private interests, but they also want a say in governmental issues affecting those interests. Thus, they back candidates for office who share their view of the world and who are willing to attend to the tiresome details of governmental service. They usually have their way. The leading citizens of a community can be seen at their vengeful best when a candidate somehow gains office who is not in sympathy with their private ends.

Citing an allegation made in the August 21 issue of Brannan's *Star* about changes made in the Record of Deeds in the alcalde's office, Councilman Jones moved that a committee of citizens be formed to investigate the affairs of the office. After Brannan and two others wrote to him in October requesting it, Governor Mason ordered an investigation to be made of Hyde's performance in office.[16] One accusation against Hyde, raised in the October 9 issue of the *Star*, was that he had been about to charge a whaling captain one dollar a day per head for holding members of his crew in the calaboose, but after the captain checked with the officer in charge of the jail and found out that the cost to the town was only eighteen cents, the alcalde backed off. In the press exchange that followed, the *Californian* published a letter from the captain asserting that perhaps Hyde's suggestion had been in jest. The *Star* replied with letters from Brannan and others asserting that the charges were indeed true and that Hyde himself had written the letter that appeared in the *Californian*.

By the end of the year, according to editorial reports, the town was beset by crime. Even the *Californian* published without comment a report from a Hawaiian paper characterizing San Francisco as a place of great immorality, where crews could not be retained on ships, where there was no order, where robberies were common, and where there was no regular administration of the law.[17] The *Star* chimed in, blaming the council for the recent escape of disorderly sailors and deploring again the infestation of the town by "idle drunken thievish Indians." The *Star*'s editor carped in late December that the town was at the mercy of burglars and violent men.[18]

For all the stated editorial concern about "robberies" and "burglaries," there is little substantive crime to be found reported in the news columns of the *Star* in 1847. There was the report of a $1,600 hotel burglary in August and another burglary in December, occasioning the editor to say that the town was at the mercy of burglars, and one criminal homicide, of which more later. The news reporter for the *Star* seems to have been genuinely surprised in November when a member of the crowd watching the drowned sailor being hauled out of the well "actually" had his pocket picked. "The thief has not been apprehended," the reporter noted, and "probably he never will." [19]

The editorial concern about crime at the time, at least on the part of the *Star*, can perhaps in part be understood in light of the fact that Brannan was pushing the appointment of Kittleman as constable and Hyde was holding the appointment up. (It is important to note, for future purposes, that newspaper complaints about crime were cast in the form of editorial comment unsupported by actual news accounts. The line between editorial comment and factual news is not always clear, but it is an important distinction to keep in mind.) The *Star* had been publishing for six months (the first half of 1847) without reporting any crime; yet as soon as an alcalde not to its liking was appointed, editorials about rampant crime began to appear.

Whatever the case, examination of the claims about the state of crime shows that much of what the editors were complaining about should be categorized more as rowdiness than as predatory crime. Unchecked rowdiness makes a community unlivable and certainly leads to predation; but for the purpose of understanding what went on in the early days of San Francisco without excusing it, it is important to distinguish between general rowdiness—which is usually directed by hoodlums at each other—and substantive crimes such as robbery and burglary—which more commonly involve innocent strangers. [20]

Despite the fulminations of the contemporary press on the state of crime in San Francisco in 1847, the concern can be traced to the political enemies of an alcalde unpopular with a powerful faction in the town. "It is clear enough," writes Bancroft of the time, "that personal enmities, business cliques, and newspaper rivalries were leading factors in the controversies," which resulted in "doubtless exaggerated statements of prevalent lawlessness." [21] In truth, the actual situation in 1847 was probably as reported by Brannan's editor writing in later years after the passions of the moment had cooled: "The historian of these times [1847] will find a barren page. It is proper to state . . . [that] there was very little drunkenness and rarely a case of disorder. The town was governed almost without the aid of a constable." [22]

CHAPTER 4

The Victors Write the History

FOR REASONS THAT WILL become evident, it served the interests of some of the leading citizens of San Francisco, the victors in the scramble for political, social, and economic ascendancy, that the Gold Rush city be remembered as having been beset by crime and disorder. (Respectable men such as those who bypassed the law to form their own tribunals of justice want historical justification.) They have been successful in their attempt to get history written to suit their ends.

One of the enduring legends in the lore of early San Francisco is that, during the years of its Gold Rush adolescence, the city was afflicted with an epidemic of criminal homicide. One version, repeated again and again in accounts of the time, has it that there were 100 murders in San Francisco in the few months prior to the formation of the first Vigilance Committee in 1851, at a time when the population of the town never exceeded 25,000.[1] Other versions claim that there were 1,000, 1,200, or 1,400 murders within a period of a few years, when the city's population was never more than 50,000.[2] Some turn the numbers around and say that there were one or more daily murders in San

Francisco and that the condition prevailed for months or years on end.[3] Commentators often add that with all this murderous carnage there was only one legal execution, "that of a miserable Spanish murderer."[4]

In fact, as this study demonstrates, the murders did not occur in anything like the numbers suggested by the legend. A better working average for the incidence of murder in Gold Rush San Francisco would be one a month, or, adjusted for variations in population, not a great deal different from the experience of many cities today.[5] But the legend has so insinuated itself into the fabric of the history of the city that the list of names of those who have reported or repeated some version reads like a roll call of distinguished regional historians.[6]

The not-so-simple fact is that the murders did not occur at all, and there are those—John Myers Myers, Roger Lotchin, and, more recently, Robert Senkewicz among them—who have tried to put the legend to rest.[7] Yet it persists. In account after account of the early years of San Francisco, some version of the legend is still invoked as an example of the rampant lawlessness that beset Gold Rush San Francisco or as an explanation of the extraordinary crime control measures taken by the citizenry of that day. Herbert Phillips (1968), Adair Heig (1982), and Curt Gentry and Tom Horton (1982) claim that there were 1,200 murders in San Francisco between the end of 1849 and the end of 1854.[8] Kevin Starr (1981) claims that "a murdered corpse or two was a morning's expectation."[9] Arthur Chandler (1977) says that, during the early 1850s, the city "averaged for months on end, about two murders per day."[10] Herb Caen, in his popular column on January 12, 1986, reports that there were 1,200 murders during the one-year period of Mayor John Geary's first term of office.[11] Alistair Cooke, on the other hand, prefers the version of the legend that there were 100 murders in the few months before the establishment of the first Committee of Vigilance.[12]

Frederick Wirt (1974), John McGloin (1978), and Charles Wollenberg (1985) have written that there were 1,000 criminal homicides between 1849 and 1856. That rate was "10 to 20 times the per capita murder rate of the early 1980s," Wollenberg adds.[13] (In fact, using the figures given in the legend and adjusting for the different populations at the two times, the per capita rate of criminal homicide for the earlier time would be closer to 80 times that of the 1980s.) If there were anything to the legend, there would be little reason to wonder why the citizens of Gold Rush San Francisco rose up in righteous indignation to stamp out criminal predators.

In discussing conditions in San Francisco at this point, it may seem as though we are getting ahead of ourselves; but, if we are to come to an understanding of how much crime actually occurred in early American San Francisco, we must look at the entire historical context in which that crime occurred. Unfortunately, there are no complete contemporary statistical tabulations that conveniently quantify the amount of crime in the early days, murder or otherwise. Myers Myers, Lotchin, and Senkewicz are correct in asserting that the legend is wrong, but just saying so is not enough. To put the legend to rest, this book demonstrates that the murders did not in fact occur, recording every reported criminal homicide in American San Francisco.

One aid in understanding how many murders in fact occurred is to examine each criminal homicide reported in the contemporary press. It has already been mentioned that Mary Williams, the most comprehensive biographer of the first Committee of Vigilance, questions the value of looking to press accounts for any idea of how much crime occurred, saying that contemporary press accounts of crime were at best "incomplete and inadequate."[14] John P. Young is even more explicit. He attributes the obvious disparity between figures in the legend and the meager reports of murder in the press to "the failure of early papers to develop on the news side, and the fact that the town was so small that its inhabitants knew all the details of an affair before they could be put into print."[15]

We are not yet ready to put those assertions to the definitive test. We shall be able to do so only after we review all criminal homicides reported in the news columns of the town's leading newspaper of the time and cross-check the numbers of murders thus arrived at against independently compiled contemporary crime tabulations. There are a number of them still in existence, incomplete though they may be. The discussion starts with the first reported criminal homicide in American San Francisco and at least mentions every criminal homicide as it occurs. (The appendix contains summary accounts of every homicide reported in the *Alta California* from the beginning of 1850 through the end of 1853, the period covered in the version of the legend from which most other versions originated.)

First, however, there is a definitional matter to be resolved. Different versions of the legend use the term "homicide" and "murder" interchangeably. The terms do not mean the same thing. Homicide is a general term for the killing of one human being by another. It includes noncriminal killings (justifiable and accidental homicides) as well as criminal homicides (murder and manslaughter). Manslaughter, simply put, is an unlawful killing in which there is no prior malice. Murder is defined as the unlawful killing of a human being with *malice aforethought*.

There should be caution about accounts of the crime of murder. Joseph Henry Jackson—who, by the way, accepts the legend of 1,200 murders having occurred in a few years—in the introduction to his *San Francisco Murders* explains why the anthology of tales of San Francisco murder omits crimes that took place in the first two decades of the city's American period and starts with a celebrated case from 1870 involving one of the shining lights of the California bar. Murders were common enough in the first two decades of American San Francisco, he says, but they were not of the sort "that produces an interesting murder case."[16] What Jackson was looking for was the stuff of romantic fiction: wealthy, celebrated, or at least interesting characters and dramatic plots, perhaps with a little mystery thrown in.

Most criminal homicides are not like that; they are squalid affairs, frequently involving uninteresting people, often drunk, who kill for little apparent reason in the heat of sudden passion—hence, by definition, manslaughters. (Killings of criminals by other criminals fighting over turf or spoils are another matter. They have always been part of the urban American crime scene but became prominent with the Chicago-style gangster murders of the 1930s and more recently have become almost epidemic as drug dealers kill each other over urban turf.) One way to get involved in a homicidal conflict in old San Francisco was to hang around saloons. American San Francisco's first criminal homicide was of that type, as were many that followed.

The first reported criminal homicide in American San Francisco was committed on November 14, 1847, in a saloon by the deep-water embarcadero.[17] (It was the first major crime on the site of the future notorious Barbary Coast.) On that Sunday evening, after a long bibulous day, a ruckus broke out in Illig's grogshop on Pacific Street, just west of Montgomery. A young sailor on shore leave from a ship anchored in the nearby cove, jostling his way to the bar to get a drink, was punched in the head by William Landers, one of a group of volunteers from the New York regiment, who were also refreshing themselves at Illig's. Landers, in the timeless way of barroom brawlers, announced that he could "whip any son of a bitch in the house." Another seaman, a mate by the name of Ward who had come by to round up members of his crew, did not agree with Lander's claim and proceeded to prove it by giving him a sound trouncing.

The outmatched Landers sought to even the odds a bit by arming himself with the rifle of another volunteer, McKenzie Beverley. Ward easily disarmed Landers and took the rifle for safekeeping to Denike's bakery/saloon down the hill by the beach near the current intersection of Sansome and Pacific streets. Aroused to action by the loss of his rifle, Beverley made his way down to Denike's at the head of a group of thirty of his fellow revelers. He demanded the return of his rifle from outside the bar; when it was not forthcoming, he fired through the door with a borrowed rifle. His shot killed an innocent bystander at the bar. Beverley was arrested by a group of citizens and taken immediately before Alcalde Hyde, who turned him over to the military authorities. He was tried in December by a military commission, found guilty, and sentenced to fifteen years' imprisonment. A few days later, however, he escaped from the blockhouse prison and was not heard from again.

Hanging around saloons was a good way to become involved in conflict. Another way, leading at least to litigation and political disputes and sometimes to personal violence, was to become engaged in land claims. At the bottom of many of the political disagreements afflicting California and San Francisco in the nineteenth century, including the one that embroiled Alcalde George Hyde, were disputes over land ownership. Time after time, such disagreements would degenerate into conflict and bloody violence, as competing claims of land ownership spilled beyond the ability of the law to contain them. For centuries, westering Americans had been in the custom of settling without question on the new lands they opened up. When they came to California, however, they found that most of the best land had already been claimed under grants from the Mexican government. Many settled (squatted) on the granted lands anyway; while claims of disputed ownership wound their way slowly through the courts, claimants often took matters into their own hands.

In San Francisco, where there was also the issue of whether the town had ever been incorporated under Mexican law in the first place, the town's right to the public lands was called into question. The problems were exacerbated during the period of hybrid military rule by the issue of the right of the alcaldes to grant or sell public lands. In easygoing Mexican times, there had not been a great demand for lots, so there was not much pressure to keep records in a businesslike way. The record of deeds to town lots was kept on a penciled map behind the bar in a popular saloon. When Americans first came, conditions did not change a great deal; as alcaldes, Bartlett and Bryant pretty much granted town lots to whom they wanted. By Hyde's time, though, it was becoming clear that San Francisco was likely to grow into a major port and the demand for lots grew, particularly those along the beach and the mudflats fronting the town.

Early in 1847, General Kearny relinquished federal claims to the beach and water lots in San Francisco and restrictions prohibiting multiple lot ownership were removed. Hyde at first sold lots directly, as had his predecessors; but in July, to raise funds for the expenses of town government, he conducted the first of a series of public auctions at which municipally owned lands were sold to the highest bidder. Disagreements over land lay at the root of the controversy between Hyde and his opponents. One faction, which supported Hyde and included the publisher of the *Californian*, favored development at Clark's Point, near the present intersection of Broadway and Battery streets.[18] The other, spurred on by Brannan's *Star*, advanced development at the "old town," the beach and mudflats fronting on Montgomery Street.[19] In February 1847, the editor of the *Star* as much as accused Hyde of being part of a clique trying to take over all the beach and water lots for speculation. Two of the accusations against him that Mason ordered investigated in late 1847 were that he had altered the map of town lots and had failed to sell lots to those who first applied for them. As 1847 ended, the investigation dawdled along.

The political controversies had quieted down by the beginning of 1848; in the first months of the year, immigration picked up and the town's population grew to about 1,000. By then, approximately 200 buildings dotted the slopes of the cove. A third hotel was under construction, and several boardinghouses, saloons, billiard rooms, and bowling alleys had been added to the town's amenities. The brackish lagoon at Jackson and Montgomery streets was being filled in, and a beginning had been made on two wharves (to keep both factions happy) —one by the deep-water landing spot at Clark's Point, the other from Montgomery Street at Clay to reach shipping over the low-water mudflats in front of the town. The council announced a sale of town lots for March to raise money to pay town expenses; fifty-two lots were sold for an average of $20 each, about the same as at the auction the year before. In April, the town's first public school opened in the new schoolhouse on the southwest corner of Portsmouth Square.

In March, the political controversies heated up again. Hyde's opponents once more lodged complaints of misconduct against him before Governor Mason and asked that he be removed from office. The governor refused their request, demanding concrete evidence of misconduct; but Hyde, disgusted with the constant political bickering, resigned on his own. John Townsend, the original choice of Hyde's opponents, was sworn in as first alcalde in early April. Thaddeus Leavenworth, who had served under Hyde as second alcalde and was later to become a political storm center in his own right, continued in that office.

The trouble began in March when Councilman Leidesdorff, Hyde's previous defender, "while warm with liquor," got in a fight with a gambler in the City Hotel over a horse race. When the case came before Alcalde Hyde and he bound both parties to keep the peace, Leidesdorff became enraged. Promising the judge that he would see to his removal, Leidesdorff proclaimed, "There is no law here but club law, and I mean to go armed and shoot anyone that offers to insult me."[20]

Again, Hyde's opponents used charges of unchecked crime in their attempt to bring him down. On March 10, Leidesdorff wrote to Mason saying that he had changed his mind about Hyde and had now formed the opinion that the alcalde was responsible for the lawlessness in the town. The same day, a large number of prominent citizens wrote to Mason asking for Hyde's removal, representing the town as "in a disgraceful state of disorder; bloody street fights of almost daily occurrence" and stating that the alcalde was openly "defied, publicly insulted on the bench, not daring to endanger his personal safety."[21] On March 18, Leidesdorff and Jones induced other members of the council (William D. M. Howard and Robert A. Parker) to join them in a letter to Mason saying that Hyde had delayed the investigation ordered by the governor and that two of the charges for which the alcalde was being investigated had been found to be substantiated.

Support for assertions of widespread lawlessness in the early months of 1848 cannot be found in the columns of either of the town's newspapers, though there was some crime reported. The *Star*, on January 5, reported the burglary of a residence in the western part of town; at the end of the same month, the grogshop/bowling alley of Thomas Smith at Dupont and Broadway was "robbed" of $500.[22] It seems that there was a fight in the place; after Smith closed down to clear out the patrons, Isaac (Red) Davis entered and stole the money. Davis was promptly identified, arrested, tried, convicted, and sentenced to two years' imprisonment. But, before the month was out, he too escaped from jail. A few days after the Smith burglary, "two individuals" in another grogshop "drank freely, quarreled highly, and of course fought violently," the *Star* reported. One of the men in the saloon fight, Cochrane by name, stabbed the other in the chest; he was arrested by a posse of citizens and brought before the alcalde for a preliminary hearing.

One of the lessons of history is that the victors write it. Governor Victoria, it will be recalled, was run out of California and was not around when the history of the period came to be written, so he could not give his side. However, the *hijos del país* remained, and it was from them that Bancroft got his version of the Rubio murder. The victors in the controversies embroiling Hyde in 1847 and 1848 also influenced the writing of the history of their time. While acknowledging that "personal enmities, business cliques, and newspaper rivalries were leading factors in the controversies," Bancroft writes, "yet so much smoke is generally indicative of more or less fire"; he continues, "it is perhaps necessary to conclude that Hyde was not altogether a model alcalde." [23] When the history of the time came to be written, it would be the version of events reported in the *Star*—the paper supported by the faction that prevailed—that dominated, not those of the *Californian*.

It is possible that the prominent citizens requesting Hyde's ouster in March were referring to Leidesdorff's outburst in court when they claimed that Hyde had been defied and insulted on the bench, because that is what Leidesdorff's behavior amounted to. But it is more likely they were referring to the Cochrane stabbing case the month before. After the preliminary hearing in the case, when Hyde ordered Cochrane into custody pending a trial, the defendant became enraged and threatened the alcalde's life. It was only at the insistence of citizens who were present, according to the *Star*, that the man was lodged in the calaboose at all. The *Californian* was much more generous to the alcalde, printing a letter in its March 15 edition that said that the man had been let go only after being relieved of a knife and then only to find a witness, in the company of an armed constable. The witness located, Cochrane was returned to jail and later found guilty in a jury trial.

But it is the *Star*'s version that made its way into the history books. According to Bancroft, whose account follows that in the *Star* almost word for word, Hyde, after the examination of Cochrane, "hinted at quarters in the calaboose." The defendant interjected that the case was bailable "and you can't put me thar [sic]." During a heated exchange in which Hyde threatened the man further with prison, Cochrane informed the court, "I was never in prison yet, and if you put me thar and want to live you had better leave this place." Hyde, "who was scarcely fit for the emergency," says Bancroft, "not relishing the aspect of affairs, would have kept the prisoner confined without sending him to jail had not the citizens and members of that town council compelled him to do so." Despite protestations elsewhere that he did not take sides in the controversies of the time, Bancroft in this instance clearly leans toward the side of those who opposed the alcalde.[24]

That is not all. It was Hyde's enemies, council members Leidesdorff and Jones, who made the assertion to Governor Mason that two charges of malfeasance with regard to town lots had been sustained by the evidence. The *Annals of San Francisco*, a frequently cited standard history of the time, picked up this version of events and passed it along.[25] The usually thorough Bancroft reports, "There is no record of progress in the investigation during the rest of the year. . . ."[26] But according to William Heath Davis, who incidentally was among those asking that Hyde be removed from office, the investigation ordered by Mason had indeed been conducted and Hyde had been exculpated of any wrongdoing.[27] For all the complaints about crime and disorder during Hyde's tenure in office, none of it seems to have attached to Constable Kittleman, Brannan's man. Despite Hyde's opposition, he was finally appointed to office; but after all the concern voiced about crime and lawlessness, he seems to have spent most of his time moonlighting as a laborer on the streets and wharves then under construction.[28] It was Hyde they were after, and Hyde they got.

In the end, while observing that the whole matter was too complicated for discussion in his seven-volume history of California, Bancroft says that "it is perhaps necessary to conclude that Hyde was not altogether a model alcalde."[29] The fact of the matter is that Hyde was more sinned against than sinning. When all was done, his political enemies. have for the most part escaped from historical criticism and somehow ended up with the lion's share of the town lands anyway.[30] The political controversies of 1848 would soon be dwarfed by events to come; what is important to our tale is that we shall meet some of the principal actors once more, in a larger arena, again in connection with accusations of political misconduct leading to unchecked conditions of violent crime.

Part II GOLD

CHAPTER 5

The 48ers

CONCERNS ABOUT SMALL-TOWN CRIME and disorder were soon to be swept aside, for a time anyway, and the petty political feuds of 1847 were all but forgotten, to be replaced by others for greater stakes, as San Francisco was catapulted to world prominence as the main port of entry for the men and goods of the great California Gold Rush.

At the end of January 1848, James Marshall, while inspecting the tailrace of a sawmill he was building for John Sutter on the south fork of the American River, found the first traces of the gold that would set in motion the Gold Rush and change forever the course of San Francisco history. When news of the discovery first arrived in the settlement on the cove, it was met with skepticism; fantastic reports of the discovery of precious metals in remote regions of the world were standard fare in the popular imaginings of the time. The first press mention of the discovery was made in the March 15 issue of the *Californian*; the *Star* followed on March 25 with a statement that gold had been found in such quantities that it had become an article of trade in the vicinity of Sacramento.

That month, a few of the more adventurous residents of San Francisco slipped quietly out of town in twos and threes to go and see for themselves. The significance of the find still did not sink in during April, and the town went about its normal business. On April 15, the editor of the *Star* went to the American River to see for himself on the pretext of other business. He returned to pronounce the whole business a sham. No sooner had he published his findings, thereby missing out on one of the biggest news stories in the nineteenth century, than a number of miners appeared in town bearing the unmistakable fruits of their success, putting an end to all doubts about the legitimacy of the find. Legend has it that Sam Brannan, always on the scene when any excitement was up, strode through the town after having cornered local supplies of shovels and pans, waving his hat with one hand and holding a bottle of gold dust aloft with the other, shouting, "Gold! Gold! Gold from the American River."[1] The local rush was on.

Workmen dropped their tools and headed for the goldfields. Soldiers deserted their posts and sailors their ships. Pupils from the newly opened school tossed aside their lessons and headed for the mines. Their teacher followed soon after. The town council suspended operations in mid-May and on May 27 the *Star* was compelled to report that the town had never been so lifeless. Stores were closed, the paper reported, and houses were tenantless. There were perhaps 150 people left in town. Some merchants stuck by their "old stands," however, and put up signs saying they bought gold. Two days later, the *Californian*, unable to hire help, suspended publication; on June 14, the *Star* followed suit.

At the beginning of June, Alcalde Townsend departed for the mines, leaving the sole civil government of San Francisco in the hands of Second Alcalde Leavenworth, who, because of the decline in public business, did not even bother to unlock his office door on weekdays. Lot owners were selling their property for next to nothing to get a stake to go to the mines, and real estate values plummeted. Thomas Larkin, merchant and American consul to California during the Mexican era, wrote in June to the secretary of state from San Francisco describing the abandonment of the town. Half the residences were locked up, he said, and storekeepers, mechanics, and laborers were all gone. The U.S. bark *Anita* had only six crewmen left aboard.[2] E. Gould Buffum reported that by mid-July there were only seven able-bodied men left in San Francisco and one store open for business.[3] It appeared that San Francisco's commercial hegemony on the bay was at an end before it was fairly started, and that henceforth the focus of urban activity would move inland to some deep-water embarcadero closer to the goldfields.

At the end of July, Governor Mason, alarmed at the depopulated state of coastal settlements, threatened to take military control of the goldfields unless citizens lent aid in preventing desertions and maintained a sufficient number of able-bodied men in the towns to protect women and children.[4] It was an idle threat. His forces depleted by desertion, he could hardly have imposed his will on those who might choose to oppose him. Less than two weeks after Mason's proclamation, news arrived of the formal adoption of the treaty ending the Mexican War, granting California to the victorious Americans. With the war's end, the few remaining volunteers who had not already deserted were discharged according to the terms of their enlistments, and Mason was left with less than two companies of regulars to exercise governmental control over California, an impossible task.

There were perhaps 800 miners working the placers in May; by late June, when Thomas Larkin visited the mines, he found 2,000 men working there. On his visit to the goldfields in July, Mason estimated there were 4,000 miners working the Sierra streams. As the news of the great gold discovery spread outward in ever-widening circles, it first reached Hawaii, Mexico, and the port cities of the western coast of South America. Soon there was a trickle of argonauts from foreign ports. By autumn, the trickle had turned into a small flood. By the turn of the season in October, there were as many as 8,000 men working the placers. Skilled miners came overland from Sonora in Mexico directly to the southern mines, as did American immigrants from Oregon. Others came by sea from Pacific and South American ports to San Francisco, the port facility nearest the mining regions; from there, they set off by launch or on foot to the goldfields.

With the first foreign arrivals in August and September, the tide of the first local rush to the mines began to turn. Residents of coastal settlements, who had rushed off in late spring and early summer with provisions for only a few weeks, began to return in August to resupply and put their affairs in order before returning to the mines. Others, having had their fill of the arduous labor at the placers and noting the enormous profits to be made in an economy of scarcity where flour could sell for as much as $800 a barrel and a pair of boots, a gallon of whiskey, or a blanket fetched $100, returned to San Francisco to trade with the expected influx of argonauts from around the world. Some, broken in health by hard labor under broiling sun in the ice-chilled Sierra streams, or sickened by nutritionally deficient diets and dissipation, made their wretched way back to the coastal settlements. There, in early September, they joined the first seaborne arrivals from foreign ports.

At the end of September, there was a return migration to the placers; but a month later, as rising waters after the first winter rains made the streams impossible to work, the tide of humanity again turned to lowland settlements and coastal towns. Some stayed in the mountains to work dry diggings, but most left the hills to await the spring when the waters again would fall. From the northern mines they made their way to the new booming city of Sacramento, and from the south they headed for Stockton, at the head of navigation in the San Joaquin Delta.

But most went to San Francisco, lured by the attractions of the already established town and the amenities it offered. The losers came to curse their luck and look for work. Those who had made their pile came to find their way home to the "states" or to wait out the winter, squandering their gold in the gambling halls and saloons of the port town. As a result, San Francisco took on new life. Real estate values skyrocketed. Available rooms were soon filled, wages were high for those who could work, and construction boomed to feed the feverish demand for housing. Some could not wait and erected tents among the more regular dwellings on the slopes of the hills leading away from the cove. The old residents returned to claim their place in the quickly burgeoning society.

Edward Kemble, Brannan's former editor on the *Star*, returned from the mines and bought the defunct newspaper from his old publisher. He also acquired the *Californian* and began publishing a joint edition in November, with the unwieldy title of the *California Star and Californian*. Edward Gilbert, who had commanded the garrison police in the Customhouse in 1847, was made editor. San Francisco had a newspaper again to signal its rebirth; in December, as if to show the town was here to stay, the school was reopened. Fueled by the return migration from the mines, arrivals from Oregon, and the first seaborne arrivals from South American port cities, the population of San Francisco grew to 2,000 by the end of 1848.

Before the gold discovery, men had outnumbered women in the town by two to one; but, as American argonauts, mostly young single men, flooded in, the gap widened greatly. Prostitutes from all over the world—like nature, abhorring a vacuum, and seeing the opportunity for business among the mass of healthy young men—headed for San Francisco in large numbers. After the gold discovery, the first women to come in any numbers arrived with the first wave of seaborne gold seekers from South American ports before the end of 1848. Some pushed on to the mining regions, but most established themselves in a tent city on the slopes of Telegraph Hill, called Chiletown, where their salable charms added to the attractions luring successful gold seekers back to the town. Prostitutes were to form an important feature in the social life of San Francisco until finally outnumbered by their more conventionally respectable sisters.

Even before the discovery of gold, military control of the criminal justice apparatus in California was tenuous. As has been noted, such government as there was operated under direct military control. By military order, alcalde courts were empowered to try minor matters, but trials for serious crimes were to be by courts-martial. As a practical matter, however, serious crimes were often tried by civil alcalde's courts. Mason, acknowledging the realities of the situation, accepted the fact but did insist that juries be impaneled and that capital sentences be referred to the military governor for approval before execution. Even so, he was compelled to censure the alcalde at Santa Cruz in August 1847 for trying an accused wife murderer on Saturday and executing him on Monday before notifying the governor.

In the spring of 1848, Mason had ordered a code of laws printed, and he intended to establish a set of courts. But the end of the war, according to his interpretation of the law, made his efforts obsolete; as the great tide of Gold Rush immigration began to arrive in California, there was little formal law to restrain its members. The adoption of the Treaty of Guadalupe Hidalgo in early 1848 ended any legal claim of the military authorities to rule. By law, at war's end, Congress was to provide a territorial government until such time as the province was brought into the Union as a full-fledged state.

One of the main themes in the history of the first years of American California—underlying the governmental confusion that contributed much to the problems of criminal disorder—was the way the national Congress, unable to decide whether the new territory should be slave or free, failed to provide a proper territorial government. Mason, in the absence of congressional action, continued to exercise de facto governmental authority in the belief that to do otherwise would result in anarchy. Military rule and that of military appointees in San Francisco would be the subject of continuing criticism in the months to come from citizens who chafed under what they considered the un-American yoke of dictatorial military oppression.

As has already been mentioned, Alcalde Townsend and most of the town government went to the mines in the summer. By August, enough interest had revived in public affairs for a group of citizens to ask Mason to appoint either Edward Gilbert or J. D. Hoppe as first alcalde in place of the absent Townsend. Mason declined, on the grounds that the end of the war removed his power to appoint local officials directly. He did, however, direct Second Alcalde Leavenworth to conduct an election to fill the office. At the August 29 election, the first for an alcalde since that of Bartlett in 1846, Leavenworth was declared the winner over Hoppe, by a vote of ninety-nine to seventy-seven. Immediately, a group of forty citizens protested the election to Mason, saying that Leavenworth had held the election on short notice, restricted the vote for the district office to residents of the town, and excluded Hispanics from the franchise.

Mason instructed Leavenworth to hold the election again, this time with at least three weeks' notice; early in October, another vote was held. Again, to the continuing dismay of his opponents, Leavenworth won. On October 9, the town council, elected along with Leavenworth, convened for the first time since the previous May and determined the boundaries of San Francisco to include the area roughly covered by the current counties of San Francisco and San Mateo—for the purpose of the administration of justice.

Leavenworth's opponents were far from through with him, however, and their struggle for control of the town government in the months that followed would constitute a principal feature of the history of 1849, significantly affecting both perceptions of and the actuality of crime and disorder during that period. As early as February, long before the gold fever caught hold, the *Star* had remarked on the existence of a band of vagabonds made up of military deserters and ex-convicts who were plundering the ranchos and missions of the remote regions of the bay area. One member of Stevenson's regiment, writing to the *New York Herald* in April about California, mentioned almost as an aside that "this, like every new colony, populated by people of a roving headstrong disposition, renders murders frequent. Mostly all carry pistols and dirk knives."[5]

In June, before closing up shop, the editor of the *Star*, speaking of the mining regions, predicted that—unless a proper government was

formed—there would be trouble from "as wild a class of unchristian-
ized fellows as ever escaped the thralldom of honest law and broke
loose upon barbarism."[6] The editor reported that such a dangerous
class was even then forming and predicted it would head north to the
mines. He proved to be correct. John Sutter, in his diary entry for
March 21, reported that he had been threatened by a band of robbers,
and his foreman at Sutter's Fort that summer commented on how the
settlement had turned from an orderly village into a brawling outpost
where "anyone who could not protect himself with his fists was un-
fortunate."[7] Mason seems to have been less observant. On his return
from the mines on July 17, the governor reported with some surprise
on the absence of crime there. Larkin warned of trouble that same
month, saying "men and passions are unfavorably changed in these
gold regions."[8]

In early October, a drunken ex-soldier named Peter Raymond killed
a man named Pfister in a dispute over liquor in Coloma. Raymond
was arrested promptly but escaped before he could be tried.[9] The
next month, a man named Pomeroy and his partner were murdered
and robbed at the mines by military deserters, who also escaped.[10] At
Sacramento, on December 6, a man was killed in a dispute over the use
of a doorway. When the alcalde, in fear of the defendant, refused to try
him, Sam Brannan did so, acting as both prosecutor and judge.[11] The
man was acquitted. In Sacramento in December, a correspondent for
the *California Star and Californian* reported that crimes were being
committed with impunity there and that three men were prostrate with
knife wounds.[12]

"Men and passions" seem to have been "unfavorably changed" in
other parts of California as well. In San Jose in mid-December, two
army deserters were seized for a highway robbery in which the victim
was shot. They were placed under a guard of ten so they could not
escape, then tried before the alcalde; before the month was out, they
were hanged.[13] At San Miguel Mission, in southern California, after
enjoying the hospitality of their host, a mixed band of army and navy
deserters returned and murdered him along with a dozen members of
his family and household. The criminals were hunted down by a body
of citizens. Two of the band were killed in the course of their arrest.
Three others were shot by a military firing squad, having been found
guilty by a quickly convened court.[14]

It was in this almost absolute enforcement vacuum in California that
people began to take matters into their own hands. At the beginning of

the Gold Rush, there were only two alcaldes to serve the entire mining region, one at Sacramento and one at San Joaquin. Arriving miners soon realized they were on their own. In the absence of established authorities, and in accordance with well-established frontier traditions, the citizens of the gold regions themselves took to convening summary courts. Juries were impaneled and miner's courts convened. Common sense was the rule of law and legal technicalities were dispensed with, even by judges with legal training.[15] A guilty finding resulted in almost immediate punishment, most often banishment, whipping, or hanging, in the absence of any jails or anyone willing to watch prisoners. By all accounts, although there were some injustices, popular justice seems to have had a generally beneficial effect at the mines in the early days. In any event, in the first year of the Gold Rush, there was no available alternative.[16]

In November, Mason determined to form a provisional government if Congress adjourned without forming a territorial government for California. News arrived in December that it had adjourned without having done so, but the governor still took no action. On December 11, the residents of San Jose met in the public square and resolved to meet in a constitutional convention in January to form a government of their own. In San Francisco on December 21 and 23, the citizens, spurred on by editorial comment in the *California Star and Californian* about the need to bring crime under control, met in Portsmouth Square and also resolved to attempt to form a provisional government.[17]

Curiously, for all its sudden rebirth as a major port of entry, in the eye of the hurricane as it were, there was actually little reported crime in San Francisco in the latter part of 1848.[18] On August 14, the commandant of the Presidio, when mustering out the remaining volunteers, wrote to Mason saying that, when the ranks of the lower classes were joined by the discharged volunteers, there were likely to be serious clashes, unless there was a military presence to support the civil organization. His assistant quartermaster echoed the same sentiments to the governor, reporting that acts of "disgraceful violence" on shipping in the harbor were almost daily occurrences and that officials "had no power to preserve order."[19]

Not surprisingly, there was little reported crime in San Francisco during the summer for the very good reason that there was almost no one in town to be either victim or criminal. Even when the population increased at the end of the year, reported crime did not increase significantly. To keep order in town after things perked up with the return migration in late summer, a number of residents formed them-selves into a volunteer militia company, the San Francisco Guard, but most members returned to the mines in late September, and the guard company, as a body, had little influence on the events that followed.[20]

Evidently Constable Kittleman had joined the summer rush with the rest of the town government; at its first meeting on October 9, the new council resolved that the alcalde should appoint a constable to assist him with his duties. If anyone was appointed, he does not seem to have left his name in the record of the time. Perhaps it was William Landers, the man who stirred up the trouble leading to the Dornte killing in 1847. His name is mentioned as being sheriff at one point in late 1848.[21] (The titles "sheriff" and "constable" seem occasionally to have been used interchangeably at the time.) So, at the end of 1848 while San Francisco awaited the flood of 49ers, the criminal justice establishment of the town consisted of a lone alcalde with ill-defined executive and judicial powers and a single sheriff or constable to carry out his orders.

There was little for them to do in the closing months of 1848. While reports of criminal homicides were coming in from all over California, San Francisco, at the center of affairs, almost got through 1848 without any reported murders. But just as the year was about to close, the murdered body of Emile Bertrand, a recently discharged veteran of Stevenson's regiment, was found on the beach on the north side of town on Christmas day.[22]

CHAPTER 6
The Rush

THE EVENTS OF 1848 were but an insipid rehearsal for those to follow. As news of the great gold strike moved outward in ever-widening circles, it arrived first, as we have seen, at Hawaii, Mexico, Oregon, and the Pacific ports of South America, and it was from those places that the first argonauts came.

Thomas Larkin's official notice, sent east in June, arrived at Washington in September; on September 20, the *Baltimore Sun* carried a news report of the discovery that was picked up and passed along by other eastern newspapers. Easterners, like those who first heard the news in San Francisco, were at first skeptical. What better way for the administration to settle large numbers of people in the newly acquired province than by conjuring up the story of a rich gold strike? By November, however, excited New York papers were all full of the story; in December, after President Polk presented Colonel Mason's report, accompanied by solid evidence of the discovery, to Congress, a gold frenzy seized the eastern United States. The mad dash to the California goldfields was on. As the news of the gold discovery spread further still, the whole world was infected with gold fever, and ships from all major ports of the world turned their prows toward California.

Entire populations were caught up in the reckless rush to get to the precious metal. Drummed on by a hysterical press, thousands upon thousands made hurried preparations to get to the gold. Those from the inland states made their way to the fringes of eastern settlement in Missouri to wait impatiently for the spring grasses to grow and provide feed for stock on the trip across the great American "desert." Less patient overland travelers struck south either to the all-weather Santa Fe trail or to the Gila trail across Mexico. Others, particularly those from the states bordering the Atlantic seaboard, made their way to eastern port cities where they took ship on hundreds of vessels, many of them unseaworthy hulks pressed into service for one last long journey around Cape Horn to California. Still others who could afford it went by steamer to Chagres on the Atlantic side of Panama and crossed the Isthmus on foot and by Indian canoe to Panama City, where they again took ship up the Pacific coast to San Francisco.

In October 1848, before the rush from the eastern seaboard had begun, the Pacific Mail Steamship Company had sent the steamer *California*, with only six of its berths occupied, around Cape Horn to establish a west coast mail run between Panama City and the newly acquired province of California. On December 1, 1848, the steamer *Falcon* left New York on a run to Chagres with its berths half empty, for the last time for years to come. By December 28, when the *California* arrived at Callao, Peru, where the gold excitement was in full sway, company agents had sold seventy berths to Peruvians headed for the goldfields, berths that had been reserved for passengers from the eastern United States to be picked up at Panama City. By the time the *California* arrived in Panama in January, it found 1,500 gold seekers from the Atlantic states clamoring to be carried up the coast to San Francisco. Additional berths were erected on the decks of the steamer, which made its overloaded way northward to California, arriving in San Francisco on February 28, 1849, with the vanguard of 49ers from the Atlantic states. North American passengers would remember that their berths had been usurped by South Americans.

The great tide of immigration from all over the world was to swell the population of California from about 12,000 before the Gold Rush to 100,000 by the end of 1849. That year, more than 40,000 immigrants came overland; the same number came by sea, half beating their way around the Horn on slow-moving square riggers, while the rest came by the Panama route. It would be almost midsummer of 1849 before the bulk of overland eastern immigrants arrived in California, directly at the placers on the Sierra streams. At about the same time, the ships making their way around the Horn, many of which had set out six months before, began arriving in San Francisco Bay in large numbers. Of the 15,000 gold seekers who arrived in California in the first half of 1849, 10,000 entered through the port of San Francisco. Of the 10,000 who landed in San Francisco during the first half of 1849, most were from Chile, Mexico, and other Pacific ports. Many of the rest were those from the Atlantic states who had come by the Panama route. San Francisco, in the first months of 1849, before the major part of the migration from the United States arrived, had a distinctly Hispanic flavor, leavened by a sprinkling of older settlers, some of them veterans of the volunteer regiment, and arrivals from the urban centers of the Atlantic and Gulf coasts.

Of the 10,000 immigrants in the first half of 1849, 200 were women. Commenting on the disparity between the sexes in Gold Rush San Francisco, the editors of the *Annals*-reported that "a very small proportion of these [immigrants] were women . . . while the vast majority of inhabitants were adult males, in the early prime of manhood. This circumstance naturally tended to give a peculiar character to the aspect of the place and habits of the people."[1]

At the beginning of 1849, the 2,000 residents of the town looked forward to the influx of humanity that would by midyear treble the town's population and before the year's end more than treble it again. The immigration that would turn the little trading village on the cove into a hell-raising boomtown attracted speculators and sharpers from around the world, bent on making a quick pile and heading away. The signs of the new prosperity were already evident. The few storehouses were soon full, and a wide array of goods littered the beaches and the beginnings of the wharfs jutting out over the mudflats—untouched by thieves, we are assured.[2] The tents of new arrivals, too busy to erect more substantial structures, dotted the hills to the north and west of the old settlement and the sand ridges to the south. Prices were high, but pockets were full. Rents and real estate values were also high, at least until late spring, when the large departure to the mines drove them down again. Prices would rise again in the fall in the boom-and-bust topsy-turvy economy that characterized the time.[3]

In January, publisher Edward Kemble changed the cumbersome title *California Star and Californian* to the *Alta California*. George

Hubbard, another veteran of the volunteer regiment, joined Kemble and Gilbert as a co-owner and member of the editorial staff. The editorial policy of opposition to the military government would continue.

Public improvements had fallen by the wayside in 1848, because of first a lack of money and later a lack of interest. But by the spring of 1849, with the knowledge that dozens of ships were making their way around the Horn, a group of well-heeled San Franciscans put together a joint stock company that in May began the construction of a wharf (called Central Wharf, Long Wharf, and later Commercial Street Wharf) from Leidesdorff Street between Clay and Sacramento streets. By the end of the year, the wharf extended 800 feet over the mudflats.[4] Observing the financial success of Central Wharf, others began to extend the streets ending at Montgomery by building wharves parallel to it.

Politically, in the first months of 1849, San Francisco was racked with discord as factions competed for power while others, who might be expected to participate in civic affairs, looked to their own private interests. Congress still continued to balk at establishing a territorial government. The Cabinet was careful not to usurp the prerogatives of Congress openly but realized that some sort of provisional government would have to be provided for the new possession, to which a great immigration was already headed. It sent two army generals to California in place of Colonel Mason. General Persifor Smith was to take command of the Pacific Military Division and General Benet Riley was to command the subordinate California Military Department and to serve as civil governor of California.

Interest in the popular movement to establish a provisional government independent of the military continued. In the end, however, the convention contemplated by the public meetings in 1848 never took place. The constitutional convention at the end of the year that resulted in the formation of a state government was the result of a military initiative.

In San Francisco, in December 1848, the town council, whose term was set to end with the year, scheduled an election in which its successors in office would be chosen. The election was held on December 27, and the newly elected council assumed office at the beginning of 1849. But the old council, citing voting irregularities, declared the election null, refused to retire from office, and called for another election in mid-January. In that election, another council was chosen; for one day at least, until the 1848 council resigned in favor of the council elected

on January 15, the town had three councils. The *Alta*, fed up with the
political shenanigans, complained that the wrangling could go on for
months "when the town is without money, when we have no police, no
organization for preventing and extinguishing fires, no jail, no court or
courts for the proper trial and punishment of offenders. . . ."[5]

While the two remaining councils squabbled over who was in
charge, yet another civil government for San Francisco was proposed
at a public meeting attended by 500 in Portsmouth Square on February 12. The assembled group resolved that both councils should resign
and that a district government called a legislative assembly should be
formed. The legislative assembly would consist of fifteen legislative
members, presided over by a Speaker, to enact laws "not in conflict
with the constitution of the United States nor repugnant to the common
law."[6] Executive and judicial duties were to be performed by three
elected justices of the peace with separate but equal jurisdiction over
both criminal and civil matters.

After an election on February 21, which, says Bancroft, "brought to
the front a very respectable body of men filled with reform projects,"
the two councils resigned in favor of the newly established district government.[7] Alcalde Leavenworth, whose differences with the legislative
assembly form the major part of the political story of the first half of
1849, did not resign. Like Hyde before him (who, incidentally, presumably having been rehabilitated, turned up as one of the proponents
of the legislative assembly), Leavenworth would preside over a time of
political turmoil. Again charges would fly that he played fast and loose
with the award of public lands and that through his incompetence or
collusion public disorder went unchecked.

Leavenworth's first public political problem in 1849 helps to explain
his historic unpopularity and bears on one of the issues that would
rise again and again until put to rest during the activities of 1851: the
security of the town jail. The council elected in January, during its few
days in office, had appointed a committee to inspect the town jail and
report on its fitness.

Bancroft, as will be recalled, says about Hispanic California that
there were then no jails. He is not exactly correct. There had been jails
in Hispanic California—they just were not much used. The *californios*
did not look to imprisonment as a preferred punishment for crime.
Secure prisons are expensive to build and even more expensive to staff.
Instead of costly imprisonment, Hispanic Californians tended, when
possible, to use fines and sentences to public works as penalties for

crimes committed by whites and whipping for Indians.[8] There was in fact a calaboose (jail) in Mexican San Francisco. In 1839, when José Antonio Galindo was sent to San Jose's jail after being accused of killing his cousin, it was not because there was no jail in San Francisco, but because there was no one there to guard him.[9] When the Americans took over in 1846, they used a calaboose maintained by the military next to the Customhouse as the town jail.[10] At first, civil prisoners were held on a contract between the town government and the military authorities. When the two constables were appointed at the end of 1847, one of them was designated as keeper of the jail.

In 1846, military authorities had erected a blockhouse near Dupont and Clay streets to ward off a feared Mexican counterattack. Later, it was used as a jail by the civil authorities. The story is told about the jail being in such poor condition that a prisoner one morning presented himself at Alcalde Leavenworth's office with the jail door on his back when he did not receive his breakfast on time.[11] In early 1848, after a spate of escapes, both newspapers lectured town officials about the inadequacies of the jail. The *Star* complained about the "unguarded and insecure prison" in March;[12] the same month, the *Californian* pointed out that the money expended filling in the foot of Clay Street (to the commercial benefit of the merchants with property there) would have paid for the construction of a substantial jail.[13]

The committee in early 1849 soon reported back that the building was insecure from the outside and that inside it was "the most awful and filthy den, perhaps ever beheld by any human being, and consequently dangerous to the health of persons therein." The recently appointed sheriff, John C. Pulis, informed them that he had received permission to place the three prisoners held there aboard some ship. When he saw the report, an outraged Leavenworth issued a warrant for the arrest of the offending council members who had prepared it. When they were hailed before him, he excoriated them for their temerity but could not make up his mind as to whether they were under charges or not. After they walked out of his court when he could not specify any charges against them, he ordered their arrest. But when the sheriff moved to comply with the alcalde's order, a number of citizens intervened and stopped him.[14]

After General Smith arrived in late February, a committee of the legislative assembly went to him and asked for his support of their government. They told him that Mason had not much involved himself in civil affairs since the peace, that the alcalde form of government was not suitable for conditions in San Francisco, and that Leavenworth had abused his office. Smith answered that while they were no doubt well intentioned, his job was to maintain the existing government until Congress should act. He also warned them that there was no precedent for the government they proposed and that if they persisted in their plan they were inviting endless litigation. He further informed them that the civil government of the district was to remain under the alcalde.

Nonetheless, the members of the legislative assembly went about their business as they saw it. At their first meeting on March 5, they elected Francis Lippett as Speaker and appointed a committee to report out a code of laws. The assembly also appointed a committee to see to the cleaning of the town jail. Later in the month, it forbade the sale of town lots; a few days afterward, it abolished the office of alcalde and all ministerial offices established by the incumbent. Myron Norton, as the top vote getter in the election for justice of the peace, was designated to serve as police judge and chief executive of the district and to take charge of all town papers in Leavenworth's possession. Norton was also empowered by the assembly to appoint two or more police officers to carry out his orders. When Leavenworth told General Smith that the legislative assembly had abolished his office, he was told not to comply with its directions and to remain in office. When General Riley arrived in April to take over as civil governor, he was less circumspect than Smith. After listening to Leavenworth's opponents, he suspended the alcalde from office on May 6 and appointed a three-man commission to investigate charges of malfeasance.

Given the press of their private business interests, the members of the legislative assembly found it more and more difficult to achieve a quorum for their meetings. Their solution was to increase the membership of the assembly to twenty-five. At an election held on May 11 under the auspices of the legislative assembly, the citizenry approved the expansion of the assembly and elected John C. Pulis sheriff along with a number of other ministerial officers.

In the face of continuing demands by the legislative assembly that he submit the town records for examination, Leavenworth stalled, saying they were not in a condition to be audited. Finally, on May 31, Sheriff Pulis, on the instructions of Justice Myron Norton, "calling to his assistance a number of the citizens," entered the alcalde's office and forcibly seized the town records from Leavenworth.[15] The next day, probably without knowing of the seizure of the records, General Riley, who frequently waffled in his support of Leavenworth, reinstated the alcalde to office. (Presumably, the committee appointed to investigate Leavenworth had come up with nothing concrete.) When Riley found out about the seizure of the town records, he issued a proclamation on June 4, telling the citizens of San Francisco to disregard the legislative assembly.

In the meantime, having learned as a certainty on June 1 that Congress had again adjourned without establishing a territorial government for California, Riley issued a proclamation on June 3 that called for an election to be held on August 1. Delegates would be chosen from all parts of the province to convene at Monterey in September to write a constitution for a state government. In the same election, officials for municipal governments organized according to Mexican law in force at the time of the conquest were to be chosen to manage the affairs of population centers of California. Members of the legislative assembly at first denied the right of the military governor to form a government and objected to Riley's proclamation denouncing them; but, after a lightly attended plebiscite on July 9, they retired from office, leaving the governmental field in San Francisco to Alcalde Leavenworth.

While all this political conflict was taking place in San Francisco, the residents of the goldfields, whose number had swelled greatly with the continuous stream of overland arrivals, were largely left to their own governmental devices. Even so, by all accounts there was less crime in the goldfields than had occurred in 1848; at least there was less editorial comment about it. Perhaps the ad hoc methods of crime control, adopted in a governmental vacuum, were having their desired effect. In January, in a settlement called Dry Diggings (later called Hangtown, and now called Placerville), three men charged with the robbery of a Mexican gambler were promptly and summarily hanged by a tipsy gathering of citizens. There was, however, the occasional report of the murder of a miner by hostile Indians or killings in barroom frays in gold camps and river towns.

As already mentioned, there was supposedly little crime in San Francisco; according to one contemporary resident who later talked to Bancroft, there was only one case of theft before October 1849.[16] In contemporary press accounts, there was somewhat more than that. In April, $700 was taken in the "robbery" of a trunk in the City Hotel; in June, a servant stole $14,000 from his "master" and left town. There was also the report of a homicide in June in the seemingly almost crime-free town. On June 21, Belden Beattie, a discharged veteran of Stevenson's regiment, entered the tent of a Chilean shopkeeper with an acquaintance; "from some misunderstanding," a quarrel erupted. The frightened Chilean pulled a pistol, and in the struggle between the Chilean and Beattie's companion that followed, the pistol discharged, hitting Beattie. He died a day later, and a warrant was issued for the arrest of the shopkeeper and the other occupants of the tent. By the time the authorities arrived to make the arrest, however, the Chileans had fled, and "the infuriated party attending the Sheriff," the *Alta* reported, "seized the tent and its effects." [17]

CHAPTER 7

The Hounds

WHILE LEADING CITIZENS of the town pursued their private business affairs in the tumultuous economy of the burgeoning boomtown, or squabbled among themselves for control of the district government, a malignant social sore festered and grew in San Francisco during the early months of 1849. In July, the town was jolted out of its apathy by riotous disorders caused by a band of hoodlums calling themselves the Hounds. Before things settled down, the first of several popular tribunals in Gold Rush San Francisco was called into existence to put down a criminal gang.[1]

The genesis of the Hounds, at the end of 1848, seemed innocent enough. From its very beginnings as an American settlement, as has been noted, San Francisco was plagued with the problem of runaway sailors. During the Gold Rush, it became almost impossible for a captain to hold his crew. Incited by tales of fabulous wealth to be found in the Sierras, entire crews (and sometimes the captain himself) would desert from arriving ships and head for the goldfields. The steamer *California*, on arrival in San Francisco in February 1849, lost almost its entire crew; a sister ship, the *Oregon*, arriving a few months later, retained a crew only by anchoring under the guns of a warship. The *Oregon* departed hastily on the return voyage to Panama, its fuel bunkers half empty. By the end of 1849, between 3,000 and 4,000 seamen had jumped ship in San Francisco, and the anchorage in front of the town was littered with almost 400 abandoned hulks.

Toward the end of 1848, when Alcalde Leavenworth, and perhaps one constable, made up the entire criminal justice establishment in San Francisco, an association of the town's merchants contracted with a group of young men to return runaway sailors at $25 a head, in order to maintain crews on the merchant ships upon which their trade depended.[2] The task, in the face of the irresistible lure of gold, was soon seen to be hopeless. Still, the group of sailor-catchers, once formed, came to the realization that they could do for themselves what they did for others. In the absence of any authority strong enough to stop them, they set themselves up as self-appointed guardians of the public peace. To fund their law enforcement activities, they imposed an unofficial tax on those who could be persuaded to pay—they organized a protection racket. Their number was soon swelled by rowdy veterans of Stevenson's volunteer regiment, beached sailors, the first arrivals from Britain's Australian penal colonies, and boys (or b'hoys) from the fighting political wards of New York City.[3]

By most accounts, the rowdy band did not call much attention to itself in the beginning. The *Alta California* reported in August, after all hell had broken loose, that at first the Hounds had done little except engage in an occasional brawl and that "to most of the community they appeared just to parade around making fools of themselves."[4] If the only newspaper in town did not pay them much notice, there were others who did. In March 1849, Vincent Perez Rosales, a recent Chilean immigrant, reported in his diary: "There is a gang of ruffians in this city called the Hounds. They are young, vicious and shameless, and seem to have sworn a mutual pact to protect one another's lives and interests. They start fights in the cafes all the time, and if anyone rises to the provocation of these united ruffians, he is beaten up."[5] As a Chilean, perhaps Rosales had more reason to notice the Hounds than did other citizens.

As noted, the first large influx of gold seekers from outside California came from Mexico and the Pacific ports of South America; in the first months of 1849, San Francisco and the placers took on an increasingly Hispanic ethnic flavor. When overland immigrants finally began to arrive at the mines from the eastern United States in great numbers, it seemed to them that many of the best claims were already taken by people who spoke the same language as those they had just defeated in a bitter war. When the steamer *California* arrived in Panama on its maiden voyage, as we have seen, impatient Americans waiting there were outraged to find out that berths had been sold to Chileans on the way up the coast. General Persifor Smith, while passing through Panama in January 1849, learned of the enmity toward Hispanic miners and, carried away by the emotions of the moment, vowed to treat noncitizens as trespassers in California. Smith did not act on his stated intention, but the harm was done; as the tide of immigration shifted the balance of the population in favor of Americans, hostile acts against Hispanic miners multiplied. American miners drove the earlier arrivals from their claims in the northern mines; many of them made their way to San Francisco, where the Hounds awaited them.

Ordinarily, it is not the established, affluent members of a society who join gold rushes. Some of the gold seekers of 1849, from both the United States and South America, were respectable young men of good family, looking for adventure or fortune; many were not. Reporting on the first seaborne arrivals from the eastern United States, the editors of the *Annals*, who were Gold Rush arrivals themselves, said they "were largely composed of the rowdy and the knavish class. They indeed had required no long time to make preparations for the voyage. Their baggage was on their backs, and their purse in every honest man's pocket."[6] And the Chileans? "This class of foreign population was generally of the lowest and most depraved character," reported the *Annals*. "The men seemed deceivers by nature, while the women . . . were immodest and impure to a shocking degree . . . washerwomen by day; by night—and if a dollar could be earned, also by day—they were only prostitutes."[7]

Given the prevailing attitude toward Hispanic immigrants, not much notice was taken when the Hounds started bullying the residents of Chiletown. They would issue from their headquarters in a tent saloon called (with some significance) Tammany Hall, located on Kearny between Clay and Sacramento streets, and go about extorting money from Hispanic immigrants, ostensibly to pay for their self-appointed law enforcement services. If a Chilean victim did not have money or refused to give it up, they might seize his goods, tear down his tent, and auction off his possessions to the highest bidder. Respectable Americans looked the other way. Emboldened by their unchallenged bullying of the Chileans, the Hounds, in the timeless way of bullies everywhere, extended their exaction to other businesses. They took to entering restaurants and saloons in large groups, eating and drinking their fill, then departing without paying.

Conditions started getting out of hand in late June after the shooting in a Chilean tent of Belden Beattie, generally considered to have been innocently in the company of a Hound who became involved in a dispute with a Chilean storekeeper.[8] By the time of Beattie's funeral in late June, measures were being taken to give the Hounds a more formal organization and respectable image; on Friday, July 13, the leaders of the Hounds met in the old schoolhouse on Portsmouth Square and drew up a constitution for a mutual aid society to be called the Regulators.[9]

Two days later, things fell apart. Sunday was the one day of official rest in Gold Rush California, both in the mines and in San Francisco. It was a day to repair one's gear, to rest, or to write letters home. For some, it was a day to heal from the revels of the night before with the hair of the dog. Sunday, July 15, 1849, dawned unseasonably warm for summertime San Francisco. Sam Roberts, boatman, sometimes pimp, and field commander of the Hounds, went with some of his friends on a Sunday outing to Contra Costa. When they returned half drunk to San Francisco in the early afternoon, Roberts went to see his Chilean woman at the Washington House opposite Portsmouth Square. (For all their announced loathing of things Chilean, the Hounds did not refrain from sexual congress with fairer members of the group.) There he found that she had taken in some custom on her own account, a German veteran of the volunteer regiment. Roberts took the man outside and beat him savagely. He then went to the Tammany Hall saloon, where he drunkenly tried to incite the denizens to attack Chiletown.

By nightfall, the idea had caught on—drunken American revelers were attacking Chilean tents wherever they found them. Roberts, with twenty other Americans, moved his headquarters to a Chilean drinking tent at Broadway and Battery streets. The Hounds ran off the Chilean customers, breaking bottles and shooting up the place. They then spread out riotously over the slopes of Telegraph Hill, smashing boats, looting Chilean tents, and raping Chilean women. Prudent Americans took to their beds. When the rioters approached the tent of Domingo Algeria, he fought back. The Hounds fired into his tent, hitting his son Ignacio in the hand and his son Rinaldo in the abdomen. Rinaldo died of his wounds a few days later.

The Hounds attack the Chilean settlement on Telegraph Hill. (*California State Library*)

The next morning was also uncommonly warm; as the Hounds, sated by their night of pillage, retired to their dens to sleep off the night of excess, other citizens crept from their tents and rooms to survey the wreckage of the night of terror. Their timidity of the night before turned to seething anger as they saw in broad daylight the results of the riot. Grumbling, they gathered in small knots and asked themselves what they could do. Sam Brannan, just about always around when excitement promised, seized the moment and mounted a barrel at Clay and Montgomery streets to address the crowd. The meeting soon grew too large for the intersection and moved to Portsmouth Square. Brannan continued his address from the roof of the alcalde's office on Clay Street. A collection was raised for the relief of the Chilean victims of the riot. When a motion was made to form a citizens' police to arrest the Hounds, 230 citizens volunteered and were promptly enrolled into nine police companies that stood guard at a meeting later that day, while officials were selected to assist the alcalde in conducting the trial of the rowdies.

Sensing the mood of the crowd, the Hounds began slipping out of town. But the citizen police fanned out; by sundown, seventeen prominent Hounds had been rounded up, examined, and placed under guard on the ship of war *Warren*. Sam Roberts was caught stowed away on the steamer to Stockton; another leading Hound was found hiding at the Mission. On Tuesday, a hastily convened grand jury returned indictments against Roberts and nineteen others for conspiracy to rape, rob, and murder, plus a variety of other charges connected with the riot. (Rinaldo Algeria had not yet died of his wounds.) On Thursday, the trial began in the schoolhouse on Portsmouth Square, presided over by Alcalde Leavenworth and two other magistrates chosen at the public meeting on Monday. Francis G. Lippett and two others served as prosecutors, and Myron Norton appeared for the accused. Over the next several days, testimony was taken about the actions of the Hounds on the night of the riot and prior occasions.[10]

By Monday, the verdict was in. Roberts and eight others were found guilty as charged; but once they were convicted, nobody seems to have known what to do with them. There was some talk of hanging, but that did not go far. There simply was no adequate jail in San Francisco—or, for that matter, anywhere in California—to hold the likes of the Hounds, so the ball was thrown to the prospective territorial governor; Roberts was sentenced to a ten-year term of imprisonment "in some penitentiary, wherever the territorial governor of California should direct."[11] The others were sentenced to lesser terms and fines. In the end, though, not much was done to the Hounds. Roberts's sentence was changed to banishment from California under pain of death should he return. Others were also exiled, some were discharged, and some seem to have been accepted to fill vacancies in the Pacific fleet.[12]

CHAPTER 8

The Unseen Hand

GEORGE HYDE, AS WE HAVE SEEN, was a victim of the politics of crime in early San Francisco. So was Thaddeus Leavenworth. The verdict of history, passed down for almost a century and a half, is that Alcalde Leavenworth was in league with the criminal band of bullies that afflicted San Francisco in the early months of 1849. Bancroft believed "there is little doubt that many of the acts [of the Hounds] were countenanced by Alcalde Leavenworth,"[1] and Eldredge notes that "Leavenworth was openly charged with being in sympathy with the Regulators."[2] More recently, James D. Hart has stated that Leavenworth resigned from office after an investigation of his sympathy with the Hounds.[3]

In account after account, the Hounds are depicted as a free-ranging gang of bullies, ignored by the better sort and encouraged by Alcalde Leavenworth in their criminal depredations. That is where the matter has rested for almost a century and a half. On closer examination, however, it seems that Leavenworth might well be carrying an unwarranted burden of guilt, more properly placed at the feet of others. If one takes a closer than usual look at the events of 1849, a different sort of picture than that portrayed in standard accounts of the time begins to emerge.[4] Francis Lippett, one of the prosecutors in the trial of the Hounds, ran up a warning flag in his opening remarks to the court. Watch out, he told them, for those who offered alibis for the accused and for the "treason," he charged, "on the part of influential men in the community who lean to the side of the prisoners and throw obstacles in the way of justice."[5]

There is a curious passage in the *Annals of San Francisco*, published at a time when the principal actors in the Hound's disorders were still very much present in San Francisco, that has gone unexplained in all the accounts since that troubled summer:

> At that period there happened to be influential parties in San Francisco . . . who considered that a gentle course of public disturbances . . . could be employed to facilitate the objects they had in view. . . . These persons . . . were known to have had secret intimacies . . . with certain leaders of the "Hounds" who undertook to promote the purposes of the former while at the same time they served their own. But the monster . . . soon outgrew the power of its protectors to keep it in bounds. . . . Fearful of committing themselves by owning a former connection . . . with such a vile association, some of the richest and most influential people in town calmly heard of all the abuses committed by their *proteges* but took no steps to quell them. It would be imprudent at this time to mention names, but the fact is so nevertheless.[6]

Thaddeus Leavenworth seems to have been a thoroughly unlikable man, unfit for the office he held, for reasons having little to do with the Hounds. He was high-handed in his treatment of the councilmen who reported unfavorably on the conditions of his jail and, in the words of the commanding officer of the Pacific Naval Squadron, "he was so unpopular he couldn't give satisfaction in anything."[7] His method of granting or selling town lots is also open to criticism, though, as with Hyde before him, some of the complaints on that score must be discounted as the rantings of his political enemies. But all of that does not make him a Hound or even sympathetic to them. Leavenworth came to California with Stevenson's volunteer regiment. He later practiced medicine in San Francisco and served, as mentioned earlier, as assistant alcalde under Hyde and Townsend. In late 1848, he was elected alcalde in his own right. His principal political opponents in 1849 were the members of the legislative assembly, that "very respectable body of men filled with reform projects."[8]

There is evidence that does seem to tie Leavenworth to the Hounds. For example, it was brought out at their trial that once, when the constable was not available, Leavenworth used Sam Roberts and some of his Houndish friends to flog a sailor convicted of pulling a knife on his captain. Former constable Thomas Kittleman testified at the trial of the Hounds that when he reported to Leavenworth having seen the Hounds robbing a Chilean tent in broad daylight early in July, the alcalde informed him that he knew all about the matter and that the culprits would be brought to justice.[9] Leavenworth does not seem to have taken any action on Kittleman's complaint—not the only time he avoided a confrontation with the bullies.

One of the charges against the Hounds brought out at their trial was that several of them had repeatedly threatened a Chilean merchant, Pedro Cueto, regarding a $500 claim that an American held against him. On three occasions, Cueto complained to Alcalde Leavenworth, who later testified that he "thought seriously about it." But when he finally went to the scene, the alcalde neglected to identify the men harassing Cueto, informing them instead that if they had a claim against anyone they should bring it to him. He told Cueto to come to his office to fill out an affidavit.[10]

On several occasions over a period of months, after eating their fill in the U.S. restaurant, a large body of Hounds walked out without paying, instructing the proprietor to bill the alcalde for their meal. On July 15, when Roberts and his men set up their headquarters in the Chilean drinking tent at the foot of Broadway Street prior to invading Telegraph Hill, they informed the proprietor that they were acting on the instructions of the alcalde to tear down Chilean tents.[11]

This is damaging evidence that on its face seems to lend support to the allegations made against the alcalde. Viewed another way, however, and with some facts added that do not turn up in the standard accounts of the time, an entirely different interpretation emerges.

In March 1849, before the depredations of the Hounds had achieved their full scope, Vincent Perez Rosales committed an unflattering word picture of Leavenworth to his diary:

> The supreme authority in San Francisco is not an alcalde as many say he is. He is only a Yankee, more or less drunk, whom they call alcalde. . . . A short time ago there was a trial between the two of the first named [Yankees]. The courtroom was full, and as both the litigants were Yankees the judge tried to reconcile them as best he could. But the weight of the evidence was so much against one of them

that there was nothing for the alcalde to do but sentence him to twenty-five lashes, for that was the minimum sentence possible in such cases. There was an immediate murmur of disapproval in the courtroom. The alcalde thought he was a lost man because he had passed such a light sentence for such serious misdeed, but while he was getting ready to admit his error and increase the dose, one of the spectators asked to be heard. "Citizens," he says, "since this alcalde is so free with punishments he passes out, I propose that the fifty strongest men here drive the alcalde three miles out of town, kicking his behind all the way." "Hooray," shouted the crowd. The alcalde, not knowing what was happening to him, left his seat and, quicker than a run, dived out the window, followed by general booing and laughter. The culprit was then let go.[12]

According to another contemporary observer, John H. Brown, keeper of the City Hotel and Leavenworth's landlord, "one evening the party with fife and drum [the Hounds] went to Leavensworth's [sic] office with a rope with the full intention of hanging him, if they could get hold of him." Brown said that he hid the alcalde in the hotel, then diverted the mob by standing them drinks at the hotel bar, for which he later billed Leavenworth.[13]

Leavenworth was not a Hound and he was not in sympathy with their cause. Indeed, he was terrified of them. Charging restaurant bills to his account and claiming his authority to tear down Chilean tents were not the acts of accomplices. They were gestures of contempt. His behavior when forced into situations in which he had to deal with the rowdy band was evasion, apprehension, and fear of confrontation. When, according to Brown, "Mexicans" reported to Leavenworth about their treatment at the hands of the Hounds, "he [Leavenworth] did all he could by talking to them, to stop such proceedings, and would have punished them, if he could have the support of the city; but he found they were too many and too strong to undertake it alone."[14] It is evident that by himself Leavenworth was not up to the task of controlling the town. Probably no one in his circumstances could have done so, particularly if, as the Annals said, they were supported by the "richest and most influential people in town." Who were these rich and influential men who supported "a gentle course of public disturbances"? There are historical references to Leavenworth's supporters as speculators and land monopolists, but one must look long and hard to find their names in the usual accounts of the time.

For some unexplained reason, Sam Brannan, always in the forefront of public turmoils, seems to have been uncharacteristically absent from any involvement in public affairs in the first half of 1849, at least until he mounted the barrel to denounce the Hounds in July. Brannan was prominently arrayed with those opposing Hyde in 1847 and 1848. While it is true that he also had extensive business interests in Sacramento and the mining regions by 1849, he seems to have been in San Francisco too. He was a member of the financial combination that erected the lucrative Central Wharf in the spring of that year. Interestingly, some of the same men (Edward Harrison and William D. M. Howard) who opposed Hyde with Brannan can also be found among the builders of Central Wharf and among the group of merchants who hired the sailor-catchers, later the Hounds. The same names appear prominently in public affairs preceding and following the operations of the Hounds. Yet while the Hounds were active, these men seem to have been strangely absent from the scene. There is room for suspicion that Brannan and his business colleagues were among the prominent men involved behind the scenes, supporting the criminal gang.

If there is reason to suspect Brannan and his friends, there is outright proof that other prominent citizens, political enemies of Leavenworth, were very much connected with the gang of bullies. Members of Stevenson's volunteer regiment, already present when gold was discovered, inevitably assumed a disproportionately prominent role in the affairs of San Francisco in the first years of the Gold Rush, on all sides of the law. Leavenworth himself, of course, was a member of the regiment. So were the members of his political opposition. Francis Lippett (formerly commanding officer of Company F) was Speaker of the legislative assembly. Myron Norton (a lieutenant assigned to Company C) was the police court judge, and Theron Per Lee (a lieutenant in Companies K and C) was one of his associate justices.[15] The senior editor of the *Alta* was Edward Gilbert, a former lieutenant of Company H who had commanded the town garrison in 1847. He was also designated as the official printer of the legislative assembly.[16] During the early months of 1849, when the Hounds were building up a head of steam, George C. Hubbard (a lieutenant in Company K) was his co-editor. In May, Hubbard sold his interest in the paper to Theron Per Lee.[17]

In the election called by the legislative assembly in May 1849 to increase its membership, Cornelius R. V. Lee (a lieutenant in Company F until he was dishonorably discharged for desertion) was chosen as a legislative member of the assembly. John C. Pulis (a sergeant in Company F), who had served Leavenworth earlier in the year as sheriff, was elected to the same office for the legislative assembly. John A.

Patterson (Company D) was also chosen at the May election as a legislative member of the assembly.[18] Not all veterans of the regiment had such seemingly respectable associations. Deserters from the regiment were among those who murdered the family of settlers at San Miguel in 1848, and some joined other gangs of bandits pillaging remote regions of California. Sam Roberts, the acknowledged field commander of the Hounds, was also a veteran of the regiment (Company E), as were many of those who followed him to Chiletown.

In the turmoils that beset San Francisco in 1849, there were many points—too many to be coincidental—where there was a connection between members of the legislative assembly and the Hounds, many of whom were also former members of the volunteer regiment. That is not to say that the overlap is complete—it was Francis Lippett, after all, Speaker of the assembly and former officer of the regiment, who warned the court to be wary of influential men who would try to obstruct justice. But the trail of evidence between the assembly and the Hounds, largely ignored for more than a century, is there to see.

When the Hounds tried to invest themselves with a semblance of respectability by renaming themselves Regulators just before everything blew up in mid-July, Cornelius R. V. Lee, former officer of the regiment and member of the legislative assembly, was elected president of the reorganized and renamed band of hoodlums.[19] And former constable Kittleman named the Lees, "brothers short and tall," as prominent among the group of men he saw tearing down Chilean tents.[20] Philip A. Higgins, a self-confessed Hound, testified for the prosecution at their trial and swore that he counted "Long and Shorty Lee" among those he would call upon, were he in trouble.

Alcalde Leavenworth testified at the trial of the Hounds, without contradiction, that on the night of July 16, after the leaders of the Hounds had supposedly been rounded up and placed aboard the *Warren*, he was approached by Cornelius R. V. Lee, who showed him a copy of the Regulators' constitution and asked to have his brother released from the ship.[21] It is more than clear that at least one member of the legislative assembly, Cornelius R. V. Lee, had more than a passing acquaintance with the criminal gang.

Sheriff John C. Pulis is another member of the legislative assembly government who turns up under curious circumstances. George Frank, the American who held the claim against Pedro Cueto, testified at the trial of the Hounds that he went to Myron Norton, police court judge in the legislative assembly government, to pay a license fee at the urging of Sheriff Pulis. While there, Frank asked Norton to see to his claim against Cueto, but Norton stalled him. So, according to Frank, he gave the claim to Sheriff Pulis for collection; when he informed a friend of this, the friend remarked, "What have you done? You have given it to the boys." Frank replied that he had given it to the sheriff. Pulis testified that it was Frank's idea that he turn the claim over to the "boys" and that he turned the matter over to "Laforte."[22] George Lefort of Company E, aka Jimmy Twitcher, was one of those named by self-confessed Hound Philip Higgins that he would call upon if he were in trouble. In any case, it was Hound Sam Roberts who showed up to collect the bill. When Alcalde Leavenworth finally acceded to Cueto's request for assistance, he asked Sheriff Pulis to go along with him to the Chilean's tent. When the alcalde went inside to talk to the men who had been harassing Cueto, the sheriff, oddly enough, chose to remain outside. Leavenworth testified at the trial of the Hounds that he had not arrested the men because he did not want to interfere with the jurisdiction of Judge Norton.

It was Sheriff Pulis, remember, who on the orders of Myron Norton went to the alcalde's office on the last day of May, before the Hounds had as yet received any notice in the press, to seize the town records from Leavenworth; even as the sheriff and his "party of citizens" were forcing their way into his office, Leavenworth hastily scrawled one last hurried entry into the town records: "Here the Hounds entered the Alcalde's office and seized the records."[23] (Written entries in business records made in a timely way are considered in law to be among the best forms of evidence; this entry shows how Leavenworth viewed his relationship with the Hounds.) At the same meeting at which Cornelius Lee was elected president of the Regulators, Pulis was chosen steward, and John A. Patterson was named treasurer.

Despite all the excitement in the first months of 1849, no hint can be found in the editions of the *Alta* for that period that any group such as the Hounds even existed. It was not until conditions had degenerated into general riot and reprisal that there is any inkling in the *Alta* that anything might have been wrong. In its August 2 edition, the *Alta* had to backtrack. The Hounds had existed since February, the paper belatedly reported, but until recently nobody knew what they were doing. They engaged in occasional street fights and brawls, but little notice was taken of them. To most of the community, it appeared that they just paraded around making fools of themselves. Later revelations showed that the depredations of the Hounds were generally well known even before the riot on July 15. Vincent Perez Rosales commented about the Hounds by name in his diary in February.[24] Former constable Kittleman testified that he watched the Hounds for more than two hours tearing down the tent of a Chilean and auctioning off the goods not two blocks from the *Alta*'s office. Yet nothing of all this appeared in any of the editions of the *Alta* before the riot of July 15.

There was one incident reported in the paper, though not identified as such, that very much involved the Hounds. In describing the shooting of Belden Beattic in its June 28 edition, the paper, as we have seen, characterized him as nothing more than an innocent bystander who was shot while a companion was having some sort of a "misunderstanding" with a Chilean shopkeeper. The next day, according to the paper, it was "an infuriated party attending the Sheriff" that seized the Chilean's tent and effects. On the occasion of Beattie's funeral, the *Alta* gushed that "the grave closed over all that remained of the faithful soldier, and the honest, the inoffensive and upright citizen. The uniform good conduct and quiet demeanor of poor Beatty [*sic*] had won for him the confidence and esteem of all his acquaintances."[25] Even after making allowances for the florid style of nineteenth-century funeral notices and the rule that it is always best to speak well of the dead, the *Alta* went too far. Beattie was in fact a Hound, and for some reason the paper failed to report on it. The writers of the *Annals of San Francisco* evidently were hoodwinked by the *Alta*'s account and claims of Beattie's innocence have been passed down over the years.[26] But he was a Hound alright.

It was at Beattie's funeral that Philip Higgins was informed that he would be accepted into the Regulators; in reporting on Beattie's shooting in August, after everything had blown up, the group that had been the "infuriated party attending the Sheriff" in the June edition was transformed by the *Alta* into a group of "Hounds," who, "outraged that anyone would fight back, assembled and sold the goods of the one who shot Beatty [*sic*] to the highest bidder." In his opening remarks as the defense attorney at the trial of the Hounds, Myron Norton appealed in racist code to the sentiments of the court, characterizing Beattie as "a companion of the men against whom there existed so much excitement."[27] Beattie was in the company of a Hound when he was shot, he was avenged by the Hounds, and it was at his funeral that the Hounds assembled to reorganize themselves into the Regulators.

Beattie was a Hound, and the editors of the *Alta* had every reason to know it. Why did the *Alta* fail to report about the Hounds before things got completely out of hand? The answer to that one is that senior editor Edward Gilbert was the official printer and close colleague of members of the legislative assembly, some of whose members were in fact in league with the criminal Hounds. Gilbert's co-editor was Theron Per Lee, judge in the assembly government. The fingerprints of members of the legislative assembly are all over the disorderly events of the time. Cornelius R. V. Lee, assembly member, clearly was a member of the Hounds, as was Sheriff Pulis, who took his orders from Judge Norton. Norton's selection as the court-appointed defense attorney for the Hounds at their trial begins to make some sense. Who better to keep them in line if they started talking about some of their betters to get themselves off the hook?

The result was that the lower-ranked members of the band were prosecuted while their leaders went scot-free. Pulis was not prosecuted, though it must have been evident at the time that he was a Hound. Neither were the Lee brothers, though one of them was actually arrested in the July 16 roundup of Hounds. Both Lees were in town at the time of the trial. Somebody was pulling strings to release Lee and it was not Leavenworth—we know of the attempt only from his account, and he would hardly have testified against his own interest. The mild sentences also begin to make sense. Nobody seems to have been punished with much severity. There were no adequate jails in San Francisco or anywhere in California, to be sure, to hold such a bunch, but residents of the mining regions had worked that problem out under even worse conditions. For a lot less than the Hounds were convicted of, criminals in the goldfields had had their ears cropped or been branded, exiled, and even hanged. In the end, the worst that happened to the Hounds was that they were ordered to leave town, but even the banishment order does not appear to have had teeth in it.[28]

Part of the kid-glove treatment of the Hounds, from beginning to end, can be explained, no doubt, by the fact that their principal victims were Hispanic. With the prevailing feelings toward Hispanic immigrants at the time, perhaps little more can be expected; but whatever the underlying reason, it was members of the legislative assembly, for certain, and perhaps other "influential parties," unnamed though they may have been, who created and nurtured the criminal gang. Yet it is at the feet of Leavenworth, as with Hyde before him, that responsibility for the criminal disorders of the time is laid.

There is a lesson in all this for students of vigilante justice. It is the victors who write the history; in the first years of American San Francisco, it was the press that provided the rough draft of that history. Like Hyde before him, Leavenworth lined up on the political side opposed to the faction supported by the establishment press. Not surprisingly, both were castigated by the leading newspaper of the day, so the distorted picture that comes down to us holds them responsible for the criminal disorders. It is the winners who have their way, and Leavenworth was not one of history's winners.

CHAPTER 9

A Real Police

THE POLITICAL DRAMA in San Francisco in 1849 was played out in front of a rapidly growing audience of newcomers. In all, 42,000 immigrants came overland to California in 1849 and a like number came by sea, most landing in San Francisco. By fall, the permanent population of the town had risen to 8,000, with a floating population of thousands more, as hordes of argonauts made their way to and from the mines (and, for some of the lucky ones, back to the "states").

Bayard Taylor, arriving in late August, found the harbor "crowded with the shipping of the world." Onshore, he said, "the town's planted and seems scarcely to have taken root, for tents, canvas, plank and adobe houses are mingled together without the least apparent attempt at order and durability."[1] The center of the town, says Bancroft, was "a straggling medley of low dingy adobes of a bygone day and frail wooden shanties born of an afternoon," extending from Broadway to Bush streets, and eastward from Montgomery Street on piles and wharves out over the mudflats to the deep-water channel.[2] The growing wharves had already begun to enclose the beached hulks and the barges pulled up to unload on the bank on the east side of Montgomery Street. Beyond the center of town, tent cities straggled toward North Beach between the cleft of Telegraph Hill and Russian Hill, and around the cove to Happy Valley and Rincon Point. The streets were filled with people, according to Taylor, "hurrying to and fro, and of as diverse and bizarre a character as the houses: Yankees of every possible variety, native Californians in sarapes [sic] and sombreros, Chileans, Sonorians, Kanakas, from Hawaii, Chinese with long tails, Malays armed with their everlasting creeses and others in whose embrowned and bearded visage it was impossible to recognize an especial nationality."[3]

Against this backdrop, Riley's promised election was held on August 1. In San Francisco, in a "spirited but orderly election," Horace Hawes was elected prefect for the district and Joseph Curtis and Francisco Guerrero were chosen as subprefects.[4] To govern the town itself, John Geary was elected alcalde to preside over the twelve-member *ayuntamiento*, which included the ubiquitous Sam Brannan. Riley also appointed Geary as judge of the first instance with original jurisdiction for both civil and criminal matters in the San Francisco district.

The now-dominant Americans could understand mayors (alcaldes) and councils (*ayuntamientos*), but the idea of prefects and subprefects was alien to their concept of governmental organization. So, though nominally the senior official in the district by Mexican law (charged with organizing the police and maintaining law and order), Prefect Hawes was relegated to the background by the Americans; John Geary, at the head of the *ayuntamiento*, emerged as the leading political figure in San Francisco in the latter part of 1849. A native of Westmoreland County, Pennsylvania, Geary had arrived in San Francisco in April with an appointment as postmaster for his service during the Mexican War. When the national administration changed soon afterward, Geary lost his job. He then entered into the auction and commission business and somehow managed to get his name on all eleven tickets for the August election. He was elected alcalde by a unanimous vote.

The Hounds riot was fresh in mind at the time of the election and the establishment of an adequate police department was one of the first priorities of the new government. "You have neither an office for your magistrate nor any public edifice," Alcalde Geary reminded the *ayuntamiento* in his inaugural address. "You are without a single police officer or watchman and have not the means of confining a prisoner for an hour. . . ."[5] San Francisco had never yet had a true police department. Two constables were appointed in 1847, it will be recalled, only to be replaced by one shortly afterward. There are several references, probably incorrect, to the existence of six police officers in San Francisco at the time the Hounds erupted,[6] but any efforts at establishing some kind of a law enforcement presence in San Francisco prior to 1849 did not result in the sort of municipal police department that modern urban dwellers would recognize.

Commentators on the social turmoil that afflicted Gold Rush San Francisco most often consider the town's problems as part of the search for order in frontier America—as an urban dimension of the westward expansion. There is some support for that view, but San Francisco can also trace part of its Gold Rush problems to a more fundamental movement in American society. As nineteenth-century America moved west, it also moved to the city. In 1790, there were only six American cities with populations in excess of 8,000; and at the beginning of the nineteenth century, no more than 250,000 Americans (5%) were urban dwellers. The United States was a rural, agricultural country and its law enforcement institutions reflected that fact. Much of the turbulence in Gold Rush San Francisco as well as in other large American cities in the mid-nineteenth century was due to the inability of urban dwellers to understand the great social changes taking place and to do what was necessary to adapt to those changes.[7]

Human settlements in preindustrial America, although the western movement was already well under way, tended to be small, stable, and ethnically homogeneous. People looked to their own resources and to their neighbors and friends when in need of help. It was not an age when the public expected government to solve its problems or resolve its conflicts. It was a time of self-help, when a man was expected, as has been noted, to "kill his own snakes." The criminal justice system, such as it was, depended on direct public participation in duties now considered the task of publicly paid officials. The idea was not far different from Bancroft's ideal of pastoral California, in which "conscience and public opinion were law and justice held an evenly balanced scale."[8] When a crime did in fact occur, the victim was expected to take a large part in seeing that justice was done (whereas today an anonymous call to the authorities passes for the exercise of one's public duty regarding crime).

There were law enforcement officers, of course: constables, such as those appointed in San Francisco in 1847, assigned to magistrates' courts. They were few in number and supported by fees paid directly for their services. A crime victim was expected to appear personally before a magistrate to obtain a warrant for the arrest of an offender. Then, with fee in hand, the victim would call upon a constable to "execute warrants already sworn."[9] Preserving the peace and enforcing the law were not viewed as the exclusive preserve of public officials; it was the public duty of all able-bodied citizens to pitch in. The general belief in self-help was even more pronounced on the frontier. As westering pioneers moved out of the settled regions, they also moved away from established institutions of government and criminal justice. It was not the timid or those inclined to depend on others who headed west. It was said that "no coward ever set out for California, and no weakling ever made it." Able to depend only on their own resourcefulness for survival in the wilderness, immigrants came to consider official intervention in their affairs as meddling.

As some Americans moved west to make a new life, others moved from the farm to the city to work the looms of the industrial revolution or to find jobs in expanding commercial centers. This internal migration was joined in the middle decades of the century by a massive immigration from Europe, fueled by refugees from Ireland's potato famine and continental revolutions of the late 1840s. The population of New York City, 130,000 in 1820, rose to almost a million by 1860. At the century's end, 26 million Americans (35% of the population) lived in cities. The massive influx of humankind into nineteenth-century American cities was attended by major social dislocations (imitating the earlier disruptions that accompanied the movement in England from farm to city of the commercial and industrial revolutions). Institutions designed for simpler times broke down. Social services, provided informally and without thought in rural and small-town America, were absent in the rapidly growing urban centers. In the end, the development of such institutions as sewer systems, garbage collection service, health insurance, labor unions, and orphan asylums would do much to make up for the loss of the natural supports of the extended family found in rural and small-town America. But for a long time—as Americans puzzled over what was happening in their cities—urban dwellers were afflicted with problems on a scale previously unknown to them.

The story of major eastern American cities in the middle decade of the nineteenth century is one of crime, pollution, and social disorder. As cities grew in size and urban cores became increasingly unlivable, early forms of public transportation (the omnibus) permitted members of the middle-class and upper-class native Protestant stock to move away from increasingly polluted city centers to the suburbs.[10] Into the vacuum came new urban immigrants, often Irish Catholic or freed black slaves. There they came in conflict in the newly congested city centers with lower-class native-born Protestant Americans who had not moved to the suburbs.

Nativist gangs, objecting to the presence of the new immigrants, rioted against the interlopers. Between 1829 and 1849, there were five major antiblack riots in Philadelphia.[11] In an anti-Irish riot in the City of Brotherly Love in 1844, nativist mobs burned down three churches in an outburst that killed thirteen people and injured fifty more.[12] The newcomers responded in kind; one upshot of the conflict was that crime and public disorders increased.[13] According to one set of figures, assaults against police officers increased 400% in Boston in the first years following the influx of large numbers of Irish immigrants.[14] It must have seemed, as it did in the 1960s, that the cities were falling apart.[15]

In view of what was happening in eastern cities, the Hounds in San Francisco were not a unique reaction to Gold Rush conditions, but a quite familiar response to the clash of cultures in a nineteenth-century urban setting. In August 1849, one month after the Hounds eruption in San Francisco, an antiblack Irish mob routed the police in Philadelphia. Institutions of social control in eastern cities, as in San Francisco —devised in earlier, easier times—were not up to the task of maintaining order in the social cauldrons the cities had become. The few constables did the best they could; but, overwhelmingly outnumbered, their best often amounted to staying out of the way of rampaging mobs. At one riot in Boston in 1825, violence continued unchecked for a week until the mayor took personal charge and put it down.[16] Very often riots ran on until the participants simply grew tired and stopped on their own.

Public ideas about self-help did not change quickly (in some quarters they still have not), but it was finally realized that there had to be some institutional accommodation to the violent circumstances. New forms of police organization were eventually developed to address the problems of crime and mob violence in American cities (modeled on those devised for the same purpose in England a decade or so before).[17] It was in the middle decades of the nineteenth century in the cities of the eastern United States that municipal police departments that would be recognizable to modern Americans were organized for the first time.[18] The new departments were much larger than their predecessors and featured military organization, with hierarchical rank structures, the better to bring a concentration of force against urban mobs. Fees for services performed could no longer be expected to fund such large forces, so the new police were supported as regularly paid municipal employees. Fittingly, it was in Philadelphia, the scene of frequent and bloody riots, that the first day-and-night police force was established.[19] Other cities followed suit; in 1845, New York City established the model for future urban police departments by consolidating a potpourri of existing police groups into a single day-and-night force, under the supervision of a single superintendent.[20]

In addition to suppressing riots and disorders, the new departments were intended actively to "prevent" crime instead of merely reacting to it, as had the constables preceding them, who made arrests only after a crime had been committed. As with other innovations, the idea of placing the police on fixed beats around the clock to prevent crime by providing a universal police presence to stop criminals before they could even get started was also adapted from English models.[21]

Such a department, thirty officers strong, under a single chief aided by an assistant chief and three sergeants, was organized in San Francisco in 1849. Malachi Fallon, a native of Ireland raised in New York City, was named the first chief of police. A former New York saloon manager and keeper of the Tombs prison, Fallon ascribed his selection as chief of the San Francisco Police Department to his "former connection with police matters."[22] (Officers were paid $6 a day, compared to carpenters and other workers, who received from $15 to $20, or to the "rougher kinds of labors," who got $8 a day.)

The ideal of a society free of crime through absolute prevention was not to be achieved in England, eastern cities of the United States, or San Francisco; but, for a time, it was thought to be attainable. The expectation that police should eliminate all predatory crime was to be voiced in the press, as we shall see, in the troubled times to come.

One popular belief about crime, later advanced by many who lived through the period, was that there really was not much criminal predation in California even after the Gold Rush had begun until after the establishment of the institutions of justice and law—the implication being that the coming of the law is what brought crime. "If contemporary evidence can be trusted," writes one commentator, "criminal conduct was comparatively rare in the mines in 1849. In the following years, when formal local governments had been established offenses were much more common": "the Forty-niner was wont to maintain,

Malachi Fallon, San Francisco's first chief of police. (*San Francisco Police Department Photo Lab*)

and probably to believe, that the coming of lawyers and law courts was responsible for the change."[23] In fact, while there was less crime in some locales in the early months of the Gold Rush, the inference that conditions were better without established law can be attributed to nostalgia. The anecdotal record of the time is mixed. According to Mary Williams, "We read, as it were in parallel columns, of bags of gold dust that lay safe in unguarded tents, and of merchandise piled high in open streets; then of robbery and murder that went unnoticed in a community where a man might drop from sight without causing a ripple of comment among his self-absorbed neighbors."[24]

There is anecdotal evidence to support a number of conclusions about the amount of crime in late 1849, depending on which of several subthemes is being advanced. One belief is that California was a crime-free paradise before the arrival of bad men in 1850. William T. Coleman, who went on to take a leading role in the later affairs of the committees of vigilance, reported that, on his arrival in Sacramento in 1849, he wondered at the piles of unprotected goods outside tents and stores. "I asked if they were left out at night and were safe. The answers were all affirmative. The doors of houses had no locks, or they were unused; the tents had no fastenings, yet there were no losses of property, as every trespasser knew that in theft he would hazard his life." Coleman attributed the crime-free state to a few summary executions of criminals throughout California. "This condition of affairs," he goes on, "continued through the winter of 1849 and the spring and early summer of 1850. . . ."[25] According to Bancroft, "As vessels arrived [in San Francisco] in greater numbers, great quantities of merchandise was discharged and piled along the beach. . . . Much of the merchandise was valuable, and all of it wholly exposed. Yet all this time there was scarcely a lock on the door of any dwelling, store or warehouse in the town of San Francisco."[26] Bancroft was assured by a resident of the time, he says, that there was but one case of theft in San Francisco before October 1849; another old resident recalled a safe containing $25,000 left unmolested outside an office on Clay Street.

Yet there is also the theme of the wild and wooly boomtown. "Fights are not unusual in gambling halls," reported Bayard Taylor, "and more than one pistol shot was heard at night."[27] Writing to her family back east from San Francisco on November 30, 1849, Mary Jane Megquier interrupted her correspondence to write, "it is now past midnight, I can hear guns firing, music, some calling for help. I think by the sound they are having a drunken row, but it is so common it is of no account."[28]

In some locales, community self-restraint or popular justice seems to have kept a lid on crime. In others, people feared to leave their dwellings. In general, public opprobrium was reserved for property crimes. Consistent with the frontier view of things, a man was expected more or less to look out for his own personal safety, and little comment was raised about violent conflicts, even those leading to injury and death. A man could carry a weapon to protect himself, but there was no secure way to protect his property. There were no banks or safes in the mining regions, so it was necessary to leave gold unguarded in an open tent while panning for more. Where the property of one is unsafe, that of all is threatened. Most instances of popular justice in the mines were therefore punishment for crimes of theft.

Crimes of all sorts probably did increase in the latter months of 1849, accompanying the great population increase in the last half of the year. And when the heavy rains of the winter of 1849–50 came early, roads to the mines became mired in mud, cutting off shipments of supplies from the coast. Some miners, unable to work the streams, headed for the cities as they had the year before. Many of those who remained had little or no income. The theft of scarce supplies was one way to survive. Similar conditions prevailed in San Francisco. Peter Burnett, soon to be the first elected governor of California, said that when he left in late summer to attend the constitutional convention in Monterey, he knew almost everyone. When he returned a few months later, he recognized almost no one. Miners, driven from the placers by winter rains, swelled the town's population to 20,000 by year's end. The lucky ones caroused through the winter. The unlucky looked for nonexistent work or sat in their dark, damp tents waiting for the rains to end.

The contemporary press record of property crime in San Francisco for the period is not great, though larger than Bancroft supposes. In mid-July, while the trial of the Hounds was going on, a man in a gambling house reported that he lost his watch to a pickpocket. No other thefts were reported in the press until late September, when the *Alta* joked about another pickpocket. In October, a young man was arrested for stealing $1,700 in gold dust and another man was arrested on Halloween for strong-arming money from a black man by saying he was a police officer. In November, a man was sent to jail for stealing several dozen bottles of wine; in late December, the *Alta* reported the sentencing of a dozen or so of the seventy thieves arrested for stealing at the scene of the first great fire. (We might ask those who argue that many murders went unreported in the press why it was that the theft of a few bottles of wine was reported.)

Part of the increase in reported crime can no doubt be attributed to the establishment of the police department. There is less chance of a crime being made known if there is no one to report it to. One type of crime—murder—did tend to be reported, police or no. It is one thing to fail to report a theft, but it is quite a different thing to ignore a dead body. The crime of murder did increase in the last half of the year in San Francisco, about as much as would be expected in a town that experienced a tenfold population increase in a year.

As has already been mentioned, Rinaldo Algeria, shot in the abdomen by the Hounds, died a few days later, the first murder statistic for the second half of 1849. In August, a Frenchman named Peter Pettit went hunting with his friend and former business partner, Joseph Daniels, on the outskirts of town. When Daniels returned alone, a search was made and the body of the murdered Frenchman was found. Daniels was arrested by Marshal Fallon, tried before Alcalde Geary, found guilty, and sentenced to hang. The next year, after regular courts were established, the state supreme court overturned the conviction because of trial errors.[29]

In October, a drunken Chilean, Cerelia by name according to the *Alta*, was refused a drink in the same drinking tent taken over by Roberts and his gang on the night of the Hounds' foray to Telegraph Hill. In the struggle that followed, the Chilean killed a black porter who was trying to eject him. The suspect left the scene before he could be arrested; on November 14, Reuben Withers killed a young man named Reynolds in the Bella Union gambling saloon. He escaped to Mexico but was returned; at a later trial in San Jose, after a change of venue, he was acquitted by a jury. On November 15, the *Alta* reported the discovery of the body of an unknown man, trussed up and shot through the chest, a mile from Clark's Point. And on the last day of the year, the paper reported the discovery of the body of Thomas Browne, "an inoffensive man," found in the bushes near the road to the Mission.[30]

As suggested by the nature of the homicides reported, the main thing that the citizens of San Francisco still had to fear was physical violence—and then only if they went to saloons and gambling houses. That was hard to avoid. Gambling and drinking were the chief entertainments of the young male boomtown society, and the locales where they took place offered the only warm, lighted, and sociable alternatives to life in a cold, dark tent. The yellowing records of the long-forgotten victims hint at the passions that prevailed in the town; contemporary observers provide support for the idea that, while the incidence of actual predatory crime might have been low, general rowdiness, which concerned the leading citizens of the town before the Gold Rush, con- tributed to later actions by the "people." Although it was prevalent at the time, no one seems to have bothered much about it.

Still, according to the *Annals of San Francisco*, Geary's administra- tion was remembered as presiding over a city "remarkable for the order which prevailed." Geary administered strict justice and firm penalties, said the annalists, which assured that though "there were people from every nation . . . no community was more harmoniously governed."[31]

On the one hand, there was the impulse to dramatize Gold Rush San Francisco as a wild and woolly boomtown. On the other, it suited the interests of the victors that the town be remembered as law-abiding in 1849, to contrast with the horrendous crime conditions a year or so later when they were forced to take matters out of the hands of the authorities. It is for these reasons that the subject of the amount of crime in late 1849 is somewhat unclear.

CHAPTER 10

Cui Bono

ARSON FIRES, and what Gold Rush San Franciscans did about them, form a prominent theme in the history/mythology of crime in the city. On six occasions between December 1849 and June 1851, the city was devastated by major conflagrations. Each time, like the mythical phoenix that adorns the city seal, the undaunted residents began to rebuild even before the ashes had cooled.

One of the legends of early San Francisco, inextricably bound up in its lore, is that the fires were set by Australian criminals bent on looting the town in the confusion attending the efforts to fight the blaze. "Many of the fires were believed to have been raised by incendiaries," said the *Annals*, "solely for the opportunity which they afforded for plundering."[1] According to the legend, the fires did not come to an end until the Vigilance Committee of 1851 drove the criminal predators from the city. Among the other objectives announced in its manifesto in June 1851 when it effectively took over the administration of criminal justice in San Francisco was that the Vigilance Committee was "determined . . . that . . . no incendiary shall escape punishment."[2]

Like the reports of 1,000 or more murders, which it often accompanies in shorthand accounts explaining the need for a Committee of Vigilance in Gold Rush San Francisco a few years later, the legend will not go away. The *San Francisco Examiner* reported in 1986:

> There were several gangs during that time which would "torch" shops and buildings if the owners didn't pay "protection" money. Worst among these groups was the "Sydney Ducks," a group of former Australian convicts. It is believed they were responsible for a large majority of the six fires that swept the city between 1849 and 1851. Sam Brannan and the Vigilantes finally broke the arson gangs in 1851.[3]

Keeping in mind that the victors at least influence the writing of the history and that their version does not always square with objective reality, we shall take another look at the causes of the great fires as we encounter them in our chronology. One thing is certain: at least by current standards, fire was quite literally out of control in mid-nineteenth-century San Francisco. Large urban fires, on a scale incomprehensible to modern city dwellers, were a terrifying reality to urban dwellers before the current century. The story of how Nero's Rome burned to the ground almost two millennia ago is well known, as is Samuel Pepys's description of the great London fire of 1666. The early histories of many of the world's great cities are marked by major fires. (Conditions grew even worse in the nineteenth century in the rush to build wall-to-wall wooden tenements to house the influx of immigrants to American cities. Only in this century has the technology been developed with which to hold major urban conflagrations tentatively at bay.)[4] By the mid-nineteenth century, little had been learned from the lessons of the past; as America moved from the farm to the city, and as urban centers grew in size and congestion, adequate fire services, like police departments, were a long time in coming.

In 1676, 50 buildings were destroyed in one fire in Boston; in 1776, 1,000 buildings burned in a New York fire. In 1788, 854 of 1,100 buildings were consumed by fire in New Orleans. St. Louis suffered a major fire in 1825, Louisville in 1827, Cincinnati in 1829, and Chicago in 1834. In 1835, 530 buildings were destroyed in another fire in New York City; in July 1849, 300 houses burned and 20 persons died in a fire in St. Louis. In 1871, more than 17,000 buildings were burned and some 250 people were killed in the great Chicago fire, allegedly started by Mrs. O'Leary's cow.

Fire protection, like police protection and the establishment of jails, is a labor-intensive and highly costly proposition; nineteenth-century Americans just were not willing to pay the price. The three essential factors upon which even a modicum of fire safety depends—an adequate water supply, a paid professional fire department, and building codes that prohibit unsafe construction practices—were sadly lacking, not just in San Francisco but in all of laissez-faire urban America at the time.

Nineteenth-century ideas about fire service—adapted from rural and small-town America, where even today they still can work—depended on volunteer fire companies, whose members, at the alarm, dropped whatever else they were doing and came together to put out the fire. In large cities the companies, each independent of the other, were merely multiplied in number. The companies might get together to elect a chief engineer, but there was really no coordinating authority to assure that the member companies worked harmoniously to extinguish fires. Indeed, competition and conflict were often the rule, rather than cooperation.

Before the advent of the automobile, the lives of most urban dwellers were restricted to their near neighborhood. In the absence of other distractions, volunteer fire stations were neighborhood social and political centers. Neighborhood pride was displayed in the trappings and equipment of the local fire companies; as cities became the home of diverse ethnic groups, the firehouse took on the coloration of its neighborhood, with political and social implications. No local politician had any chance of being elected unless he was connected to one of the fire companies. The natural competition between companies to be the first at a fire often translated into violence as companies fought each other while buildings burned to the ground. Indeed, fighting between gangs of firehouse rowdies was one of the main reasons for the need to develop municipal police departments.

In Gold Rush San Francisco, where all the sins of nineteenth-century urban America were writ large, little thought was given to establishing a proper fire department until after the first of the great fires. There was a start on building cisterns to store water to battle fires, but little was accomplished at first. Nothing was done to enact or enforce anything like a building or fire safety code. Wooden frame construction predominated in the hastily thrown up structures in the early Gold Rush years, often with canvas ceilings and walls through which stovepipes were thrust directly. The result was that once a fire started, whatever its cause, there was little chance of stopping it before it burned itself out. According to one contemporary observer, writing in August 1849 to his wife back east:

> I consider the risk alone of fire here exceedingly great. The town is but one great tinder box, and a fire once commenced at the windward side would be certain to burn the whole of it to ash, and this I predict will sooner or later be its fate. The material is all of combustibles, very dry pine, with a large proportion of canvas roofs; no engines, I mean fire engines; no hooks or ladders; and in fact no water (except in very deep wells) available where it might be most required. Many people have their all at stake under these circumstances. Is it not enough to make a prudent man tremble?[5]

In the pathology of fire as crime there are a number of classic causes of arson. Currently, about 42% is arson as vandalism, according to *Firehouse* magazine; 23% is attributable to arson for revenge; 14% to arson committed by pyromaniacs; another 14% to arson for profit (insurance fraud); and 7% to arson to cover up another crime.[6] In Gold Rush San Francisco, the most common explanation put forth for the fires, as we have seen, is that gangs of Australian criminals set the fires so that they could steal in the confusion, while building owners in the path of unstoppable fire tried to move their property out. "Investigations showed clearly," says Herbert Asbury, "that at least four [of the six] conflagrations had been started by gangs of fire-bugs led by two former convicts from Australia. . . ."[7]

Australians, as mentioned earlier, were among the first argonauts, and those who came were not always the most law-abiding residents of even that rowdy British colony. After losing its American colonies as a dumping ground for felons with the success of the American Revolutionary War, Britain had cast about for an alternative place to send its growing number of convicts. At first, abandoned hulks were pressed into service as prison ships; but as England's southern ports became littered with decaying wooden jails, it was decided instead to transport convicted prisoners to the far side of the world, to New South Wales (Australia) and Van Diemen's Land (Tasmania). Beginning in the last years of the eighteenth century, thousands of British convicts were shipped out to the previously unsettled antipodean colony. By the middle of the nineteenth century, there was perhaps a majority of non-convict settlers (free settlers, and the descendants of guards and former convicts) in the land down under, with a strong leavening of convicts and ticket-of-leave men (parolees). When news of the gold strike in California spread, Sydney, Australia, was one of the Pacific ports it reached, prompting a large number of immigrants, many of them recent ex-convicts, to strike out for California. Using skills learned in Sydney harbor, many of them took work in the early years in San Francisco as boatmen, ferrying passengers and lightering goods, in the early years, from the deep-water anchorage beyond the mudflats in front of the town to the beach near Montgomery Street. Some of them joined the Hounds, and part of the enmity they felt toward Chileans can perhaps be understood (if not excused) as economic competition. Sam Roberts, the field commander of the Hounds, though not an Australian, was a boatman and no doubt shared their feelings toward the Hispanics. One of the Hounds' actions during their raid of Chiletown was to smash the boats of their Hispanic competitors.

In the years leading up to the establishment of the Vigilance Committee, Australians would figure prominently in the annals of crime in San Francisco. There is no question that Australian ex-convicts were well represented among those arrested for stealing at fires, but that does not necessarily mean they set them. Looting is a phenomenon that often accompanies the confusion following many types of disaster. Opportunistic criminals soon see the possibilities for committing theft in the aftermath of floods and earthquakes as well as fires. That does not mean they caused them.

As a matter of fact, as we shall see as we go along, most of the six great fires that afflicted Gold Rush San Francisco were probably started by accident. But another idea has been advanced that bears analysis. Viewed one way, the great Gold Rush migration can be seen as the transportation of a great number of customers from all parts of the world to the west coast of North America. Eastern merchants, sensing correctly that great profits were to be made in the goldfield economy of scarcity, shipped massive amounts of goods around the Horn in anything that would float. Not knowing what was needed in San Francisco and the goldfields, they cleared their warehouses. If they guessed right and sent items that were scarce but in demand, there was a fortune to be made. According to the chaotic individualistic business practices of the time, shippers jealously guarded their manifests from each other. The resulting economic history of Gold Rush San Francisco is the story of boom and bust. With scarce goods and full-pocketed miners, business was good, and fortunes could be made on one voyage. When, however, as often occurred, several ships showed up bearing the same goods, they became a drug on the market and fortunes were lost.[8]

As mentioned, the arrival of the *Belfast* in late 1848 with a store of goods depressed prices by 25%. With the flood of humankind that followed, prices again rose in the first of a cycle of wild economic fluctuations. Rents and prices declined in the spring of 1849 as the populace returned to the mines, but they rose again a few months later with the arrival of thousands of summer gold seekers in advance of the hundreds of merchant ships making their way slowly around the Horn. As news of the tremendous profits to be made reached the East, shipload after shipload of merchandise was dispatched to California; by the fall of 1849, ships began to pile up on each other in San Francisco harbor at the same time that out-of-work miners, driven away by the high winter waters, began to arrive in town. Prices in the glutted market fell below cost. Still, with unemployment high, much went unsold, and there are reports of bales of goods used to fill in the holes in the mud-choked streets during the rainy winter of 1849–50.

Much of the loss did not fall on local merchants, however, because a great deal of the merchandise did not even belong to them. Eastern shippers sent the goods "blind" on consignment to commission merchants in San Francisco who acted as their agents for a percentage of the profits. If the merchandise was sold above cost, the profit was shared by the eastern shipper and the San Francisco commission merchant. If goods were lost at sea or sold below cost, the San Francisco merchant was not personally out of pocket. In fact it was very much in the economic interest of San Francisco merchants that gluts be reduced by whatever means so that the profits on remaining goods would increase. Vincent Perez Rosales explains how it was accomplished. Commenting in his journal about the arrival of unwanted goods, he says, "Nobody, however, was discouraged. Even the lowest-priced items could be given scarcity value by arranging for convenient fires. We saw such fires break out all over town day after day, posing the danger of a general conflagration."[9]

Journalist George Wilkes, later publisher of the *National Police Gazette*, who was present in San Francisco during most of the great fires, was even more explicit:

> The warehouses of San Francisco were glutted to the roofs; but the precious commission merchants of San Francisco could not make returns to their Atlantic shippers; and then came the terrible conflagrations which gave them a clear balance sheet. . . . "Thieves, thieves, incendiaries!" shouted the merchants. "Hang them! Hang them!" echoed

the ignorant and the timid—"they have set our city on fire." And they did seize and hang several poor devils . . . though nobody benefited but the merchants of San Francisco.[10]

The fact that a few contemporary observers suggested that the commercial establishment was responsible for the fires that plagued the town does not mean that they were culpable any more than unsupported allegations against Australian criminals prove that they were responsible for the blazes. But there is a demonstrable correlation, as we shall see, between the incidence of disastrous fires and the fluctuating economic conditions in San Francisco. To be fair, we must at least consider the intriguing possibility that some members of the commercial establishment were perhaps involved in contributing to the holocausts that helped bring the Vigilance Committee into existence to punish the arsonists.

The first of the major fires in Gold Rush San Francisco broke out in the early morning hours of December 24, 1849, in a building at the corner of Kearny and Washington streets, across from Portsmouth Square. The fire started at 5:45 A.M. on the second floor of Dennison's Exchange Saloon; fed by canvas walls and ceilings, it spread quickly to nearby buildings. "There was no wind," wrote an early historian, "but almost all the houses were mere shells, ceiled and walled with cotton cloth papered or painted, and very inflammable. No fire department or fire company existed; and nothing at all effective to stop the flames was or could be done. . . ."[11] Before the disorganized citizenry could mount an assault on the fire, fifty buildings valued at $1,000,000 lay in smoking ruins. In the confusion that attended the fire, criminal opportunists took advantage of conditions and looted where they could. Seventy thieves, many of them recent Australian immigrants, were arrested for stealing salvaged goods, no doubt lending a measure of credibility to the belief that they were in the habit of setting fires so they could steal.

The Christmas Eve fire of 1849 seems to have been caused neither by Australian criminals nor by merchants with glutted storehouses. If there is anything to an account left by John H. Brown, who lived in the town at the time, it was set as revenge for a racial affront. The issue that stalled the establishment of a territorial or state government in California was the congressional dispute about whether California should come into the Union as slave or free. Californians had answered the question for themselves by inserting a clause in their proposed constitution at Monterey prohibiting slavery in California. That does not mean that blacks were particularly welcome.[12] It is true that in the topsy-turvy society of Gold Rush California, men who had been doctors in the "states" could be found digging ditches while former laborers made fortunes in real estate; while a black man might be found getting his shoes shined by a white man, the conventions of centuries were not to be wiped away in a day.

According to Brown, the only contemporary who seems to have left an account of the origin of the fire, there was an unwritten rule in San Francisco about serving blacks in white saloons.[13] The custom prevailed that a black man could be served one drink—but just one— in one of the "better" white saloons. He was then expected to depart. In December 1849, Dennison's Saloon was taken over by a southerner named Thomas Bartell (or Battelle). Evidently Bartell did not subscribe to the custom, for when a black man entered and ordered a drink, the new owner beat him senseless. The black man vowed vengeance, said Brown, and was seen in the vicinity of the saloon on several occasions just before the fire. He bided his time, according to the account, and on Christmas Eve morning, 1849, he burned the place down—along with a good part of the rest of the town.

CHAPTER 11

Ayuntamiento

ACCOUNTS DEALING WITH CRIME and criminal justice in Gold Rush San Francisco most often skip from the affair of the Hounds in 1849 to 1851 and the events leading up to the formation of the Vigilance Committee. There is usually some sort of transitional comment, like that found in the *Annals of San Francisco*, to the effect that after the Hounds were suppressed, good order prevailed for a time. "Col. Geary went into office as alcalde soon after the affair of the 'Hounds,'" reported the contemporary *Annals*:

> From that time until the office was abolished [May 1850] the city was remarkable for the order which prevailed, and its comparative freedom from the commission of heinous crimes. The city comprised people of every nation, class and sort, many of whom had for months been exercising an unrestrained course of villainy and rascality, yet no civilized community has ever been more harmoniously governed. . . .[1]

The way the story usually goes, it was only after the establishment of a municipal government according to American forms, and the abolition of the office of alcalde (and those of the members of the *ayunta-*

miento), as good citizens returned to their private affairs, that predatory criminals became emboldened and in the end visited a criminal reign of terror on the town. According to this version of events, the business leaders of the *ayuntamiento* government managed the town well, but they soon returned to their private affairs. In their neglect, the governance of the town was taken over in the spring of 1850 by professional politicians who looted the treasury to line their own pockets and presided over the general deterioration of civic conditions. It was only when the business leadership wrested direct control of affairs back from the incompetent and corrupt politicians through the agency of the Committee of Vigilance that conditions again improved. It is true enough that crime did increase in the latter part of 1850; but it is also true that much of what occurred during the *ayuntamiento*'s tenure in office had a bearing on criminal justice issues that emerged later, and its members' role went far beyond simple neglect.

The long-forgotten factional political squabbles of the *ayuntamiento* government of 1849–50 would be worthy of no more than a footnote in the criminal justice history of San Francisco were it not for the fact that the council was dominated by some of the same businessmen who had criticized earlier regimes—one of whom would lead the movement that flouted the legally constituted government that followed them in office.

From the beginning of American attempts to establish a municipal government, the principal financial support for the town government, and the principal source of political disputes, was the sale of public lands. The legislative assembly had tried unsuccessfully to impose a license tax as an alternative source of revenue; in August 1849, the prefect vetoed a business tax ordinance passed by the *ayuntamiento* on the ground that it taxed the small merchants disproportionately in favor of the large. (It was finally approved later in a modified and much reduced form.) So, in October, *ayuntamiento* member Sam Brannan offered a resolution in council that water lots belonging to the town be sold at auction and that the proceeds be used to provide public wharves, a city hospital, and a city hall. Several hundred lots were sold at public auction in November. In the meantime, G. Q. Colton, appointed justice of the peace by Prefect Hawes, assuming what he considered to be the rights of a justice of the peace under Mexican law, also took to selling town lots, some of which had already been granted to others. The Colton grants set in motion title disputes that lasted for years. Justice Colton sent the money he obtained from the land sales east, and he soon followed it.[2]

On December 31, Prefect Hawes demanded an accounting from the *ayuntamiento* of all the lots it had sold. The *ayuntamiento* responded by asking the governor to suspend Colton from office, along with Hawes, who had appointed him. On January 3, 1850, the *ayuntamiento* conducted a sale of 400 beach and water lots that realized $635,000 for the town coffers, to be paid into the treasury in installments over the next ten months. When he received no response from the *ayuntamiento*, Hawes complained to the governor, who, on February 15, decided to suspend the further sale of town lots in San Francisco. Again, on February 28, Hawes demanded an accounting from the *ayuntamiento* of all land sales and asked specifically how many lots had been bought by members of the *ayuntamiento*. He also wanted to know how many lots *ayuntamiento* members owned on the line of the wharf they proposed to build on California Street with money from the land sales.

His suspicions were well founded, for the records showed that members of the *ayuntamiento*, Sam Brannan notable among them, had received 120 lots in the land sales they had ordered, and that they appropriated $300,000 of the payment received to build a wharf along a line where they held 50 lots.[3] Knowing where the wharf was to go, *ayuntamiento* members had insider information on which lots to buy; then they used the proceeds from the sale to construct a wharf at a location that benefited their investment. At first, the governor backed the prefect; but in the end, he suspended him as requested by the *ayuntamiento*. Hawes moved to have the governor impeached; but later, when a municipal government according to American forms was provided, the matter was finally forgotten.

Geary, in his inaugural address, in addition to his remarks about the absence of police, had reminded the *ayuntamiento* that "[you] have not the means of confining a prisoner for an hour."[4] Apparently, the old blockhouse jail was never put into good condition because the legislative assembly, during its attempt to run the town government, rented rooms to serve as a jail, and the Hounds were imprisoned on a warship while waiting for their trial. In the closing months of 1849, Marshal Fallon used space in the schoolhouse on the square as a place to hold prisoners. Heeding Geary's reminder, the members of the *ayuntamiento* set about providing a jail for the town. First they approached the military governor and asked him for a loan to build a

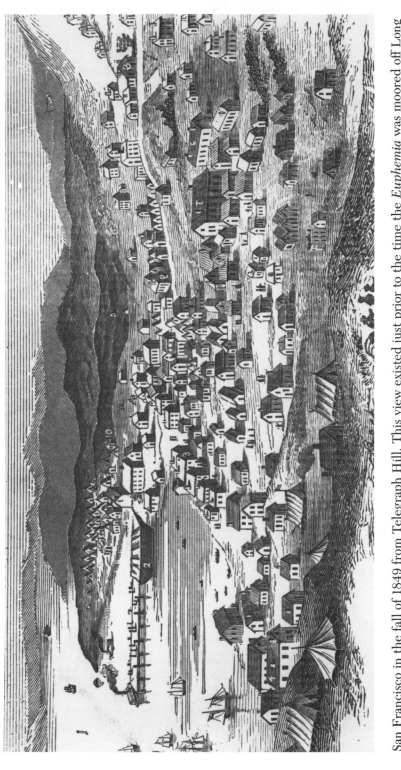

San Francisco in the fall of 1849 from Telegraph Hill. This view existed just prior to the time the *Euphemia* was moored off Long Wharf near the *Apollo* (shown with dark hull marked "2"). (*California State Library*)

jail. He informed them that by law he could not lend them money but that he would give them $10,000 if they came up with matching funds and agreed to use the money to build a district jail and a courthouse.[5] Instead, the *ayuntamiento* decided to act on its own.

In October, Sam Brannan reported on the purchase of the brig *Euphemia* for $3,500 from William Heath Davis, another member of the council, to serve as a temporary town jail. After alterations that brought its final cost to almost $8,000, the prison brig was anchored off the Central Wharf at Battery Street.[6] Nobody seems to have raised an eyebrow at the two members of the town council, both of whom had criticized their predecessors in office for fiscal shenanigans and had turned down a gift of money to buy a jail, when they arranged for the town to purchase a ship owned by one of them, at a time when the harbor was choked with abandoned hulks to be had for the taking. Two years later, the insecure conditions of the town jails would be one of the reasons given for the necessity of calling the Vigilance Committee into being.

Geary had also announced to the *ayuntamiento* in his inaugural address that "you have neither an office for your magistrate nor any public edifice." In the years following the American conquest, town offices had bounced around. Alcalde Bartlett used a house on Montgomery Street. Bryant used space in the Customhouse on Portsmouth Square until displaced by the military. Hyde and Leavenworth used a building on Clay Street opposite Portsmouth Square, and the legislative assembly used the schoolhouse on the square as its headquarters. The old schoolhouse came to be known as the Public Institute because of its use as a general-purpose public meeting room. Abandoned as a school during the Gold Rush, it was later used to conduct church services and theatrical performances; it was there that the Regulators held their organizational meeting and that the Hounds were tried. As has been mentioned, the building was used by Fallon as a jail and later as a civil courthouse; but by the end of 1849, the town had outgrown the capacity of the structure to serve as a multipurpose governmental office building.

Alcalde Geary settled himself in a building that was later used as a justice court on the upper side of the square. In February, with money in hand from beach and water lot sales, the *ayuntamiento* resolved to consolidate governmental offices into one building, the American Hotel, at Stockton and Broadway streets "to promote," says Bancroft, "the lot speculation of certain members."[7] Confronted by public criticism of improper expenditures to buy the city hall, the *ayuntamiento* appointed a committee from among its members to investigate the matter. The committee never did file a report, and the council later moved into the new city hall. Other branches of the town government declined to move in, however, saying that the location was too far from the town's business section.

In early April, two members of the council committee formed to investigate the purchase of the city hall found another location, the Graham House, at Pacific and Kearny streets—named after its owner, *ayuntamiento* member James S. Graham, who also served as a member of the investigating committee. An appropriation for $150,000 to purchase the four-story building was hastily rushed through the *ayuntamiento;* on April 5, the police department moved in as the first tenant of the new city hall.[8] On May 9, the building was formally inaugurated as the home of all city and county offices, a function it was to serve until it burned in the great fire of May 1851. The courts, council, and police had rooms on the upper floors. Its ground floor was a jail thought to be "suitable for years to come."[9]

In the aftermath of the December 1849 fire, the *Alta* editorialized in January that it believed there were arsonists in town and suggested that the police department should be increased in size. If the *ayuntamiento* did not want to do it, said the paper, the merchants should organize a night watch on their own to be on the lookout for fires. There was no need, because the *ayuntamiento* promptly passed a resolution to increase the force; by February 21, it had been enlarged to fifty members. The very next day, however, Sam Brannan reported as chairman of the Finance Committee that, due to a deficiency of funds in the treasury, the department should again be reduced to thirty members. The situation resolved itself with the coming of spring, when a number of officers quit the force to rejoin the return migration to the goldfields.

The financial peccadillos of an obscure temporary town government in Gold Rush San Francisco—not really extravagant, given the standards of municipal morality of the time—would, as stated, be worthy of little interest, were it not for some of the members and the events that followed. Sam Brannan was the moving spirit of the *ayuntamiento* government of 1849–50. It was Brannan who personally moved the sale of town lots that redounded greatly to his financial benefit and that of other members of the council. He also appropriated the funds from the sale to erect a wharf near lots he owned, which also benefited him and his friends financially. Then he had the chutzpah to announce that the town could not afford to pay for an adequate police force. It was

The prison ship *Euphemia*. (*California State Library*)

Brannan who engineered the purchase, from a fellow *ayuntamiento* member, of a wooden hulk to serve as an escape-ridden jail. Brannan participated in two insider deals to acquire city halls, the second of which housed another sievelike wooden jail. Yet this is the governmental body applauded by Bancroft for leaving a surplus in the treasury at the end of its tenure "and no bad blot on their public character." [10]

Little more than a year later, when the "good" people of San Francisco rose up to rid themselves of municipal corruption, in part because of the inadequacies of the police and their inability to hold prisoners in the crackerbox jails, Sam Brannan would serve as the first president of the Committee of Vigilance formed to do the job.

Part III **THE YEAR
IN BETWEEN**

CHAPTER 12

Here Come the Democrats

THE DELEGATES CHOSEN in the August election called by Governor Riley met in convention at Monterey in September 1849. Over the next few months, without the approval of the national Congress, the members of the constitutional convention formed a state government for California. In October, they presented a constitution to Governor Riley, who informed his superiors in Washington that unless ordered to do otherwise he intended to turn the government of California over to elected civilian officials. He immediately set an election for November 13 to ratify the constitution and to elect the state officials it provided for. On a rainy day in November, California voters slogged through the mud and rain to ratify the constitution overwhelmingly and to elect a governor and members of a bicameral state legislature. On December 17, the legislature met in the newly designated capital, San Jose, where, on December 20, Peter Burnett was sworn in as the first civilian governor of American California. General Riley thereupon tendered his resignation as governor, ending direct military control of governmental affairs in California.

The rush of gold seekers continued. Thousands arrived from around the world: from Europe and Asia, Mexico, South America, and Pacific ports. As immigration from the eastern United States achieved full flow, Americans came to dominate the Gold Rush population numerically. By the spring of 1850, between one-half and two-thirds of the 100,000 Californians were from the United States. By year's end, California's population reached 150,000. During 1850, San Francisco's population would fluctuate between 20,000 and 40,000 as residents made their way back and forth to the mines. The pattern set in earlier years continued. In summer, when weather in the Sierras was warm and the rivers were low, the population in the mining regions increased while the towns declined. During the winter, the urban population again rose as the miners moved out of the Sierras ahead of the rains.

Business cycles followed a similar pattern. Business was heaviest in the spring when up-country merchants laid in stores to supply the summer increase and again in the fall when they stocked up before the rain closed the roads to the mines. In 1850, the volume of goods arriving continued to exceed the needs of Californians; although San Francisco appeared bustlingly prosperous to outward appearances, depressed economic conditions continued.

In the first session of the newly elected legislature, the lawmakers set about organizing a state government. They divided California into counties; established a court system, consisting of a supreme court, district courts, county courts, and justice courts; and enacted a set of penal laws and laws establishing civil procedure. In designing a court system, the legislators looked, quite naturally, to models in established states. While such courts might work elsewhere, their inability to deal with conditions in Gold Rush San Francisco would lead in part to the establishment of the Committee of Vigilance a year later.

On April 1, 1850, elections for county officials were held throughout California. In San Francisco, Roderick N. Morrison was elected county judge to preside over a court of sessions, comprised of the county judge and two associate justices, Edward (Ned) McGowan and Harvey S. Brown. John C. (Jack) Hays, a former Texas Ranger who had distinguished himself in the Mexican War, was elected county sheriff.

The formation of a state government brought party politics to California. In October 1849, Alcalde Geary had chaired the first Democratic party convention in San Francisco. The meeting of the party that was to dominate the politics of the state and the city for most of the decade convened at first in Dennison's Exchange Saloon at Kearny and Washington streets, but the size of the attendance forced a move to Portsmouth Square.[1] Whigs, the other dominant national political party at the time, though already in a fatal decline, followed suit. In the early 1850s, they would provide the chief formal political opposition to the dominant Democratic party in California and San Francisco.

Not everyone came to California to mine gold. Some, failed politicians at home, came to get in on the political ground floor. One was William Gwin, a former congressman from Mississippi who arrived in San Francisco in the summer of 1849, just in time to serve as a judge in the trial of the Hounds. He became a leader of the proslavery Chivalry ("Chiv") faction of the Democratic party and was later elected to represent California in the U.S. Senate.

Another was David C. Broderick. The son of an Irish stonecutter, he was born in Washington, D.C., but raised in New York City. Before he was twenty-one, he was the foreman of a volunteer fire company and later operated a saloon, involving himself in local New York politics. Unable to break through the old guard at Tammany Hall, he joined the rush to California, arriving in San Francisco in mid-June 1849. He went into the lucrative business of minting badly needed coins; by the end of 1849, he had sold out at a handsome profit.

Broderick distinguished himself in fighting the fire of December 1849—as mentioned, almost an essential requirement for anyone with political aspirations in the nineteenth century—and was shortly thereafter made foreman of the Empire Fire Company, the first volunteer fire company organized in San Francisco. In January 1850, he was elected to fill a vacant seat in the new California legislature. He spent the rest of his life in politics, leading the opposition against both the Whigs and the Chivalry faction of his own party. He was elected president of the State Senate in 1851; in 1857, he won a seat in the U.S. Senate. In the early 1850s, Broderick was the foremost Democratic politician in San Francisco to oppose the forces that came in conflict with the established authorities.

The inability of nineteenth-century urban Americans to establish adequate police and fire services early was symptomatic of a more general inability to understand and deal with the great social changes facing them. In a similar way, mid-nineteenth-century urban Americans tried to govern themselves according to obsolete practices that may have been suitable in an earlier, simpler time, but were found to be totally wanting in the rapidly changing cities of the day. Before the growth of cities, the public will could be expressed directly in meetings

State Senator David C. Broderick. (*California State Library*)

held in public squares, attended by all who might be interested in the issue at hand. Officers were selected, discussion was open, resolutions expressing the will of those assembled were formulated on the spot, and committees were appointed to carry them out.[2]

As cities grew in size and neighbors became strangers, the old ways no longer worked. Public meetings of the entire electorate became unwieldy assemblies, unable to get any work done. The stage moved indoors into the back rooms as political parties assumed the function of managing the electoral process. In the absence of any central register of voters, the party that could get the most votes into the ballot box from any source was assured of victory. The result was that municipal politics in the latter part of the nineteenth century often degenerated into a physical contest between opposing gangs of bullies, representing the various factions into which the cities had split, trying to see who could stuff the most votes into the ballot boxes. Exercising the franchise before the institution of the secret ballot and firmly enforced election laws was often not an occupation for the weak or timid.[3]

Before adjourning in April 1850, the legislature had enacted a charter for San Francisco, providing the town, for the first time, with a city government according to American forms. The government was to be headed by an elected mayor and a bicameral council with eight aldermen and eight assistant aldermen elected from the eight wards into which the city was divided. There was to be an elected recorder (police court judge) with the jurisdiction of a justice of the peace for offenses committed within the city limits, and an elected city marshal to supervise the police department. Elections were to be held yearly, and the mayor and council were empowered to fix public salaries and to establish and regulate a police department and a regular night watch.[4] At a city election on May 1, 1850, the voters of San Francisco approved the charter and elected officials to replace the *ayuntamiento* government. John Geary was elected the city's first mayor, Malachi Fallon was elected city marshal, and Francis Tilford was elected judge of the recorder's court.

Devastating fire, as we have seen, was a prominent fact of nineteenth-century urban life, not just in San Francisco but in growing cities everywhere. As in other cities and with other needed institutions, the laissez-faire response was not up to the requirements of the task. After its election in 1849, the *ayuntamiento* had authorized the acquisition of two hand pumpers from the "states," but no attempt was made to establish a formal fire-fighting capacity until after a large part of the town had burned down in December while the residents tried to figure out what to do. Prodded to action by the disaster, the *ayuntamiento*, in January 1850, appointed Frederick Kohler, Broderick's partner in the minting business, as fire chief, with instructions to organize a fire department. He assigned the three engines in town to three hastily organized volunteer companies, the Empire, the Protection, and the Eureka, manned by former firemen from eastern cities.

In late January, someone—probably, said the *Alta*, one of the "most desperate scoundrels of England who have been serving the Queen" —set a fire on Washington Street above Kearny, occasioning the call for a night watch to protect against fire, with the results already noted. Several other fires were reported, but none got out of hand; as people became absorbed with their personal affairs again, interest in completing the formation of a fire department dwindled.

Fire commanded attention once more in the early morning hours of Saturday, May 4, 1850, when the U.S. Exchange Saloon, erected on the site of Dennison's Exchange, burst into flame. Again the fire spread rapidly against the feeble efforts of the embryo fire department to contain it. By midday, an area three times the size of that burned in the December fire was engulfed and $4,000,000 worth of property lay in ruins. The main victims of the December fire had been gambling halls near Portsmouth Square; but in the fire of May 1850, it was the stores of merchants that were burned. Immediately, it was conjectured that arson was the cause. Perhaps so, for in his confession a year later, one of the Australian criminals hanged by the committee supposedly told his interrogators that he had heard rumors that another Australian, Billy Shears, had set the May 1850 fire. No reason why he might have done so is offered. Whatever the motive, and whoever may have started the fire, it was the merchants themselves who benefited. At the time of the fire, according to press reports, due to disorganized shipments from the East, there was sufficient lumber on hand to rebuild the town thirty times over.[5] A few days later, the value of the lumber that survived the fire had increased fourfold.

The May fire rekindled interest in the establishment of a fire department, and the previously designated volunteer companies were formally organized. The city council passed an ordinance requiring citizens to help at fires; authorizing the excavation of artesian wells; providing for the erection of cisterns; and ordering householders to keep a number of waterfilled buckets at the ready.

On June 14, fire struck again. In the third and largest fire so far,

400 buildings burned before the flames could be stopped. According to press reports, the fire started accidentally in a faulty chimney of the Sacramento Bakery, but again rumor circulated that the fire was the work of arsonists. A contemporary observer with no axe to grind, Francis Marryat, who had arrived in San Francisco by ship on June 14 while the fire was still burning, reported, "This fire was attributed to incendiarism but when the general carelessness that existed is considered, it is quite probable that it resulted from accident."[6] Again it was the merchants and large property holders who benefited from the disaster. Depressed prices rose as stocks were destroyed by the fire. "Some of the largest losers by the recent fire will in the end be the greatest gainers," reported the *Alta*. "The opening of Commercial Street will enhance the value of the land abutting thereto . . . to an extent greatly exceeding the value of the buildings destroyed."[7]

"A vast amount of the property destroyed was in the hands of commission merchants and heavy losses will fall on shippers in New York and New England," the paper pointed out, while warning with later implications that the result would be that eastern merchants would in the future refuse to ship goods on commission but would demand cash with orders. It was likely, the paper went on, that the commission business would decline.[8]

Press reports of predatory crime, while not approaching the amounts of later periods, increased to a measurable degree in the first half of 1850. There were four reported burglaries in the six-month period and two muggings. For some reason, criminal homicides declined to three. Two of the burglaries were of commercial premises. In one, the thieves had entered by "false keys" and removed more than $5,000 from a safe. In the other, more than $5,000 in jewelry was taken from a store. Two others were residential burglaries, thefts from trunks in hotel rooms. In January, the second reported mugging in San Francisco was committed in Portsmouth Square. An arrest was made. The next occurred in March, when three men held up a man bringing wood to the city and robbed him of $10.

On March 3, two Frenchmen leaving a brothel on Pacific Street at Dupont were accosted by three Chileans. After an angry exchange of words, one of the Chileans stabbed one of the Frenchmen and fled before he could be arrested. One of his companions, Francisco Ramirez, was arrested and later convicted of manslaughter.[9] In May, Daniel Matthews was arrested on Pacific Street for the stabbing death of a sailor during a quarrel. By the time his case was called in district court, though, Matthews had skipped on $4,000 bail. In early June, Domingo Basquez (*sic*), a fourteen-year-old Chilean, was arrested for fatally stabbing a man in a dispute over a cigar. After the man was stabbed, but before he died, Basquez was convicted of aggravated assault.[10]

The amount of predatory crime reported in the press, while on the rise, seems almost absurdly small for our perception of conditions in a boomtown with 30,000 people. Either the crimes happened and just did not get into the papers, as suggested by Mary Williams and others, or our perception of life in boomtown San Francisco needs modification.

With the exception of murder, some crimes of predation probably did not make it into the papers. Even today, with sophisticated methods and a public conditioned to reporting crimes, many crimes still go unreported. Victimization surveys, conducted to verify the completeness and accuracy of FBI-gathered statistics, show that even today as much as three to ten times more crime occurs than is reported to the police. A national crime survey in 1975 showed that as little as 26% of property crime was reported and 47% of violent crime. The great majority of commercial burglaries and robberies are reported, however.[11] While it is fair to assume that nineteenth-century San Franciscans, unaccustomed as they were even to dealing with a police department, were probably less inclined to report crimes to the authorities, it is also fair to conclude that most homicides did come to official attention. (Modern victimization surveys do not even consider the crime of criminal homicide in their analyses for the very good reason that there is little variance between actual and reported offenses.) The fact of the matter is that nineteenth-century San Franciscans simply were not subjected to anything like the amounts of crime to which modern city dwellers have become inured.

Other than the fact that knives were perhaps more commonly used as weapons of assault in nineteenth-century criminal homicides (firearms before the invention of the center fire cartridge were a less certain proposition), the motivations and means of murder were largely the same as in any age. Other types of crime, however, took different forms. Burglary was a much more difficult crime to commit in the nineteenth century than it is today. It is common now for residential areas to be largely uninhabited during the day, while people are away at work, and for commercial areas to be untenanted at night after businesses have closed. It is a relatively simple matter, as many doped-up amateurs have discovered, to find a building that is uninhabited to steal from with virtual impunity.

Nineteenth-century burglars, on the other hand, had to be professionals, particularly in Gold Rush San Francisco, with a less clear-cut line between living and working areas than in other cities. It was more common then for residential premises to be inhabited during the daytime and for commercial houses to be used as sleeping quarters at night. One of the factors working in favor of the burglars was that, before the invention of the telephone, householders, particularly those who had no immediate neighbors, were on their own when burglars came to call. On some occasions, gangs of burglars would openly break into inhabited dwellings, knowing there was no way for the occupants to raise a cry. Altogether, it took a level of skill, daring, and stealth not found among the generality of modern thieves to be a burglar in the nineteenth century. Accordingly, burglary occurred less frequently. In a similar way, robberies were rarer before the proliferation of the automobile. Once away from the immediate scene of a crime, the motorized robber of today can quickly lose himself in a maze of streets. It was not so simple for the nineteenth-century robber, who had to get away on foot.

But why did crime increase at all in the first months of 1850? Part of the rise may have been due simply to a reporting increase. In December, the *Alta*, the chief source of day-to-day crime statistics, went from a weekly to a triweekly format. It is possible that some crimes that had gone unreported before, murder always excepted, were now put in to fill the pages of the more frequent editions of the paper. It is also true that economic conditions were bad; some people, given no other alternative, will steal to eat.

As yet, the press—and presumably the public—was not particularly concerned about predatory crime. In January, the *Alta* reported that there was no place in the world with such a population and so little crime. A few months later, the paper again said, "Despite its variety a better regulated society never existed" and that "there was no business for the well arranged and indefatigable police, ever on the alert to secure the black sheep from the flock."[12] Still, an ominous note was struck in April, prefiguring some exciting times to come, when a householder in the Mission came home to find a burglar in his house, a recent escapee from police custody. The burglar fired upon the householder, who aroused neighbors who helped him subdue the criminal after a violent struggle. "The people of the neighborhood were so incensed against the rascal," reported the *Alta*, "that the administration of instant and summary punishment was seriously contemplated." In the end, the neighbors turned the burglar over to the regular authorities.[13]

CHAPTER 13

Crime Wave

IN MID-1850, REPORTED PREDATORY CRIME in San Francisco increased, no matter how one counts it. The following table compares the number of crimes reported in the *Alta* for the second half of 1850 with the two preceding six-month periods.

Comparison of Reported Crimes

	July/Dec 1849	Jan/June 1850	July/Dec 1850
Criminal Homicide	6	3	13
Robbery	1*	2	18
Burglary	0*	4	49

The population of San Francisco in the last six months of 1849, during which there were six reported criminal homicides, one robbery, and no burglaries, ranged up to 20,000. During the first half of 1850, when there were three homicides, two robberies, and four bur-

---

*A number of robberies and burglaries were committed during the rampage of the Hounds, but they were not reported separately in the press.

glaries reported, the city's population, swelled by wintering miners, is variously reported to have been between 25,000 and 40,000.

During the last half of the year, however, in which there were thirteen criminal homicides, eighteen robberies, and forty-nine burglaries reported, the population actually declined to about 21,000 in September after gold seekers returned to the mining regions. By the end of the year, the population of San Francisco rose to about 30,000; but during the period during which the reported incidence of serious crime increased precipitously, the number of San Franciscans was actually about the same as it had been during the preceding period, so the increase in reported crime cannot be traced to any great increase in population during the periods of comparison.

We have to consider the possibility, as mentioned earlier, that the increase in crime was not real but was instead due to improved reporting methods. The *Alta* had been published as a weekly paper, under one name or another, since the American conquest. After the *Californian* was absorbed by the *Star* in late 1848, San Francisco was a one-newspaper town for a while, but the great profits to be made in publishing a newspaper soon attracted competition. The *Pacific News* started as a triweekly in August 1849; by early 1850, it was published daily. The *Alta* became a daily in January 1850 and was joined by its main competitor, the *Herald*, another daily, on June 1. On July 1, the daily *California Courier* commenced publication. By July, then, there were four daily papers competing for the news business in San Francisco. The increase in reported crime might be attributable to improved reporting.

Not so—criminal homicide, as already asserted, is the crime affected least by changes in reporting techniques. Most murders, then and now, occur on the spur of the moment without any serious planning. The excitement surrounding the crime or the presence of the dead body soon draws official interest in most cases. The incidence of reported murder in San Francisco approximately doubled in the last half of 1850 over the highest previous six-month period, even though the rate did not begin to approach the numbers set out in the legend.

In early July, Louis Bernal, a native of Mazatlán, shot Carmelita Bertrand in the head in a saloon at Broadway and Stockton. The jury at his first trial found him guilty and recommended mercy, but his attorney moved for a new trial on a technicality; at his second trial, he was acquitted. In early August, the *Alta* reported that two Indians beat a third Indian to death in a drunken row at the Mission; in September, according to the paper, another Indian was cut to death by two men named Philip Santiago and Rito Carlan. Several days later, a "Mexican" died in the hospital after having been stabbed in a fray. On October 16, a Chilean woman, Big Mouth Mary, killed Louise Taylor, an Australian immigrant, in the same saloon where Carmelita Bertrand had been killed in July. A few days later, a black man, not named in the press, was found at the Mission, dead from multiple stab wounds.[1]

In November, Jack Smith was shot in a dispute at the Verandah Saloon; a few weeks later, another man was killed under almost similar circumstances at the El Dorado Saloon across the street. On November 26, a man named Arthur O'Connor killed a recent Australian immigrant named Michael McMahan in a flare-up at the Rendezvous Saloon. Later in the month, John Bolton killed John Toby on the bark *Salvador* in the harbor.[2]

On December 1, a ten-year-old, Charles Boyle, shot a seven-year-old to death on the Mission Road. Later in the month, a man, determined by the coroner's jury to have "died by violence at the hands of another," was found floating at the foot of Washington Street. On December 30, the robbed and murdered body of a man last seen playing cards with two others in a saloon was found on California Street.[3]

It should be noted that at least seven of the homicides involved liquor or saloons, lending credence to Bancroft's later observation, despite the concerns of the vigilantes about public assassination, that "at no time in the history of the country need any well behaved man, minding his own business and avoiding drinking saloons, have greatly feared for his life."[4]

Reported robberies jumped from two in the preceding six-month period to eighteen in the second half of 1850 and that is no statistical aberration. One was reported in July, then none until September, when there were three. Four were reported in October, three in November, and seven in December—three times more in one month than in all of the first half of the year. Burglary also went up. In each month of the last half of 1850, the press reported more burglaries than in the entire first half of the year. There were six each in July and August; twelve in September; seven in October; and nine each in November and December.

But do these numbers reflect reality or are they the result of improved reporting caused by the presence of competing news gatherers? Criminologists agree, even those who question traditional methods of counting crime, that criminal homicide tends to be well reported. Using murder as a general index of what was going on, we can safely say that crime was going up. Murder was increasing, and the press was reporting that very real increase. There is independent evidence that corroborates the fact that the day-to-day press did a thorough job of reporting serious crimes. According to one tabulation cited in another newspaper of the day, and apparently extracted from court records, 741 police cases were brought before Geary's court in the seven months between August 1849 and March 26, 1850. Of that number, four of the cases are listed as homicide. The daily editions of the *Alta* for that period reported five homicides, a close match.[5]

Another independent tabulation, covering part of the same period and extending later, was a report issued by the grand jury in August 1850.[6] According to the report, there were seven arrests for murder in San Francisco between November 13, 1849, and August 1, 1850. During the same period (if we are allowed to fudge by one day), the daily editions of the *Alta* reported an identical number of homicide arrests. So there were more crimes to report and the paper was reporting them. What was going on?

One of the reasons offered for the growth of crime in modern cities is the veil of anonymity that a vast aggregation of people, all unknown to each other, provides, behind which strangers can commit crimes they would not dare to in smaller, stabler societies where they would be easily identified. Mid-nineteenth-century eastern cities, as mentioned earlier, were already taking on that sort of anonymous character; one result was an increase in crime and disorder that led to the formation of modern municipal police departments.[7]

In San Francisco, the emerging urban problems of America expressed themselves in their most pronounced form. If the move toward a modern, highly mobile, anonymous society can be said to have been under way in eastern cities, it was represented in its most advanced form in Gold Rush San Francisco. In the sense of its exposure to urban crime, San Francisco can be said to have been the first modern American city.[8] Not surprisingly, its institutions of government were not able to deal with the crime conditions confronting them. Peopled by a polyglot assemblage from around the world, with conflicting cultures and value systems, San Francisco could not easily establish a cohesive sense of community. As thousands of strangers, many of them sick, dispirited, and penniless, streamed back and forth through the city, it is no wonder that many of them turned to crime. Neither is it surprising that the justice institutions of the new city were puzzled by the conditions that confronted them.

By the spring of 1850, the easy pickings at the goldfields had ended. The placers were pretty well worked out; mining methods to extract gold from dry diggings and buried quartz deposits became more complicated. The work to get gold became more arduous. Competition increased as more and more argonauts arrived in search of the increasingly scarce metal. A year before, a miner averaged $16 a day; but by 1850, the average take tailed off to between $3 to $5 a day. Times were bad.

The legislature, that same spring, urged on by American miners, enacted a law calling for a tax on foreign miners. The law required that all miners who were not American citizens must pay a $20 monthly tax to continue to work the goldfields. The law had the effect, no doubt intended by its proponents, of driving foreign miners from the mines. There are foreigners and then there are foreigners, though, and the tax of 1850 was enforced chiefly against those who were nonwhite. Chinese miners, accustomed to centuries of extortion at home, said nothing and paid.

Other groups were not so docile. In regions where their comparatively low population numbers permitted the tax collectors to enforce the law, Hispanic miners were effectively denied the right to mine. Many took to the high road and formed bandit bands that plagued the remote areas of the state for years, giving rise to legends of Robin Hood–like characters such as Joaquín Murietta.[9] Many others headed home, some by way of San Francisco; while they contributed more than their share of the murder statistics, killing each other in barroom scrapes, they do not seem to have contributed much to the general statistics on predatory crime.

Part of the increase in crime in the latter part of 1850 can no doubt be attributed to the arrival of increasing numbers of immigrants from Australia. Technically, they also came under the provisions of the law; but, as white men, they were generally overlooked by the tax collectors. But a combination of the Americans' suspicions of all foreigners and the Australians' tendency to fall back on the criminal skills that had sent many of them to Australia in the first place soon resulted in the appearance of more and more Australian names on court dockets. The extension of wharves over the mudflats in front of the town by the spring of 1850 reduced the need for boatmen to lighter goods in from the deep-water anchorage, putting many Australians out of work. With the coming of bad times, American hackmen organized themselves in an effort to put their Australian counterparts out of business.[10] Not so surprisingly, many turned to crime.

The city was doing what it could about crime. The police department was reorganized in July as provided for in the new charter. The council, by ordinance, organized the city into three police districts: the First extended from California Street to Rincon Point (with a station house at First and Mission streets); the Second, embracing the main business district, from California to Pacific streets (with a station house in the city hall at Pacific and Kearny); and the Third from Pacific Street to North Beach, including Sydneytown and the Latin Quarter (with a station house on Ohio Street, now Osgood Place). Each of the districts, in line with progressive police thinking of the time, was staffed with a captain, an assistant captain, two sergeants, and a number of officers (fifteen in the First District, eighteen in the Third, and thirty-one in the Second, covering the business heart of the city). In the face of obviously increasing crime, the strength of the force was set at seventy-five men. The three district captains were to be paid $10 a day, and other ranks received $8. Payday was twice monthly.

Under the new American government, Geary's alcalde court was replaced by a regular judicial system. The legislature appointed Levi Parsons to the district court in San Francisco with trial jurisdiction for most penal offenses. As already mentioned, County Judge Roderick N. Morrison, elected in April, formed the court of sessions with associate justices Edward (Ned) McGowan and Harvey S. Brown, with trial jurisdiction for other offenses. Francis Tilford's recorder's court was an examining court for more serious offenses and a trial court with jurisdiction for breaches of the peace and violations of city ordinances.

The organization of the courts serves to point up that San Franciscans and Californians—indeed, nineteenth-century urban Americans generally—did not comprehend fully the great social change that was affecting their cities and also helps to explain some of what went wrong the following year. When the legislature organized the California court system in the spring of 1850, it looked, as might be expected, to existing American models. Trial jurisdiction even for such relatively minor crimes as petty theft was reserved for the district courts, the usual practice in judicial systems of the period. Recorder's courts sat merely as examining courts in these cases. Such an arrangement might work in small-town America, where crimes of all types were infrequent;[11]

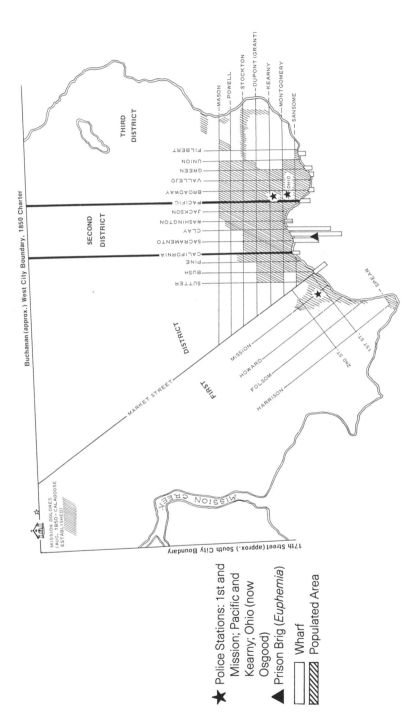

Police districts in San Francisco in late 1850. The three districts would later be reduced to two and then to one. (*Tom Mulkeen*)

but in Gold Rush San Francisco, with crime and arrests on the rise, prisoners awaiting trial in district court on minor charges piled up in the flimsy wooden jails, which simply could not hold them all.

In April, five men escaped from the prison brig; in August, a man allowed liberty from the prison ship, after his original accuser had left town, was arrested for extortion in a nearby saloon. In September, five more men escaped from the station house jail in the city hall acquired a few months before by the *ayuntamiento* government. The attitude that allowed a convict to go free to conduct private business, along with the flimsy construction of the jails, reflected a simpler society that failed to reckon with the new reality of urban life in San Francisco.

The June 1850 fire gave fresh impetus to the organization of the fire department. In July, the department was formally organized by charter; in September, the members of the volunteer fire companies elected Frederick Kohler chief engineer of the combined companies. On September 17, 1850, the fourth great fire struck. It began in the Philadelphia Saloon on Jackson between Dupont and Kearny streets and destroyed 150 buildings before it was put out. Contemporary accounts attribute the fire to a faulty flue; there was no suggestion at the time that it was the work of arsonists.

But if there was no one to accuse for that specific fire, establishment critics, looking for someone to blame for the generally disorganized conditions, settled on governmental officials and eventually cited their inability to control all types of crime as an excuse to replace them. The charter council elected in May to replace the *ayuntamiento* government was given a few months of grace, but it soon ran afoul of the real establishment in the town. In the end, the council would be saddled, along with the courts, with historic responsibility for conditions that caused the creation of the Vigilance Committee the next year.[12]

Mayor John Geary, partner in a commission business and hence a member of the merchant establishment, has escaped the opprobrium of history. Indeed, he is generally remembered as the one bright spot in the otherwise blemished record of public officials of the time.[13] One has to dig through the footnotes of standard histories to find any criticism of the popular mayor—there you will find material suggesting that he was every bit as venal as his contemporaries. "Geary's demeanor is not wholly spotless," William Heintz reminds us, citing an obscure footnote found in Bancroft:

> His unassuming manners and ability, and his veto of many obnoxious measures, gave an eclat to his official career, which served greatly

to gloss over several questionable features, such as amassing some $200,000 [the equivalent of $4,000,000 in current money] in less than three years, not derived from trade; illegally buying city lots; countenancing the purchase of the useless city hall on Stockton Street and other doubtful transactions connected with the disposal of city property.[14]

Sometimes a hint that things are not as they seem slips through.

As with the governments of Hyde and Leavenworth before it (but, strangely, not that of the *ayuntamiento*), the basis of criticism of the 1850 council was founded in economic policy affecting the interests of the commercial establishment. Revenues from the lot sales authorized by the *ayuntamiento* were quickly expended on wharves that benefited members of the authorizing body and on the planking of streets, generally approved by the public as a welcome alternative to the mudhole conditions that prevailed during the winter of 1849–50.

The value of town lots had declined in the economic downturn, and the city council was reluctant to resort to land sales in a depressed market as a way of raising revenue to run the town. So it enacted an ordinance to raise funds by the imposition of a tax on the businesses of the city. Included in the tax bill was a salary provision that would set the pay for the mayor and recorder at $10,000 a year, that of the marshal at $9,000, and that of each member of the common council at $6,000. The response was instantaneous and direct. The "people," goaded on by Sam Brannan and other business leaders, took to the streets in mass public meetings, vociferously repudiating the council's action. The issue of exorbitant council salaries is brought up time and again to describe the outrageous behavior of the 1850 council. In sum, the costs, even if enacted at the highest level, would not begin to approach the amounts garnered by the *ayuntamiento* at the public trough. There is little mention of the real bugaboo of the commercial establishment —the proposed business tax. In the face of spirited opposition, the business tax did not pass; to pay the city's bills, the council resorted to the issuance of scrip to be redeemed by future municipal revenues. The scrip on which the city agreed to pay prevailing rates of commercial interest (as much as 3–8% a *month* in the wildly unstable boomtown economy) soon depreciated to a fraction of its face value.[15]

The financial condition of the city was such that police officers had not been paid since the preceding February. A recurring theme throughout the Gold Rush era was that police officers went for months on end without being paid and then received their pay in badly depreciated scrip. The citizenry might want a large police department to put a stop to crime, but it was unwilling to pay for one. One result of the infrequent paydays was a tremendous turnover in personnel, as high as 100% in a year. (Another factor to account for the turnover was the lack of job security. When an administration changed, it was common practice to replace almost the entire department with men loyal to the new regime.)

Critics of government did not immediately resort to charges of crime and lawlessness to bring down their opponents. In September, when the five men escaped from the station house jail, the *Alta* could still joke about the prisoner in the jail "downeast" who complained that he was going to seek lodgings elsewhere if his jailer did not keep the sheep from entering his cell. Meanwhile, the newspaper continued to defend the police, saying that they were equal to the police in any city in the world, and chided the department's critics who said that the officers should resign if they did not like getting their pay in scrip depreciated to 40% of its par value. On November 30, the grand jury commended the marshal and his men for the good work they were doing. Nevertheless, some police officers were accommodating themselves to their lack of pay by going into business for themselves. Shortly after his July appointment, Officer Day was fired by the mayor for "filching" money from an immigrant. After his appointment to the force in November, Officer Phineas Blunt, assigned under Captain Lambert in the First District, commented to his diary, "This morning I took my first lesson from Captain Lambert of this station house, [sic] he told me that by good management I could make my expenses independent of my regular pay as a policeman. I look upon Mr. Lambert's suggestions as not justifiable by honest men. I am surprised at his suggestions, but perhaps I ought not to be surprised at anything in California."[16]

There were some, though, who were beginning openly to consider alternative measures of maintaining social control.[17]

CHAPTER 14

A Preview

By 1851, BOOMTOWN SAN FRANCISCO had begun to lose some of its rough edges and to take on the look of a more settled community. Most of the immigrants of the early Gold Rush years had come to California intending to make their pile and return home. Many had done so; much of the human movement through San Francisco was of successful gold seekers returning to the "states." Others, however, had taken a look around, seen the potential of California, and decided to stay on. Some sent for their families; the rough dress and habits of earlier years began to disappear, perhaps in part due to the influence of increasing numbers of "god's own policemen"—women. Gone were the tents of 1849, at least in the commercial core of the city, replaced in many cases by more substantial brick structures to house families and merchandise and, it was hoped, to impede the spread of disastrous fires.[1] Houses were under construction on Powell Street out toward the Presidio; a plank road, being built to the Mission along the old Mission Road, stimulated real estate development south of Market Street. Central Wharf and its competitors continued their spread out over the mudflats in front of Montgomery Street. To all appearances, the city was thriving.

San Francisco remained the main point of entry for men and goods coming to California; but immigration was down and fewer successful miners came to San Francisco in the winter of 1850–51. The weather was drier than the year before, the roads to the mines remained open, and the "rising towns of Sacramento and Stockton offered all the attractions of dissipation closer at hand."[2] For all the apparent prosperity, the local economy was depressed. Goods sent by eastern shippers continued to stream in, glutting the market. Prices and profits were driven down, and unemployment was widespread. Public gambling houses declined even as drinking saloons increased in number. Hordes of the unemployed lounged in the streets of the city. For free entertainment they crowded into the law courts around Portsmouth Square; at the hint of any unusual occurrence, whether a fistfight or a runaway horse, hundreds would materialize on Portsmouth Square to find out what was going on.[3] The *Alta* on February 11, 1851, reported that idleness was widespread, that hundreds if not thousands crowded the courts of justice, and that hundreds would materialize instantly at any noise or fight on the plaza.

There were ten burglaries reported in the press in January. On January 3, burglars entered the store of James Dows on Washington Street and blew his safe containing $5,000. The same night, an office on Commercial Street was burglarized of some business papers. In mid-month, Captain Howard of the First Police District lost $2,500 in gold from his lodgings in a firehouse. The discriminating thieves left a like amount in scrip behind. About the same time, fifty-six ounces of gold were taken from under the pillow of a man sleeping in a rooming house. On January 19, Juan Espinosa entered a house on Pacific Street and stole $1,080 belonging to José Sepulvia. Late in January, R. S. Watson frightened off thieves with gunfire after they had dragged the safe out of his company office. On January 25, a physician on Pike Street (Waverly Place) lost $250 to a prowler; the next day, a North Beach sausage maker lost $2,800.

On February 1, burglars took the safe containing $500 from a store on Stockton and Green streets to the corner, where they blew it open. On February 5, a man and his wife grappled with burglars who entered their bedroom on Bush Street. On February 14, instruments were reported stolen in the burglary of a store at Sansome and Jackson streets; the same day, a man named Christofer Kane was arrested for burglariz-

Portsmouth Square in 1850. The vigilantes were to hang their first victim from the crossbeams of the Custom House on the right. (*California State Library*)

ing another store. A few days later, burglars stole $300 from a trunk on Montgomery Street and $1,000 in silver from a man on Powell Street. On February 3, two hoodlums tried to mug Officer Bernard Blitz on his beat at North Beach and ended up in jail for their trouble. The next day, a man was beaten and robbed of $170 on Dupont Street; on the occasion several days later of "one of the most atrocious and daring highway robberies ever heard of in California," in which a man was robbed of his rifle on Mission Road, the *Alta* commented that when a man cannot walk on a public highway in broad daylight without fear of robbery or murder, "it's time we should be stirring."[4]

The press honeymoon with the criminal justice authorities was at an end; the next robbery in San Francisco would plunge the city into two days of excitement, prefiguring the events of the summer to come. It had rained a bit on the evening of Wednesday, February 19, and there was little foot traffic on the streets at 8:00 P.M. when two men entered the store of Charles Jansen at Montgomery and Washington streets. The men at first feigned interest in buying some blankets; when Jansen bent over to take some from a lower shelf, one of the thugs struck him down with a slung shot.[5] They took $2,000 from his cash drawer and promptly escaped.[6]

The next morning, the papers raised the cry. The crime was "one of the most barefaced cool and audacious robberies which the annals of any country give a history," proclaimed the *Alta*. "Who is safe when the store of a peaceable citizen can be entered and the proprietor almost murdered?"[7] The press seized upon the case to trumpet a litany of all that was wrong with the justice system. There had been a rash of recent crimes about which nothing had been done, the papers reported. Criminals were hidden by their friends from the police, who did little to catch them. The thieves, if they were caught, used their loot to pay pettifogging attorneys who got them off. "Is it worthwhile," asked the *Courier*, "if caught, to offer them [the criminals] a trial in our courts? Is it not better to make examples of them, if found, by hanging them at once?"[8]

By Friday, the police had two suspects in custody, both of them Australians. One of them was a man who gave his name as Windred or Wildred. The other was identified as James Stuart (aka English Jim), a well-known Sydney criminal. Stuart, a native of England, had been sent to the Australian penal colonies about fifteen years before at the age of sixteen on a conviction for forgery. He had arrived in California in November 1849 as part of the first great rush; by the time of the arrest for the Jansen robbery, he was well known to the authorities in Sacramento and the northern mines for his many crimes. In October 1850, he had been tried in the mines for the theft of $4,000—it was only due to the intervention of the authorities that he was not lynched. He then escaped, allegedly murdered a man in Marysville, and moved on to Sacramento, where he became involved in a horse theft ring. He was arrested several times for theft; on one occasion, while being held on the prison brig in Sacramento, he was recognized by a resident of Marysville as the wanted murderer from that city. Before the transfer papers could be processed, however, he managed to get himself released from jail; it was an officer from Sacramento who pointed Stuart out to the San Francisco officers on Central Wharf, where he was arrested for the Jansen crime. The only hitch was that the man arrested said that he was not Stuart—he gave the name of Thomas Berdue and swore that he knew nothing of the crime with which he was charged. At a preliminary hearing in justice court on Friday, conflicting testimony was given about the identity of Stuart/Berdue. Nevertheless, both he and Windred were held on a charge of robbery.

The next day, about noon, Stuart/Berdue and Windred were escorted under police guard to the house where Jansen was recuperating. There the victim tentatively identified the arrestees as his assailants. On the way back to the courthouse, the crowd accompanying the police (no doubt largely made up of the courthouse loungers and those who were accustomed to hang around the town square waiting for something to turn up) hooted for the release of the prisoners so that they could be summarily dealt with. As the group crossed Portsmouth Square, a rush was made on the guard to seize the prisoners, but the officers fought it off successfully. The examination of the prisoners continued that afternoon in the justice court at the top of the plaza while as many as 5,000 excited citizens milled around outside. Adding to the excitement was an unsigned handbill circulating among the crowd, calling attention to "the series of murders and robberies that have been committed in this city, without the least redress from the law. . . ." Lynch law was offered as the only never-failing remedy. "Are we to be robbed and assassinated in our domiciles, and the law to let our aggressors perambulate the streets . . . ?" the handbill continued. "If so, let each man be his own executioner. Fie upon your laws! they have no force. All those who would rid our city of robbers and murderers will assemble on Sunday at two o'clock, on the plaza."[9]

But the "people" were not satisfied to wait until the following day.

As the judge announced adjournment of the examination until the following Monday, the cry was raised—"Now is the time"—and a rush was made to seize the prisoners. Fortunately for the prisoners, it so happened that the Washington Guards, a private guard company, had been drilling on the occasion of their namesake's birthday; Recorder Tilford, having heard threats of a possible lynching, asked them to stand by in their armory next to the justice court.[10] When the rush was made to seize the prisoners, the Washington Guards held the populace at bay while the police spirited the prisoners into the judge's chambers. The crowd was thwarted in its attempt to seize the prisoners and began gradually to disperse; but as dusk fell, between 6,000 and 7,000 angry men assembled around the city hall jail a couple of blocks away. Mayor Geary, Recorder Tilford, the ever-present Sam Brannan, and others addressed the excited crowd; it was finally resolved that a committee of twenty men would be appointed to assure that the prisoners did not escape. Another committee of twelve was appointed to work with the authorities on the best course to follow.

The mass public meeting was adjourned until 10 A.M. the following day; the committee of twenty went to see the prisoners, while the committee of twelve retired to a room in the recorder's court to deliberate. Committee member Sam Brannan wanted to hang them outright. "These men are murderers, I say, as well as thieves. I know it and I will die or see them hung by the neck," he said.[11] The chair called him out of order; about all the committee could agree on was to adjourn to Portsmouth Square in the morning to report that the prisoners were still in custody. Before the meeting adjourned, Brannan offered a resolution that would have recommended to the public meeting the next day that the prisoners be hanged on Monday. The motion failed.

On Sunday morning, more than 8,000 men gathered in Portsmouth Square. It was one of those false spring days that visit San Francisco in February. It was clear and warm after a drizzly week, just the sort of day for outside activity like a hanging. The *Alta*, the only paper published on Sunday, perhaps alarmed at the momentum of events, cautioned that lynch law, once let loose, could get out of hand. Brannan delivered the majority report from the committee of twelve; Recorder Tilford, Judge Parsons, and Mayor Geary also addressed the crowd. The mayor proposed that twelve citizens be selected to sit with the examining justice the following day, but the crowd was not having any of it. William T. Coleman, a young commission merchant, came up with a solution more acceptable to the crowd. According to his later account, Coleman's idea was that the people should form a court of their own and try the prisoners that very day. If innocent, they would go free; if guilty, they would hang before sundown. The crowd, he stated, wildly shouted its approval.[12]

Another committee of twelve was appointed to make the necessary arrangements; while the committee met, a handbill containing Brannan's recommendation of the previous night to hang the suspects summarily was circulated among the crowd. Thinking the paper contained the recommendation of the committee just appointed, members of the crowd made a move to seize the prisoners, but they were forestalled by cooler heads. It was to be an exciting day.

The trial, strictly an extralegal affair except for the presence of one judge who agreed to serve as counsel for the defense, convened at 2:30 P.M. in the recorder's courtroom at city hall before a citizen's jury of twelve members. The defendants, for their own safety, were not present at the trial but were held under a heavy police guard in the marshal's office upstairs. As the trial proceeded through the day, virtually the entire population of the city milled around outside the city hall. At 7 P.M., while the jury was out interviewing Jansen, who was still too disabled to attend the trial, members of the crowd—many no doubt warmed by spirits from one of the nearby saloons—waited in the chill night air on the streets around city hall. Becoming impatient that no resolution had been reached, they decided to take matters into their own hands. They moved on the station house to take the prisoners but were again turned away by Marshal Fallon and his men.

The jury returned, and the trial resumed. After hearing more testimony, the panel retired to deliberate; it was not until nearly midnight that its members finally reported their findings. The jury was split nine to three in favor of conviction. Outraged by the unexpected verdict, the crowd in the courtroom went wild. Brannan and others called for the names of the dissenting jurors so they could be hanged along with the prisoners. The jury, pistols in hand, backed away into the jury room. After a time, exhausted by the late hour and emotionally drained by the excitement of the long day, the crowd began to drift away. There were several attempts through the night by one determined group to break into the jail and rescue the prisoners, but they were repulsed by a 200-man guard posted by Mayor Geary.[13] The next day, Stuart/ Berdue and Windred were spirited away by the authorities for their own safety, but by then the excitement was over for a time, and the citizens of San Francisco resumed their usual weekday occupations.

The defendants were tried separately in district court the following month, and both were convicted as charged. Windred was sentenced to ten years' imprisonment and Stuart/Berdue was given fourteen years for the Jansen robbery and sent to Marysville to stand trial for murder.

The fact of the matter was that Berdue and Windred were telling the truth all along. Berdue was not Stuart—who indeed had committed the Jansen robbery—and neither Berdue nor Windred had anything to do with the crime for which they were tried.[14] But for the courage of a few jurors and the steadfast resistance of the authorities, Brannan and other hotheads would no doubt have caused the hanging of two innocent men. The question for us, though, is: what kind of circumstances could plunge the people of the city into a fevered state of excited outrage and cause them to bypass the regular institutions of justice in such a cavalier fashion? The limits of the town's toleration had been reached, Mary Williams suggests: "The crime itself was no more heinous than many that had passed unnoticed, but the victim was so well known and so popular that his misfortune roused unusual indignation."[15]

It seems, when crime reports such as those at the beginning of this chapter are pulled out of the context of daily life, that there was quite a lot of crime just before the Jansen robbery. Viewed another way, however, particularly when compared to later urban experience with crime, there does not seem to have been so much after all. All the reports of crime for that period amounted to about one criminal homicide a month,[16] one burglary about every four days, and less than three robberies, of one sort or another, a month. That is the sum total in putatively crime-ridden San Francisco, where murder was reportedly a daily occurrence.

George Stewart is closer to the mark: "There has been a tendency among historians to exaggerate the amount of crime before the attack on Jansen, and to consider that this attack was merely the last straw." By way of explanation, he suggests that "the present affair coupled robbery with violence in a way which was out of the current pattern of crime."[17] Indeed, a close reading of the *Alta*, published almost uninterruptedly under one name or another since 1847, reveals only one report of a robbery with violence (as defined by the penal code) of a commercial property until at least the end of 1853—the Jansen robbery.

Simply put, the crime of commercial robbery did not occur in Gold Rush San Francisco. The Jansen robbery can be said to be the introduction to San Francisco of a criminal phenomenon that would become an urban commonplace. But at the time, in supposedly wild and woolly

San Francisco, it was totally outside the experience of the citizens. No wonder they went wild. Always in the background, sometimes coming to the fore, is the suspicion that members of the commercial establishment, through the vehicle of a compliant press, furthered the belief that crime was rampant to justify their acts. That hypothesis also helps to explain the sentiment fostered by the press and the leadership of the movement to hang Jansen's suspected assailants.

Jansen was not just any victim. He was not some woodcutter returning from the Mission or some drunk who got mugged making his way home from a low dive—he was a member of the commercial establishment. He was well known and popular, as Mary Williams asserts.[18] He was, according to George Stewart, "a solid citizen . . . and other solid citizens immediately began to think 'I might have been the victim.'"[19] It was members of the commercial establishment, some of whom had taken the lead in the movement against the Hounds, who dominated the public meetings and made up the committees that tried Berdue and Windred. They were not reacting to some abstract concern about crime—they were responding to an attack on one of their own. It was the loungers about Portsmouth Square who provided the crowd, the Greek chorus calling for lynch law. They milled around in the square and made rushes to seize the prisoners, but it was the commercial establishment of the city and colleagues in the press who were calling the tune.

CHAPTER 15

Officialdom under Fire

THE THREAT OF A LITTLE summary justice in the Jansen affair seems to have had an effect on the robbery rate in San Francisco, at least for a while. There was not another robbery of any sort reported after the Jansen crime until May 15. Three robberies were reported that month and two in June. Overall, the robbery rate, while certainly more than the town was accustomed to tolerating, was down compared to the preceding six-month period.

Comparison of Reported Robberies

Month	1	2	3	4	5	6	Total
Jan/June 1850	1	0	1	0	0	0	2
July/Dec 1850	1	0	3	4	3	7	18
Jan/June 1851	0	4	0	0	3	2	9

The lesson does not seem to have extended itself to burglars, though. Ten burglaries were reported in the *Alta* in January and seven in February. March, with seventeen reported burglaries, was the highest month up to that point in the experience of Gold Rush San Francisco. There was little question in anyone's mind who was committing them—the names of Australian criminals appeared with increasing frequency on court dockets. When the police, having been tipped off in advance, sprang a trap on several thieves breaking into Colonel Stevenson's property on March 17, they arrested George Adams, William Watkins, and several other well-known Sydney thieves. After that arrest, the number of burglaries declined. There were six reported in April, eight in May, and five in June. Still, there were more in the first six months of 1851 than in all of the preceding year.

Comparison of Reported Burglaries

Month	1	2	3	4	5	6	Total
Jan/June 1850	0	0	0	3	0	0	3
July/Dec 1850	6	6	12	7	9	9	49
Jan/June 1851	10	7	17	6	8	5	53

Even before the Jansen robbery, the critical attention of the commercial establishment had been turned on government officials. San Francisco city officials in the first months of 1851 are chiefly remembered for having contributed to the conditions that eventually brought the Committee of Vigilance into being. Bancroft describes the scene:

> In the mad race of money-getting, office-holders as well as others were troubled with the itching palm. Gold dust was abundant; every one appeared to be getting rich; business men were not always over-scrupulous in the means employed for the acquisition of wealth; San Francisco was a mighty metropolis in embryo; why should not her officers make money with the rest? So they voted themselves large salaries, built and bought extensively, let contracts to supporters at double current rates, stole the public lands, imposed heavy taxes on the people and swelled the public debt until the young city groaned beneath the weight.[1]

Little more than a month after the May 1850 election of the council, according to the *Annals*, "the community was kept in a state of excessive excitement" about a council plan to raise revenue by means of a tax on business that also included a healthy salary for members of the council. "The proposed aldermanic allowance seemed monstrous and unjust," reported the *Annals*, "from the fact that the city was then much embarrassed in pecuniary affairs, and that certain most obnoxious and heavy taxes were proposed to be laid upon the inhabitants."[2]

Less than a year later, as the council's term was coming to an end in the spring of 1851, the city was heavily in debt. Total civic expenditures between August 1, 1849, and November 30, 1850, a period that embraces the term of the *ayuntamiento* and a few months of the 1850–51 council, were $1.5 million. In the next three months, another half million was spent. Extraordinary expenses had been incurred, according to the *Annals*, to pay for "grading and improving the public streets, building certain wharves, the purchase of expensive premises for corporate purposes, the monstrous salaries claimed by boards of aldermen and other municipal authorities, the heavy outlay attending the hospital, fire and police departments. . . ."[3] According to the *Annals*, speaking of the city officials of 1850:

> In various ways they trafficked in scrip and always to their own advantage. The tax-collector, for instance, refused to receive scrip in payment of license duties and other city taxes . . . while instead of paying into the city treasury the *cash* which was actually received, he only handed over his own comparatively worthless paper, purchased with the city's cash for that express purpose. . . . Considerable fortunes were thus gained by sundry officials. . . .[4]

When the steamer *Oregon* arrived in San Francisco on October 18, 1850, with the news of California's admission into the Union as the thirty-first state, the city erupted in an impromptu celebration lasting for days. A more formal celebration with parades and speeches was also planned for later in the year. As part of that celebration, commemorative medals of gold were struck for presentation to the mayor, city department heads, and members of the common council. When news of the medals leaked out, the press seized upon the issue; as politicians backpedaled away from any involvement in the matter, the papers excoriated the council for its extravagance.[5] The issue of the medals has since become standard fare in accounts attempting to show the council's venality and its contempt for the public welfare.

The justice system also came in for its share of press criticism. "At that period of which we write," said the *Annals*, "the tribunals of justice were considered altogether insufficient for those dangerous times, and many of the individuals connected with them incapable and corrupt."[6] As to the attorneys who practiced before the courts, the day after the Jansen robbery the *Alta* expressed the widely held belief that "the highwayman uses his loot to pay pettifogging attorneys who get him off. Such attornies [sic] are father to the thief and the murderer."[7]

Bail was easy to obtain. Many defendants were allowed to go free on their own recognizance; even if money bail was required, it was a simple matter for a defendant, like the accused murderer Matthews and many others, to post bail then slip quietly into the confusion of the Gold Rush populace.[8] But even if an accused criminal should come to trial, he still had little fear of being convicted. Respectable citizens avoided jury duty and, commented the *Alta* in April, no one was "so debased" that he did not have friends who would hang around the courthouse hoping to be called by the sheriff to be on a panel when regularly called jurors failed to show up.[9] If by some chance a defendant was tried and convicted, there was still a good chance he would go free. The existing jails were wooden sieves and the construction of a new county jail on Broadway, begun late in 1850 under the administration of the court of sessions, was delayed time and again because of the lack of funds to complete it.

In early April, two of the arrestees from the Stevenson burglary in March, William Watkins and Jim Briggs, escaped from the station house jail. Watkins was promptly recaptured, but he escaped again soon afterward in a mass breakout with other confederates from the Stevenson job, including George Adams, who cut their way through a two-inch plank at the back of a cell and bored through the brick foundation of the city hall.[10] William Windred, under sentence for the Jansen robbery, escaped with them and left for Australia soon afterward.

In the wooden station house jail, fifty or sixty prisoners were being held in six cells designed to hold half that number. Every few mornings, until the county jail was finally completed in the summer under the auspices of the Committee of Vigilance, newspaper readers were greeted by a story of another escape. Prisoners slipped out while their guards were looking the other way, made false keys to open the locks of their cells, or dug their way out. There were no more jokes about sheep invading cells or about prisoners carrying jail doors on their backs. The easygoing times were gone, and the lackadaisical procedures of an earlier day no longer worked. Crime was up—and it was no laughing matter.

For months on end, construction of the county jail went forward in fits and starts as money apparently disappeared down a judicial rat hole. In April, in the face of accusations that he had profited personally from the construction contracts, Judge Morrison resigned from office. After his resignation, his two former associates on the court of sessions scheduled an election to fill the vacated office. The state legislature, in the meantime, enacted a law to fill the vacancy by legislative appointment. In the election, one claimant to the office was chosen by popular vote and another appointed by the legislature. Both showed up in court and proceeded to hold each other in contempt.[11] In the end, the legislative appointee, William Campbell, prevailed, but not before the public was treated to the spectacle (at a time when the town seemed to be under concerted attack from predatory criminals) of two claimants to a judicial office, each using the powers of that office to unseat his opponent.

District court judge Levi Parsons also contributed his bit to the judicial farce. After the *Herald* criticized Parsons for practices that, in the editorial view, would encourage crime, the judge held its editors in contempt of court. One editor refused to pay the fine assessed, and the judge remanded him to custody in the station house jail. A crowd of 4,000 led, as might be expected, by Sam Brannan marched to the jail publicly to visit the imprisoned editor and to repudiate the action of the judge. Another court freed the editor.[12]

The press honeymoon with the police was also coming to an end. The *Picayune* in January 1851 remarked that the police were sensitive to the slightest imputation of fault on their part but that "out of the immediate vicinity of gambling or drinking saloons, a policeman is scarcely ever to be found, day or night." Crime was increasing, the editor said, but criminals were not being detected and sent to court in proportion to the incidence of crime.[13] The next month, the *Alta* complained that twelve or fifteen officers of the seventy-five-officer force did all the work of the department.[14]

The *Alta*, citing the disordered state of affairs, had been after its readers since the beginning of the year to elect a good government. As the April election neared, Sam Brannan and a group of business colleagues put together an independent slate of candidates for the spring election; but before the election, the slate was withdrawn. It was the regular slate of Whig candidates that swept the April 28 municipal election, in which a new charter limiting the authority of the council to expend money was also approved. Mayor John Geary had declined to run for another term; the Democratic mayoral candidate, recorder Francis Tilford, was beaten by Charles Brenham, a popular steamboat captain. Whig Robert G. Crozier soundly defeated incumbent Democrat Malachi Fallon for the office of city marshal, and Whig Royal H. Waller was elected recorder. Whig Frank Pixley was elected city attorney, and Whig candidates also carried a majority of the council seats. As the time of the Vigilance Committee approached, then, it was not pro-Broderick Democrats who held the reins at city hall. Significantly, for reasons that will become evident, it was the Whigs, members of the party of business, who controlled the town government.

The historical belief is pretty well set that the public officials in the early months of 1851 contributed much by their own actions to the need to establish a Committee of Vigilance. It is true enough that the officials were not angels. They probably measured up to common standards of municipal morality of the day, particularly as found in San Francisco. But there is more to the history of disturbed civic affairs in the spring of 1851. That story usually gets lost, however, in the rhetoric surrounding the excited events that followed. The charges of council extravagance in purchasing medals to honor themselves received almost daily attention in the newspapers of the day, but it was never fully ascertained who ordered them in the first place. On one occasion, the man who made the medals said they had been ordered by the historically popular Mayor Geary.[15] The man later recanted and said he could not remember who ordered them. It is the council, however, that has carried the historical burden of blame.

As noted earlier, it was little more than a month after the election of the council of 1850, according to the *Annals*, that the city was "much embarrassed in pecuniary affairs." The public coffers, then, already had to have been empty when the council charged with extravagance assumed office. The question naturally arises as to what happened to all the money from the recent lot sales made by the *ayuntamiento*. It certainly did not go to pay aldermanic salaries. Even at the highest rate proposed, the salaries would have cost no more than $66,000 a year. As it was, in the form the ordinance finally passed in January 1851 over Mayor Geary's veto, the salaries could have cost no more than $20,000 for the year. That is a very small part of the $2,000,000 in civic expenditures made in the seventeen months from August 1, 1849, to the end of February 1851 cited by the *Annals*.

More pertinent to an understanding of the city's failing financial condition were expenses cited by the *Annals* for paving and grading the streets.[16] Street paving and grading was an expensive proposition, but one that had strong public support. Memories of the quagmire conditions experienced in the rainy winter of 1849–50 were fresh in everyone's mind. The establishment of police, fire, and medical services was another costly proposition (see chapter 25). Nineteenth-century city dwellers were just becoming aware of the high costs of what are now considered essential city services, and they did not like it.

If we want to find some real extravagance, we should look to the cost of "building certain wharves" ($300,000) and "the purchase of expensive premises for corporate purposes" ($150,000), which directly benefited members of the *ayuntamiento* government. But there is little mention in contemporary criticism of the officials of 1850–51 that the seeds of financial disaster had been sown and nurtured by the 1850 council's predecessors in the *ayuntamiento* government. Lotchin has it right: "Land sales raised large amounts, but the merchant-business [read *ayuntamiento*] council had squandered much of this money."[17] It was members of the same group, the big landlords and merchant leaders of the city, who led the massive tax protest in the summer of 1850 that led to the financially disastrous issuance of scrip.[18] Yet again, it was the council that was blamed, not the leading businessmen who caused it all to happen.

It is also true, by current standards of professional propriety, that criminal justice practitioners were not particularly honest. Neither were they probably any worse than the average for their time in urban America—yet other cities did not degenerate into vigilante violence. Perhaps members of the court of sessions were playing fast and loose with public funds set aside to build a county jail.[19] But the larger part of the problem of construction delays can be traced to practices forced on the government by the leading businessmen of the town. The tax revolt, as has been discussed, resulted in the issuance of scrip that depreciated greatly in value. Contractors working for the city thus inflated costs by two or three times when paid in scrip so that they would not be the losers; that is the principal reason that money to build the jail was found to be insufficient.

The impression comes through, if one looks a bit beyond the standard explanations of what occurred, that the Gold Rush turned San Francisco into a full-sized social laboratory of the changes then affecting American cities. Much of the difficulty encountered by the authorities in San Francisco was not so much attributable to their venality or inefficiency but rather to being in the midst of a social revolution they did not understand. In examining the issues facing the criminal justice apparatus of the town, we can see that those responsible for adapting to the new conditions just did not understand what was going on. They tried to make the changes, but it was a question of too little and too late.

The easygoing bail procedures do not so much point to essential incompetence as to the fact that courts were trying to employ a system that had worked well in preindustrial America but was inadequate to the needs of a changing city. It might have been alright to let a man free on his own recognizance in small-town America because there was really no place for him to go; but in the anonymity of the boomtown, such releases were an invitation to escape. Drawing jurors from among people around the courthouse, a practice embedded in the law, also might have worked well in small-town America. In a small community with a stable population, the decision of a jury selected in that manner could be expected to adhere closely to the prevailing ethos of the community. (It had better—they would have to live with both their decision and their neighbors.) But in a boomtown of strangers with an as yet ill-formed community of values, there was little incentive to bring in convictions. The idlers who made up the juries actually had more in common with the average defendant than with his accuser.

The editor of the *Alta* had the beginning of an understanding of the problem. In April 1851, the paper counseled the legislature to do away with the system that required the sheriff to call for jurors from persons around the court. What was needed and recommended was a standing panel of 200 permanent, respectable citizens from whom jurors would be drawn.[20] (In August 1850, the *Alta*'s editor had commiserated with the sheriff when he complained that he could not get "intelligent" juries. When the sheriff produced a list of delinquent jurors with the editor's name on it, the editor went before the district court and was excused on the grounds that he was a member of a volunteer fire company. He then advised others to join fire companies as a way of avoiding jury duty.)

Beyond any charges of venality, the problems with the courts suggest systemic administrative problems. As already mentioned, police court judges by law were not given trial jurisdiction for even minor crimes of theft. While higher courts presumably concerned themselves with more weighty matters, petty criminals unable to make bail began to pile up in the flimsy jails. The legislature eventually changed the law to give primary jurisdiction to the recorders for crimes of theft, but by then events had taken on a life of their own.

People at the time were puzzled at the inability of the courts to handle the business before them, partly because they were in the midst of a social change they could not fully understand. Looking back on the practices of Tilford's court from the vantage point of forty-six years later, the *San Francisco Chronicle* in 1896 described court procedures in 1850 and wondered at the judge's ability to handle the load. "Instead of telling one's troubles to the warrant clerk in those days," reported the *Chronicle*, "the complaining witness went before the judge in open court and 'made information.' This was written down in long hand on blue legal cap [*sic*] paper, and after being duly considered by the Judge a warrant was ordered issued."[21] These procedures were in effect in 1850 (and 1851) but later changed as the press of business demanded it to provide administrative assistance to the courts. The courts in the early 1850s continued to use procedures more suited to the courts of 1847, before the rapid urbanization of the community.

In point of fact, as seen in the above crime statistics, the courts were faced with a new set of conditions that neither they nor their critics in the press fully understood. John Geary might have been able to dispose of his 741 criminal cases easily enough in seven months (that is about 4 cases a court day). Recorder Tilford in the later period, however, with 2,051 cases in eight months (or 9 cases a court day), was faced with a new order of things. Without the assistance of a prosecuting officer (none was appointed until 1856), he was expected to handle twice the case load of his predecessor.

Perhaps it is true that the presiding judge of the court of sessions profited from the jail building scheme, and that is certainly the judgment of history, but he was not in it alone. Prominent members of the soon-to-be-organized Vigilance Committee were deeply involved in the matter; despite later protestations of critics to the contrary, the methods employed pretty much represented the common business practices of the time.

Judge Parsons was probably as arrogant as history reports him to be, and he certainly did not read the mood of the day. But perhaps something else was also at work. Courts nowadays, confronted with a steady stream of cases, sit continuously. But in preindustrial America, and much of the rest of the world, where crime was a less frequent occurrence, they conducted sessions only when there was a need for their services. In Gold Rush San Francisco, as in mid-nineteenth-century urban America generally, the increase of predatory crime suggested that sessions should be continuous. Mired in the old way of doing things, the judges worked at the same old leisurely pace. The legislature in 1851 realized that something needed to be done—one of its enactments was that the San Francisco district court should conduct a special May term to catch up with the criminal case backlog. Parsons cavalierly went about his business according to the dictates of his own opinion, trying civil cases while criminal defendants stewed in jail or took their leave. Interpreted one way, his holding of newspaper editors in contempt for affronting him personally can be construed as another example of judicial arrogance. But viewed another way, the same action could be interpreted as the reaction of a man under stress from press attacks on an issue neither of them could fully comprehend.

One of the statistics brought up later to justify the establishment of the Committee of Vigilance, and repeated in nearly every account of the time to show the sorry state of criminal justice in Gold Rush San Francisco, is the record of dispositions of the 184 criminal cases brought before the district court between April 30, 1850, and May 23, 1851.[22] On its face, the report carried in the *Herald* is surely damning: 68 of the 184 were discharged, 21 escaped, 6 died, 2 received pardons, and 9 remained in custody. Of the remaining 78, 40 probably forfeited bail, the paper said, and the rest were unaccounted for, though more than 20 had been convicted and sentenced.

How many of the holes in the statistical picture were attributable to lost prisoners and how many to faulty record keeping is not known; if the latter is the case, our predecessors had about as good a conviction rate as the modern justice system.[23] What the tabulation does show is that the justice system in 1851 was being confronted, perhaps for the first time in the experience of much of the citizenry, with a phenomenon that has now become a part of everyday judicial life.

One of the smoldering issues today confronting the criminal justice system is the fact that for some reason or another (plea bargaining, crowded prisons, judicial laxity) too few criminals seem to make it to jail. (Citizen disapproval of conditions has resulted in a decade of legislation calling for mandatory sentences for certain crimes in California; this in turn has resulted in what has been called a crisis in jail overcrowding.) The merits of the argument as to whether not enough people are going to jail aside, current raw statistics look much like those of 1851. One modern study of a nationwide sample has shown, for example, that for 2,780,000 index crimes (crimes selected on the basis of their likelihood of being reported), 727,000 arrests were made (about 26%). Of those arrested, 160,000 (22%) were convicted and sentenced to jail, and 63,000 (less than 9%) actually went to prison.[24] The percentages at corresponding stages are not a lot different when current figures are compared to the 184 cases in San Francisco in the early 1850s. Our predecessors in 1851 were unwittingly getting a look at the future—and they did not like it.

CHAPTER 16

The Last Straws

GOLD RUSH CALIFORNIANS, as is becoming evident, did not fully understand the great social upheaval of which they were a part, but they certainly knew that something unusual was going on and that institutions of government were not up to the task at hand. The familiar system of common law, while well adapted to older, better-regulated communities, said the *Alta* on one occasion, just did not work in the heterogeneous society of Gold Rush California.[1] The editor did not have a specific remedy in mind at that time but thought something more summary than the laws in force was needed.

The 1851 legislature did what it could. The foreign miners tax was repealed, not out of any feelings of ethnic altruism but to improve business conditions by providing a larger pool of customers. A new charter, passed by the voters in the April 28 election, was enacted for San Francisco, as has already been mentioned; among provisions extending the city limits and reorganizing the city government, it not only prohibited salaries for aldermen but also restricted the authority of the council to expend funds.

The legislature also provided for a county board of supervisors to manage county business in place of the court of sessions, and, to help the city in its fiscal crisis, established a funded debt commission. The commission took control of all city property with authority to rent or sell it to retire the public debt, and it issued city stocks paying 10% per annum interest, which it exchanged for higher-interest but less stable city scrip. In the end, the city was to work its way out of debt. Changes in substantive law as well as the manner in which it was administered were also enacted. In January, Governor Burnett resigned his office and was replaced by Lieutenant Governor John McDougal. In his farewell address to the legislature, Burnett said that one way to bring crime under control in a society with no adequate alternatives was to assess the death penalty for serious crimes of theft. The legislature agreed— for several years, grand theft and armed robbery were capital crimes in California.[2]

Recorder's courts were given jurisdiction over petty theft cases; the district court, as mentioned, was ordered to conduct a special May term to catch up on the backlog; and all serious criminal matters with the exception of murder, manslaughter, and arson were removed from the jurisdiction of the district court and turned over to the court of sessions. Early in May, a large number of cases were transferred from the district court to the court of sessions. With all the changes and with a new business-dominated Whig city government in office, it might be expected that conditions would improve. But they did not. Like a vessel under way, the urban problems did not respond immediately to the reversal in direction. The changes would come, but not before the city was plunged into violent disorder.

Business in the spring was still bad. Real estate declined from a total value of $16 million in 1850 to $10 million the following year. Ships full of goods continued to arrive, and the glut grew. According to the *Annals*:

> The commerce and imports of San Francisco were very great during 1851—too great indeed for profitable trade . . . most kinds of goods were a dead loss to the owner. In the palmy days of '48 and '49, all were purchasers, at any price: now everybody sought to sell, at no matter what sacrifice. . . . Enormous losses were sustained during 1850, and especially 1851, by foreign shippers. The commercial people in San Francisco generally acted as agents on commission for others, and didn't often import as merchants on their own account. The losses therefore on merchandise did not so very much affect individual citizens, while

to the general public it was a positive gain to have an unlimited supply of goods at low prices.[3]

So the only casualties from the surfeit of goods were the profits of local merchants. Day after day, the press reported on the continuing glut, saying that profits would have been good were it not for the overstock of merchandise.[4] "We can see no chance for improvement until the markets are materially relieved of the surplus on hand," commented the *Alta* on April 24. "We want a general clearing of the market," complained the paper on April 26, before any good could be realized. They were soon to get their "clearing."

In March, a 270-pound firebell was installed in the Monumental Engine Company at the head of Portsmouth Square; on the evening of May 3, even before the new city administration was sworn in, the bell announced the start of the fifth and greatest fire to afflict San Francisco until the disaster of 1906. The fire started in the upstairs room of a paint store on Clay Street across from Portsmouth Square and spread quickly to other nearby buildings even before the Monumental Engine Company could drag its pumper the few feet across the plaza. The chief engineer of the department and many of the city's firemen were away in Sacramento when the fire struck, and no coordinated assault was brought to bear on the conflagration. By the time the fire had burned itself out, twenty square blocks, or three-quarters of the business section of the city, were in ruins and from twenty to one hundred people (the accurate number was never established) had been killed.

In the immediate aftermath of the fire, it was attributed to accident, which is probably the case. But as the magnitude of the conflagration became known, public wrath grew, and stories circulated that the police had been investigating plots to burn down the town. Within a few days, the belief crystallized, according to the *Alta*, that little doubt remained that the fire had been set "by an incarnate fiend for the purpose of robbery."[5] The *Courier* shortly afterward complained that "immigrants from Sydney have been able to burn the city over our heads four or five times. . . ."[6]

By the time Bancroft got around to telling the story, it had turned into a plot to burn down the entire region. The May 1851 fire in San Francisco, according to California's foremost historian, "was the work of incendiaries as several previous fires were, and as was the burning of Stockton two days later." A house on Sacramento Street had been

The great fire of May 1851. (*California State Library*)

set on fire at the same time, he says, and arsonists had burned Nevada City a few weeks before. "All this was but one scheme concocted by rascals in convention assembled for the simultaneous annihilation of the chief cities of Northern California."[7]

The legend persists. Both the *San Francisco Examiner* and the *San Francisco Chronicle* in March 1986, reporting on the discovery of the archaeological remains of a building destroyed in the 1851 fire, attribute it to arson by Australian criminals. Even more recently, a writer in 1987 reports: "On May 4, 1850, most of San Francisco was destroyed in a great fire. One year later to the day [the latter fire actually started on May 3], a gang of thieves with the improbable name of Sydney Ducks, guided perhaps by a misplaced sense of yearly ritual, started a fire in a building on Portsmouth Square. The fire spread, and once again almost all of San Francisco burned to the ground."[8] In actual fact, the fire was probably an accident. Parker's *Directory*, published in 1852 only a year later, after the passions of the moment had cooled but while many of the principals were still present, said so without contradiction: "This fire, though by some ascribed, as usual, to design, is now generally charged to accident or carelessness."[9]

Accident or arson, the merchants had their "clearing" and prices rose by 15 to 20% after the fire. Charges against the Australians continued to fly. On May 17, the *Alta* reported in some detail on an attempt to burn the city hospital. And in reporting on a fire thought to be arson on Pike Street on May 31, the paper said that alarms of fire can be expected any time "when we have a band of desperadoes in our midst, who have long gone unwhipped by justice." Whoever, if anyone, was setting the fires, local merchants benefited and Australian criminals were blamed.

It is true enough, however, that some Australians were not acting in any way to disabuse the people of that notion. It must have seemed that the town was being flooded with Australian criminals. In May, according to the *Alta*, reporting the arrival of a ship from Australia, 700 more Australian immigrants were on the way. The *California Courier* in June said that immigration the previous month was greater from Sydney than from the Atlantic states and that Australia was serving as little more than the transshipment point of English prisoners to the United States.[10]

This was also the period, remember, according to one version of the legend, during which "it was notorious" that "at least one hundred murders had been committed within the space of a few months."[11] If so, the leading newspaper in town certainly never mentioned anything like that in its news columns. Reported murders, in the first six months of 1851, occurred at about the same rate as during the preceding six months. As shown in the following table, reported criminal homicides actually decreased in the first six months of 1851 in San Francisco.

Reported Criminal Homicides

Month	1	2	3	4	5	6	Total
Jan/June 1850	0	0	1	0	1	1	3
July/Dec 1850	1	1	2	2	4	3	13
Jan/June 1851	2	0	2	1	2	2*	9

With minor variations, the rate of about one criminal homicide a month was to continue throughout the early years of the 1850s.

On January 21, 1851, Hosea Fernandez killed a French sailor in a drinking and dancing saloon at Pacific and Kearny streets. A week later, a mock serious scuffle in another saloon between Charles Barnett and Charles Bartley degenerated into an impromptu duel with pistols in which Bartley was fatally wounded. In March, the headless body of a man, presumed to be a murder victim, was found floating off Central Wharf. Also in March, "Captain" Elijah Jarvis was murdered almost on his doorstep in the Mission. William Slater, a young man who had threatened him after a fight a few days before, was arrested for the crime.[12]

In April, the bound body of a murder victim was found on the dock at the foot of Sacramento Street; in May, William Lawley shot and killed his girlfriend in the street at Jackson and Kearny before turning the pistol on himself. Later in the month, the badly beaten body of a man recently released from jail was found floating off Rincon Point. On June 1, the poisoned body of Frank Brewer, a recent arrival flush from the mines, was found in the street at Montgomery and Pacific. Three newfound friends, Australians, were promptly arrested for the crime; two were brought to trial. On June 22, Samuel Gallagher shot and killed a gambler he found in bed with his woman in a brothel on Merchant Street.[13]

That is the total number of criminal homicides for the first half of 1851 reported in the news columns of the *Alta*. In the editorial columns it was a different story. On February 24, at the height of the Jansen

---

*Does not include the man hanged by the Vigilance Committee or two men stomped to death at the June 1851 fire.

excitement, the *Alta* complained editorially that there had been 500 murders in California and that no one had yet been executed. Where the figure came from is not apparent—nor does the paper mention any period during which the 500 crimes were supposed to have occurred.[14] Perhaps we should mark the figure up to the excited rhetoric of the moment; one month later, after things had quieted down, on the occasion of the discovery of a headless body off Central Wharf, the same editor remarked that days, even weeks, could go by without necessity of recording any "sudden or violent" deaths.[15] The fact of the matter is that murders did not occur in anything like the numbers put forth in the legend. But the men of 1851 were not the sort who were given to reflective statistical analysis.

Immediately after the April 28 election, Crozier replaced Fallon as marshal; according to the custom of the time, Democratic members of the force were promptly replaced with worthy Whigs. If it was hoped that a change in the police administration would reduce escapes, those hopes were misplaced. The jails were still wooden sieves, and no administration could have been expected to eliminate escapes without a new facility.

Even as the stage was being set for the course of action that eventually corrected the conditions faced by the city, public and press perceptions about those conditions worsened. While the citizenry waited for the completion of the county jail, the old jails filled to overflowing and spilled over. On May 5, five prisoners escaped from the station house; on May 8, another dozen followed in their footsteps. On May 12, two prisoners escaped from the prison brig. On May 13, the mayor reported to the council that the prison brig *Euphemia*—the temporary expedient of 1849—had been sold for $70 to pay a judgment against the city. The prisoners on the brig were moved to the already crowded station house; by the end of the month, according to the *Alta*, there were sixty-six prisoners in the city hall jail, "such as no white man, however criminal, ought to be incarcerated in. . . ."[16]

In mid-May, concerns about fire and crime prompted the establishment of a volunteer police force. Authorized by the council and sworn in by the mayor, the group took to patrolling the streets of the business district to protect against fire and crime. In June, however, things seemed to fall apart. On June 1, the *Alta*, reporting on the robbery of Captain Hunt, reminded the people of the flagpole in Portsmouth Square and suggested it be used to hang some of those who infested the city, setting fire to buildings and robbing people. On the same night, the poisoned body of Frank Brewer was found in the street, $10,000 was taken in the burglary of a jewelry store, and a man hit in the head with a slung shot ran screaming into the station house.

On June 2, Benjamin Lewis, an Australian, angry that he was being evicted from his room on Central Wharf, set it on fire and fled. He was caught soon afterward by a nearby police officer. Twelve hours later, a member of the volunteer police reported that he had come upon four men trying to set fire to his house on Commercial Street. The same day, nine prisoners, George Adams (again) and other well-known Australian criminals among them, escaped from the station house jail. On June 3, there was an attempted burglary of another jewelry store, but the thieves were driven off by people in the store. The burglar of another store on Broadway Street, a young Australian, was caught by a crowd of passersby the same day and almost hanged. In the end, the angry crowd turned the culprit over to the police.

At Lewis's arraignment on June 3 in the recorder's court, thousands thronged the city hall and the streets outside. When a fire rig drove by at noon in response to a false alarm, a rush was made to seize the prisoner to shouts of "lynch him." Public officials addressed the crowd. Mayor Brenham was hooted, as was Marshal Crozier, when he informed the assemblage that Lewis was not in the station house but was safe in custody elsewhere. If so, the crowd wanted to know, "Where's [George] Adams? where's the prisoner?" Sam Brannan suggested that Lewis be turned over to the volunteer police. The mayor called on the Washington Guards to be ready, the marshal said he would deliver the prisoner to the sheriff the following morning, and the district attorney assured the crowd that a trial would follow within twenty-four hours.

On June 4, the suspect arrested in the $10,000 jewelry store burglary the previous Sunday was released at the request of his attorney without a court hearing.[17] When an indictment was presented in district court against Lewis, Judge Parsons, on the motion of the defendant's attorney, quashed the indictment on the grounds that the grand jury had been illegally convened.[18] On Saturday, June 7, a suspected attempted arson of a wharf was discovered. Fires had apparently been set beneath the California Street Wharf at several locations but had burned themselves out. The "people" had had enough, and the press was with them.[19]

The editors knew what to do about conditions if the justice system did not. The *Herald* in early June editorialized that, if Lewis was guilty and the law did not hang him, lynch law should prevail.[20] A few days later, after the attempt to set fire to the California Street Wharf, the *Alta* reported that there was a gang of criminals in town bent on its destruction. It was time, said the paper, for the citizens to rouse themselves.[21] On June 8, a correspondent for the paper, calling himself "Justice," offered a two-point program to correct conditions: the establishment of a committee of safety to board every vessel arriving from Australia to screen out undesirable immigrants (transgressors should be shot down "without mercy") and the appointment of a committee of vigilance of twenty men from each ward to hunt out hardened criminals. The criminals should be given five days to leave the city, after which time "a war of extermination" would be carried out. The *California Courier* announced, in a later edition, that "where the guilt of a criminal is clear and unquestionable, the first law of nature demands that they be instantly shot, hung or burned alive."[22] The "people" were to prove themselves worthy of their charge.

Part IV VIGILANCE

CHAPTER 17

Lex Talonis

PRIVATELY ADMINISTERED JUSTICE and justice administered outside the regular bounds of law or custom, of which vigilantism is one form, are as old as human history and as fresh as yesterday's news story. Hammurabi, the Babylonian lawgiver of four thousand years ago, is chiefly remembered for his retributive dictum "an eye for an eye, a tooth for a tooth." His legal rule is frequently cited as a practice to be emulated by those who think we have gone soft on crime and as a primitive barbarism by those who would mark how far we have come. Less well known is his true purpose in imposing such a seemingly harsh code. Hammurabi's draconian measure was intended to convince his subjects that they should leave the punishment for private wrongs to the state. He was trying to wean them from an older and even harsher code, the Lex Talonis, the law of personal or family reprisal. It was only by the imposition of harsh penalties for crime, he believed, that he could expect his subjects to put aside their old ways and leave the administration of justice to governmental officials.

When a man named Bernard Goetz shot four youths he thought

were about to mug him in a New York subway and when a distraught father, Jack Spiegelman, gunned down his daughter's accused killer in a San Francisco courtroom, both were giving expression to that same primitive, elemental impulse that lies just beneath the thin veneer of manners, customs, and law we call civilization. "Vigilante shooting," trumpeted the press of the nation; while officials clucked their pro forma protestations, most Americans understood the frustration behind their acts—and they approved.

Over the millennia of human history, the impulse toward self-help justice has taken many forms. In tribal Saxon England, from which our common law system of legal procedure eventually evolved, there were no formal institutions of criminal justice, so community-administered justice was actually the legal norm. When a criminal was discovered in the commission of a crime, the "hue and cry" was raised and all members of the community were expected to respond. They joined together and ran the culprit down. Punishment was swift, certain, and harsh.[1] The Sicilian Mafia, a kind of shadow government, imposing its own brand of law and justice, was a response to the same impulse, growing as it did out of resistance to the eleventh-century Norman conquest of southern Italy. So were the feuding Kentucky hill families who settled their own accounts in the disorganized era following the Civil War and frontier lynch mobs, meting out summary justice beyond the pale of eastern settlements. Even today we read of the reestablishment of South American "death squads" in the suburbs north of Rio de Janeiro. Comprised of private security guards, off-duty police officers, and common thugs, and financed by businessmen sick of rampant crime that the authorities cannot control, the bands of gunmen hunt down and summarily execute persons believed to be common criminals.[2]

The first notable Vigilance Committee in the United States dates from 1767 in the South Carolina back country. When crime rose in the enforcement vacuum following an Indian war, responsible citizens banded together as Regulators and, in a two-year campaign against crime, brought the bandits to heel.[3] Lynch law, "the practice or custom by which persons are punished for real or alleged crimes, without due process of law," found, and finds, expression in many times and places. But vigilantism, a distinctively American phenomenon, goes beyond the strictly summary nature of lynch law. What distinguishes vigilante movements from lynch mobs, in the words of the definitive historian of vigilante justice, is the regular (though illegal) organization and existence for a definite (often short) period of time.[4] In practice, the line is not always so clear.

Fueled by revolutionary sentiments set in motion by the conflict that ended British rule of the American colonies, vigilante justice became a common feature in the life of westering nineteenth-century Americans. As Americans moved into the frontier, in the aftermath of the Revolutionary War, they often outran the institutions of justice. Perforce, the people had to do for themselves. Quite literally, the gallows was the first public edifice erected in many frontier settlements. Though such summary public justice is generally thought to be exclusive to the American tradition, there was at least one instance in Hispanic California. Near Los Angeles in 1837, after Gervasio Alipas murdered Domingo Feliz with the aid of the victim's wife, a board of public security was hastily formed, comprised of "the most respectable men of all classes." It pushed the regularly established authorities aside, judged the suspects guilty, and executed them before an impromptu firing squad.[5]

In the governmental vacuum that followed the American takeover of California, accommodations to the absence of adequate institutions of justice were made. Even before the Gold Rush, Californians were in the habit of looking to their own resources when it came to the imposition of punishment for crime. In 1847, it will be remembered, Colonel Mason had occasion to caution the alcalde of Santa Cruz for executing a wife murderer without clearing it with the governor. With the discovery of gold and the rush of humankind that followed, the meager institutions of justice were taxed far beyond their limits, particularly in the more sparsely populated regions of California. The "people" responded by taking matters into their own hands. It was a posse of citizens who ran down and killed the San Miguel murderers in 1848. In January 1849, three men who had robbed a Mexican gambler at Dry Diggings (later Hangtown, now Placerville) were tried before a hastily convened jury of twelve and hastily dispatched at the end of a rope.[6]

During the next few years, popular justice constituted an understandable feature of life in the mining regions of California. At the outset, there was little else that could be done. The tide of Gold Rush immigrants totally overwhelmed the feeble existing institutions of justice. Furthermore, human settlements were small and transitory, moving to take advantage of the latest strike. There was no tax base to support a jail or justice system, and even less of an inclination to do so. Settlements were geographically isolated from each other; it was an easy matter for a criminal to disappear on the way to trial in the county seat. If by some happenstance a criminal was held for trial, there was a good chance that witnesses had moved on.

Imbued with the American tradition, exacerbated by the frontier experience of having to rely on their own resources, the argonauts established a justice system of their own without much thought. Upon the discovery of a crime and the arrest of a perpetrator, the nearby citizens would immediately form themselves into a court, choosing a judge and jury from among the assembled crowd. With only a nod to the niceties of the law, they would try, sentence, and punish convicted offenders on the spot.

In the absence of jails or any other means to hold prisoners securely, the penalties for crime ran toward corporal punishment. Whipping and banishment, with or without mutilation by cropping an offender's ears or nose, were meted out to first offenders for minor crimes. Hanging was usually reserved for what were considered more serious crimes or repeat offenders. No doubt there were injustices perpetrated, particularly when the crowd was, as was often the case, "warmed with liquor." There are stories, perhaps apocryphal, of grave injustices. According to one account, a man was tried for stealing the horse of another from the front of a saloon. Later, after the man had been hanged, the horse was found at the rear of the saloon where its owner had mistakenly tethered it in the first place. On another occasion, when an ad hoc jury finally returned a verdict of guilty, its members were informed that the "people" approved because the defendant had been hanged half an hour earlier.

There was no alternative to popular justice in the mines, at least until the state and county court systems were well established, jails were built, and the extremely mobile population of the early Gold Rush years had settled down. On the whole, the citizens did what they had to do according to the conditions of their time and place. The tendency favoring popular justice did not restrict itself to the mining regions, however. It was the same sentiment that dominated public thinking in the formation of the response to the depredations of the Hounds —and it was to make up a prominent part of the mental furniture of nineteenth-century San Franciscans, even after regular institutions of justice and law enforcement existed.

In April 1850, after a court system had been established, and on the eve of the charter election that would provide the city with a fully articulated American city government, the neighbors of a burglary victim in the Mission, as already noted, seriously considered lynching the culprit. By September, the *Alta* suggested lynch law as a remedy to cruelty to animals. In October, against the backdrop of two reported recent lynchings in the mining regions, the editor informed his readers that he was becoming more and more a friend of Judge Lynch on the grounds that villains had no fear of the police or the courts.[7] Yet, by the end of November, the paper was able to report on improved social conditions in the city as "the wild turmoil and chaos of a border life . . . is fast changing to the concordant harmonies of an organized society"; when an attorney, in a letter to the editor, suggested lynch law as a solution to the problem of arson, the editor demurred. By year's end, however, the paper editorialized that the "horrible increase of robberies and murders without any apparent dread of detection and punishment is frightful." The editor warned that, if the authorities did not take action, the community would take the administration of law into its own hands: "They will sleep no longer."[8]

In early January 1851, a crowd of bystanders in Portsmouth Square attempted to seize and hang a pickpocket that an officer had in tow; early the next month, a crowd on Central Wharf was prevented only after a struggle from lynching a man who had shot a pieman.[9] As part of its criticism of the police department that month, the *Picayune* recommended that members of the California Guard be asked to patrol at night, but only if they were allowed to control themselves, "and they be permitted to take their own way in the treatment of public offenders when discovered."[10]

In February, the *Alta* felt constrained to explain to its readers back east the need for lynch law in the mining regions. There were no jails in the remote areas of the state, the paper pointed out, and transportation of criminals to widely separated courts was difficult. The trials were usually fair, said the paper; as the mining portion became more settled, the usual forms of law would take over and summary justice would decline. As we have already seen, that was not the way things went. Instead, the more settled regions, with "the usual forms of law" already in place, emulated their fellows in the mining regions. In February, as already related, San Francisco was whipped into a whirlwind of excitement by the Jansen robbery, and two men came close to being hanged by an outraged popular tribunal. A couple of days later, there was a "bit of lynching" when William Wilson, caught stealing clothes in an auction house, was set upon by other customers who gave him a sound thrashing before turning him over to the authorities.[11] Soon thereafter, there was a report of a summary hanging in Stockton; in Sacramento, the citizenry broke into jail, where the suspect in a shooting was being held, took him out, and hanged him. The original victim recovered.

In a summary of events published with an eye on eastern readers, the *Alta* bemoaned criminal conditions in the city and commented that people had found it necessary to rise in several parts of the state, supersede the forms of law, and constitute new courts from among themselves. Easterners should not be too quick to condemn, for they did not understand conditions in California, the editor cautioned. The state was peopled in part by the scum of Europe and Australia who would as soon burn the town and murder as eat. It was next to impossible to catch them or convict them if caught. Lynch law was not the best law, said the paper, but better than none.[12]

In March, at the public meeting looking into the conduct of Judge Parsons, William Coleman, dissatisfied with the way Berdue's trial was moving through the regular courts, tried to interest the crowd in taking over the case. He was ruled out of order. The same month, a horse thief was hanged on the Cosumnes River; a few days later, five more were hanged elsewhere in the mining regions. At the end of the month, Slater, the accused murderer of Jarvis, was moved from the station house jail to a warship for his own safety. Sensing the temper of the times, several attorneys declined to take his case. A few days later, as the prisoner was being escorted under police guard along Kearny Street, a group of horsemen from the Mission tried to ride them down. Marshal Fallon's officers fought them off and succeeded in getting Slater into the police station. Some tried to whip up the crowd, but their efforts came to nothing. It was not yet time.[13]

The press position about the suitability of lynch law is ambivalent throughout. In lulls between notable crimes, or if a crime, though notable, occurred at a distance, the papers tended to counsel moderation. At the end of April, when the French of San Francisco made plans to go to the Mokelumne River where their countrymen were being ousted from the mines, the *Alta* counseled patience, saying that the Americans would straighten things out. In May, when a group of Napa citizens entered a jail and hanged a man awaiting a hearing before the supreme court, the paper commented that the lynching was cruel and unjustified.

The paper was less tolerant of criminal misconduct closer to home, however. In April, on the occasion of one of the multiple escapes from the jail, the *Alta* commented that the money to try and convict criminals might as well be thrown away, "unless the people take the matter into their own hands and execute summary justice." Early in May, in the aftermath of the great fire, when feelings were running high, a vessel without port clearances arrived with a number of Sydney passengers, some still bearing the shaved heads of prisoners. "The aiders and abettors of this outrage deserve to be lynched," said the paper. "Our people must take this matter in hand."[14] After "Captain" Hunt was mugged in San Francisco on the last day of May, the paper reminded the people of the flagpole in Portsmouth Square and suggested it be used to hang some of those who infested the city, setting fire to buildings and robbing people. Despite the existence of a full-fledged justice system in San Francisco, it is clear that by the end of May the town, its leading citizens, and the public press were all ready to imitate their counterparts in the less-populated mining regions.

CHAPTER 18

John Jenkins

ON SUNDAY, JUNE 8, two young merchants were discussing crime conditions in the city and decided to visit Sam Brannan in his office at Bush and Sansome streets. There, with Brannan, they decided to convene a larger group on Monday at the California Engine Company station house down the street at Market and Bush to get their thinking on what could be done about lawless conditions. Notes were sent to 100 responsible men who could be trusted to keep the notice of the intended meeting in confidence. On Monday afternoon, 40 of the invitees convened in the engine house, agreed that something had to be done, and appointed a committee to draft a constitution for a group to be formed to eradicate crime. Later that evening, 100 of the leading men in San Francisco gathered in Brannan's building on Bush Street. At that meeting, they chose a name for their association: the Committee of Vigilance.

On Tuesday, those San Franciscans who did not already know about it were informed by the morning press that Judge Parsons had quashed the indictment against Lewis and had put his case over until it could be heard by the July grand jury. That night, the same 100 men convened again in Brannan's building, formally adopted the constitution presented, and entered their names in the rolls of the Committee of Vigilance. By 9 P.M., their work for the day completed, most went home. Some lingered.

Even as the members of the new organization were signing their names in the rolls of the Committee of Vigilance, a Sydney immigrant, who has come down to us with the name John Jenkins, made the last and biggest mistake of a presumably long and spotted criminal career. At 8 P.M., George Virgin, a shipping agent, left his upstairs office on Central Wharf to see to a ship's departure. He was not going to be gone long, so he did not lock his office door. In any event, he had previously taken the money from his strongbox and given it for safekeeping to the barkeeper downstairs.[1]

After Virgin left his office, Jenkins—by all accounts an exceptionally powerful man—entered, put the strongbox in a sack, heaved it over his shoulder, and made his way back down the outside stairs. Virgin, having remembered something he had forgotten, returned to his office just as Jenkins was leaving the area with a sack over his shoulder. Quickly realizing that he had been burglarized, Virgin raised the alarm as Jenkins was casting off in a small boat from the end of the wharf. Jenkins rowed briskly across the cove toward Sydneytown, but he was cut off by boatmen aroused by Virgin's cries, who angled against his line of flight. After a violent struggle, the outnumbered thief was finally subdued. Jenkins was taken to the shore and given a sound drubbing by his captors, who then started to walk him to the station house. En route, the escort party met a recently enrolled member of the Committee of Vigilance who suggested that the prisoner be turned over instead to the new crime-fighting group. Jenkins was thus taken to Brannan's building, where a few members of the committee remained.

Just before 10 P.M., the citizens of San Francisco were treated to a curious tolling (double taps at one-minute intervals) of the bell of the California Engine Company on Market Street, which was picked up by the Monumental Company at the head of Portsmouth Square. The members of the Committee of Vigilance hastened from around town to Brannan's building while nonmembers wondered at the unusual turn of events. While a crowd of the curious milled around outside Brannan's rooms, members of the newly formed committee, apprised of the circumstances of Jenkins's arrest, tried to figure what to do with their prize. Their confusion was put to an end by shipmaster William A.

Howard, who moved to the front of the room, placed his pistol on the table, and exclaimed, "Gentlemen, as I understand it, we are here to hang someone."[2] Procedures for an immediate trial were devised. The entire committee would serve as the jury with Sam Brannan as judge and another member as prosecutor. No defense counsel was allowed, but the defendant was to be permitted to speak in his own behalf.

In the two hours it took to arrange for and conduct Jenkins's "trial," while the crowd waited patiently if somewhat noisily outside to find out what was going on, Captain Benjamin Ray, commanding officer of the Second Police District, tried to gain entry to Brannan's building. He was told to wait. At midnight, the "trial" completed, Brannan exited his building and addressed the crowd still waiting in the vacant lot across the street. He pointed out the impotence of the regular courts and taunted them for their submission to rule by criminals. He told them that the criminal had been taken, tried, convicted, and sentenced to hang by a unanimous vote of his judges. Brannan asked the crowd to approve the sentence. He was greeted by a resounding chorus of "ayes," punctuated with a sprinkling of negative votes.[3]

There was some sentiment to wait until dawn to execute the sentence in the full light of day, but in the end the committee decided to hang Jenkins immediately on Portsmouth Square as an example to other criminals. Just before 2 A.M. on June 11, the prisoner was taken from Brannan's rooms, surrounded by almost the entire committee formed into four columns, twenty ranks deep. The escort lashed a rope around its outside files to prevent anyone from breaking into the ranks to free the prisoner. With Jenkins in the center, his arms pinioned behind him, the group moved out like some outsized caterpillar toward Portsmouth Square, accompanied by the jeering crowd and the tolling of the death knell on fire company bells.

As the escort party and its prisoner made their way along Montgomery Street, an advance party was sent ahead to rig a block to the flagpole in the square. When the hanging party reached Clay Street at Kearny, Captain Ray and a group of his officers attempted to seize the prisoner but were turned away. As the party entered the square, state senator David Broderick mounted the bed of a wagon, called for the sheriff, and, hearing nothing, exhorted the crowd to rescue the prisoner for the law. A rush was made to do so; in the attendant confusion, two officers slipped under the rope and almost reached the prisoner, but they were also defeated, turned away at gunpoint. The struggle for the prisoner turned into a general melee. One end of a long rope was placed around Jenkins's neck, the other end over a beam of the old Customhouse; he was dragged by his neck for over a hundred feet while his outnumbered rescuers held onto his legs. He was probably dead by the time he was hauled aloft. (Shipmaster Ned Wakeman is said to have put the rope around his neck.)

With Jenkins hanging from the Customhouse beam, Sam Brannan, always ready with the apt phrase, cried out, "Let every lover of liberty and good order lay hold of the rope."[4] Many complied; during the early morning hours, lighted by the gambling halls around the square, whose fevered activity continued unabated throughout the night, Jenkins remained hanging from the beam. Several attempts by police officers to cut him down were rebuffed until finally, as the sun was coming up, coroner Gallagher was allowed to take possession of the body. One lover of liberty later reported that while holding the rope of the executed thief he had his pocket picked.[5]

The general public and, at least officially, the press as yet had little specific information about what was going on. The editor of the *Alta*, when the paper went to press in the early morning hours of June 11 while Jenkins was still hanging a block away in the town square, thought that the execution had been conducted by an organization supported by influential men to visit punishment on a notorious criminal. The editor was uncertain about details but vaguely supportive of the action taken, and he trusted that the outcome would be beneficial.

More was to come out at the inquest convened by coroner Gallagher on the same morning. Captain Ray testified that he had gone to Central Wharf the night before to investigate the theft of a safe and was informed that the prisoner had been taken to Brannan's. He then told of his efforts to take charge of the prisoner. David Broderick testified that he went to Portsmouth Square to help the authorities stop the execution but was unsuccessful. He called out for the marshal and the sheriff, he testified, but heard nothing from them. Afterward, though, he said, he saw several men at the bar of the Union Hotel across from the square, Brannan among them, claiming credit for the hanging.[6]

While the coroner conducted his inquest at city hall, a large public meeting was organized in Portsmouth Square. Speeches approving of lynching were greeted by general cheering; but when one voice, that of an attorney named Clarke, was raised in protest against the summary execution, he was seized, roughed up, and threatened with hanging himself before order was restored. The meeting was then adjourned; Clarke, disheveled and bruised, was followed home by the hooting crowd.[7] That afternoon, the *Picayune* had more details. The paper, clearly favoring the actions of the committee, placed Brannan at the center of the affair and reported that Jenkins was the keeper of a notorious dive and the associate of Australian criminals.

By the next day, June 12, public support seemed solidly behind the committee. So was the press. Apologists for the committee are quick to point out that the press almost unanimously approved of the actions of the committee; only the Democratic *San Francisco Morning Post* opposed the actions of the vigilantes—and it expired in November. It was politic for members of the press to support the aims of the merchant class, and well they knew it. In 1856, the *Herald*—which had strongly supported the 1851 incarnation of vigilance, having been given the exclusive advertising business of the city's auctioneers a few months before—came out in opposition to the second establishment of the committee. The auctioneers immediately withdrew their advertising and copies of the paper were burned in the streets. The *Herald* limped along for a time in a reduced state, but its business was effectively ruined by its opposition to the committee.

The coroner's inquest reconvened on Thursday, June 12; Sam Brannan, while a bit vaguer about his participation than he supposedly had been at the bar of the Union Hotel, nevertheless testified that the object of the body was to protect the life and property of fellow citizens and to see that they were not troubled by burglars, incendiaries, and murderers. The same day, the committee took the initiative away from the authorities and published a proclamation containing the statement of purpose, to which was appended a list of the names of 183 of the most prominent men in the city, primarily leading merchants, who collectively accepted responsibility for Jenkins's hanging.

The public meeting again convened on Portsmouth Square on June 12; when Broderick, who had brought a large number of friends with him this time, spoke in opposition to radical proposals put before the crowd, he was jeered by the assemblage and threatened with hanging. A rush was made by members of the crowd to take the platform away from Broderick's forces, but they held the stairs. Broderick then declared that a motion to adjourn had passed and left with his friends. Others took control of the platform but adjourned without taking further action.

When the coroner's jury (with former alcalde Thaddeus Leavenworth as foreman) rendered its verdict the following day, it found that Jenkins had met his death in a preconcerted action at the hands of a Committee of Vigilance. Those responsible, according to the jury, were the 9 identified by the inquest during its own inquiry and the 183 who claimed responsibility. There the matter rested. Given the evident mood of the town, it is highly unlikely that any grand jury would have found against the prominent citizens involved. There was no grand jury anyway; it had been suspended until the July term.

The public gathered again on Portsmouth Square; while a motion to declare the Vigilance Committee the official agents of the people failed, the chairman entertained a motion to adjourn *sine die*, with the comment that he was satisfied to leave matters in the hands of the men named in the published membership list of the committee. A few days later, Broderick's Law and Order faction announced another meeting for Sunday, June 22, but Mayor Brenham suppressed the circulation of the meeting notices. We do not know whether Broderick would have gone forward at that time anyway; on the date scheduled for the meeting, nature, in the form of the sixth great fire, again visited disaster on the city.

The Central Wharf burglar, the criminal who triggered the formation of the committee, was tried, hanged, and is chiefly remembered by the name he gave to the committee, John Jenkins. Perhaps in the attendant confusion it did not matter, especially to the dead thief, that Jenkins was not his name.[8] "His real name . . . was Simpton," reported the *Picayune* on June 11, the day he was hanged. "He was well known to the police, having for some time kept a notorious *crib* on Dupont Street, called the *Uncle Sam*." After his demise, no in-depth inquiry was made into his identity. (Perhaps the man hanged had adopted his name from that of a noted Australian bushranger hanged several years before. John Jenkins had become something of an Australian folk hero in 1834 after his conviction for the murder of a local barrister and newspaper editor. In a statement in open court, Jenkins was openly contemptuous, behavior imitated by the man who was hanged by the vigilantes in San Francisco.)[9]

According to statements later made to the committee by habitués of Sydneytown, who seem to have accepted the committee's use of "Jenkins," the man hanged had sold the *Uncle Sam* to a man and wife named Connally early in May 1851. A few days later, Connally died suddenly and unexpectedly, and Jenkins/Simpton was reported immediately to have begun consoling the bereaved widow. The executed criminal had come from Australia's penal colonies, said the *Picayune*— "he was known there as a desperate man, having been transported for

life for arson and an attempt at murder."[10] That is about all we know
of Jenkins, or whatever his name was. It is tantalizing to speculate,
though, and perhaps appropriate, that there is more to the story than
we have been told. One of the problems with trying to take a fresh
look at events during the period of the Vigilante Committee's ascen-
dance is that most of the surviving documents are the committee's own
records, which, as might be expected, relate events from the sometimes less than totally objective perspective of those who took over the
governance of the town and set about hanging criminals.

Most of the remaining records of the committee are based on secret
testimony taken before the extralegal tribunal, with no opportunity
given for cross-examination of witnesses. It would be idle to suggest
that the committee fabricated testimony out of whole cloth; it is apparent from cross-checking the testimony that is preserved that the
committee had a pretty good idea of the large picture. But there are
also indications, as noted below, that it ignored or modified facts that
did not match its view of events.

Given the people he is known to have associated with, Jenkins (or
Simpton, or whoever) was no choirboy. Still, some intriguing questions
remain unresolved. First of all, there is little doubt that he committed
the burglary of Virgin's office; he was caught in the act. But if he
was such a well-known criminal, it is curious that, unlike others of his
ilk, his name, either as Jenkins or Simpton, does not appear among
those who were frequently being arrested at that time.[11] If, as reported
in the contemporary press, his real name was Simpton and Jenkins
was an obvious alias, why did the committee accept its use by his
supposed former cronies as his name weeks after the hanging? We shall
probably never know for sure; but consider for a moment by what name
we would now know Berdue, the man falsely accused of the Jansen
robbery, had he been hanged as the "people" wanted.

Curiously, in all the many accounts of the night of great excitement
culminating in a public hanging on the main square, there is no mention of the whereabouts of the mayor, city marshal, or county sheriff,
the three officials responsible for keeping the peace, enforcing the law,
and suppressing riots. No one seems to have wondered about their
absence from such exciting events.[12] San Francisco in 1851 was still a
walking city. An omnibus service had been started to the Mission; but,
for the most part, San Franciscans lived, worked, and played at loca-
tions within easy walking distance of each other. Brannan's building
at Bush Street near Market and Portsmouth Square, half a mile away,

markcd the effective limits of the city center. At 10 P.M. on June 10, a peculiar tolling was heard from the bell of the fire company at California and Market, picked up by the bell of the company at the head of Portsmouth Square. Vigilantes, accompanied by curious citizens, streamed toward Brannan's building. The trial, attended by noisy excitement outside, was conducted over the next few hours, followed by a clamorous torch-lit parade across town, accompanied by the tolling of the death knell on fire company bells.

Yct with all this public clamor, the three principal officials charged with maintaining order—Mayor Brenham, Marshal Crozier, and Sheriff Hays—were apparently nowhere to be found. One is forced to conclude that their absence was no accident. It is fairly evident that the officials charged with keeping the peace must have known what was going on and, due to either sympathy with the cause or outright complicity in the scheme of the commercial leaders of the city to take over the management of the justice system, made themselves scarce. For one reason or another, no one heretofore has remarked upon their absence during the critical events of June 10.

In the following months, as the Vigilance Committee took testimony in its secret conclaves, it would hear and record evidence claiming that Marshal Fallon had been part of the criminal gang. He, along with several other police officers, is listed by the leading historian of the 1851 Committee of Vigilance as a principal member of the criminal gang afflicting the city.[13] While he was certainly not without fault, as discussed below, that judgment is perhaps a bit harsh. One thing is for sure. Fallon was all cop; had he won the April election and been in office on the night of Jenkins's hanging, we can be sure that he would have been one of the first on the scene to marshal his forces and take the prisoner back. We have seen how his men fought off the attempt to seize and hang Berdue, who was innocent of the crime with which he was charged, and to seize Slater, also innocent. It would not have been left to individual officers, had Fallon been in office, to try against insuperable odds to retake the prisoner on their own.

Hall McAllister, a prominent attorney who had served as a prosecutor in the trial of the Hounds and went on to a distinguished career before the California bar, was present in Portsmouth Square the night of Jenkins's hanging. He testified at the coroner's inquest that he and a large part of the crowd opposed the illegal hanging and that, if the authorities had mounted an organized attempt to rescue the prisoner, he would have joined in. Broderick, it will be remembered, had called for the sheriff on the night of the hanging, but it is not recorded that he ever replied. Whatever his other faults, if Marshal Fallon had been in office that night, he would have been on the scene, we can be sure, and history might well have taken a different turn. But the party of business was in office, and it is their account of events we now read.

CHAPTER 19

The Committee Takes Charge

BEFORE JENKINS WAS ARRESTED on Tuesday, June 10, 100 San Franciscans had signed the rolls of the committee organized to combat crime in San Francisco. By Thursday, following Jenkins's hanging and the excitement that accompanied it, 183 of the leading citizens of the city claimed membership. In the next few days, hundreds rallied to the cause, swelling the membership to 500. By June 18, the committee had outgrown Brannan's building and moved to new quarters at Battery and California streets to accommodate meetings of the full membership. At the end of that exciting summer, the committee claimed a membership of more than 700.[1]

Who were these "influential men" who took it upon themselves to extirpate predatory crime from San Francisco? At their head as first president of the committee, as would be expected, was Sam Brannan, real estate operator and merchant, second to sign the rolls. He was beaten to the honor of being first by former naval officer and businessman Selim Woodworth. Others, chiefly merchants, bankers, and auctioneers, quickly got in line behind them. There was Jonathan

Stevenson (#101), real estate operator, who had brought the New York regiment of volunteers to California. There was James Dows (#170), the wholesale liquor merchant who had been burglarized in January; and R. S. Watson (#12), the merchant who the same month drove off the thieves trying to steal his safe. He was the "Justice" who on June 8 wrote the scathing letter to the *Alta* calling for vigilante justice.[2]

Bankers Eugene Delesert (#439) and Felix Argenti were members, as was James King of William, who would go on to greater fame a few years later when his death in a shooting scrape triggered the organization of the second Committee of Vigilance. (Argenti, #187, and King of William, #186, were not among the first 183 whose names were published on June 12, but they were among the first of the next group who signed up.) So were commission merchants William T. Coleman (#96), who had risen to prominence in the Jansen affair and would later head the Executive Committee of the 1856 Vigilance Committee, and Joshua Norton (#339), who in a later incarnation would reign as the self-proclaimed Emperor Norton of the United States and Protector of Mexico.[3] George Oakes (#5), one of the two young businessmen who got the committee going, signed up at once. His friend James Neall, Jr. (#178), waited for a while. Prominent merchant William David Merry Howard (#287), Brannan's ally from the earlier disagreements with Alcalde George Hyde, was a member.[4] So were the seafaring allies of the merchant class—shipmasters like William A. Howard (#102), whose timely gesture helped get Jenkins's trial started, and Edgar (Ned) Wakeman (#91), who placed the rope around Jenkins's neck.

Shipmasters were an invaluable, perhaps indispensable, part of the committee. The merchant leaders of the city were a hardy lot; they had braved the rigors of the frontier to come to San Francisco, after all. But hardiness is one thing; hanging a man is another. Shipmasters, their seaborne colleagues, on the other hand—given the conditions under which the maritime service was run in the nineteenth century—were perfectly suited to the work that lay ahead. Commercial seafaring was a hard business before the middle years of the present century. Crews were often pressed into service by crimp gangs, requiring, or so it was thought, harsh treatment by tough captains and bully mates to maintain discipline. There was no taste of democracy or law at sea. A shipmaster was a law unto himself, with just the sort of temperament to enforce the summary measures called for by the Committee of Vigilance.

In his autobiographical *Roughing It*, Mark Twain admiringly recounts an experience of one sea captain of that era that gives some

insight, embellished with Twain's characteristic humor and irrever-
ence, into the way merchant mariners dealt with matters of crime
and criminal justice in their province. Interestingly, Twain's model for
the character, under a thinly disguised pseudonym, is the same Ned
Wakeman who strung the noose around Jenkins's neck.[5]

Some time after the events of the summer of 1851 in San Francisco,
Captain Wakeman took his vessel to Peru's Chincha Island, where
there were no courts, officers, or government of any kind at the time.
When Bill Noakes, the bully mate of another trading ship, after losing
a fight with Captain Ned, killed Wakeman's black friend and first mate
in front of a number of other shipmasters, Captain Wakeman took it
upon himself to arrest and punish the culprit. Says Twain:

> Early in the morning Captain Ned called in all the sea captains in the
> harbor and invited them, with nautical ceremony, to be present on
> board his ship at nine o'clock to witness the hanging of Noakes at the
> yardarm!
>
> "What! the man has not been tried." [one of them interjected]
>
> "Of course he hasn't. But didn't he kill the nigger?" [said Ned]
>
> "Certainly he did; but you are not thinking of hanging without a
> trial?"
>
> "*Trial*! What do I want to try him for, if he killed the nigger?"
>
> "Oh, Captain Ned, this will *never* do. Think of how it will sound."
>
> "Sound be hanged! *Didn't he kill the nigger?*"
>
> "Certainly, certainly, Captain Ned—nobody denies that—but—"
>
> "Then I'm going to *hang* him, that's all. Everybody I've talked to
> talks just the same way you do. Everybody says he killed the nigger,
> everybody knows he killed the nigger, and yet every lubber of you
> wants him *tried* for it. I don't understand such bloody foolishness as
> that. *Tried!* Mind you, I don't object to trying him, if it's got to be done
> to give satisfaction; and I'll be there, and chip in and help, too; but
> put it off till afternoon, for I'll have my hand middling full till after the
> burying. . . ."[6]

In the end, Wakeman bowed to the concerns of his more sensitive
colleagues and agreed to try the man before he hanged him. A quickly
thrown together jury unanimously found Noakes guilty, after Wakeman
warned two of the mate's friends who were on the panel that they
would also go home in a basket if they failed to vote right. Dispensing
with the need for a sheriff, Wakeman climbed a tree himself, rigged a
halter, and hanged the man. "When the history of this affair reached
California," Twain concludes, "it made a great deal of talk, but did
not diminish the captain's popularity in any degree. It increased it,

indeed. California had a population then that 'inflicted' justice after a fashion that was simplicity and primitiveness itself, and could therefore admire appreciatively when the same fashion was followed."[7] (Captain Ned Wakeman was not one to put much stock in legal technicalities in any matter that touched him. He came to California in the first place one jump ahead of the law. The captain of a river steamer in New York, when he heard that his property was about to be attached in a legal proceeding, he loaded his vessel with fuel, slipped out of the harbor without calling attention to himself, and made his way around the Horn to California.)[8]

Although most members of the committee were prominent merchants and shipmasters, the trades and common workmen were represented, if to a slight degree. John Sullivan (#269), the boatman who captured Jenkins, was allowed to join.[9] But those who were not part of the leadership of the merchant/shipmasters establishment were excluded from membership on the committee's ruling board. Soon after the formation of the Vigilance Committee, its leaders realized that the body was too large to operate effectively as a committee of the whole. So the group was divided into two parts, a twenty-member Executive Committee, which ordered, and a General Committee comprised of everyone else, which obeyed. According to Bancroft, an unabashed supporter of vigilantism, the Executive Committee was "the central power round which all interests revolved. It was the inquisition, the privy council, the secret spring that moved the ponderous machinery. . . . All power was lodged in them; all secrets were lodged with them; all orders emanated from them. . . ."[10]

As to the General Committee, however, "every member of the association was bound to obey [the Executive Committee] unquestioningly, unhesitatingly, and as blindly as a common soldier obeys his commanding officer"; "each member of the general commitee . . . knew his place, knew exactly what to do when an alarm sounded; and further than that he knew nothing. He could well keep the secret which was never entrusted to him."[11] In effect, then, twenty men, meeting in secret, made life and death decisions about the fate of suspected criminals in San Francisco in the summer of 1851.

A 100-man vigilante police force, half again as large as the regular city police, was formed, under the leadership of Jacob L. Van Bokkelen, who reported directly to the Executive Committee.[12] Left largely to its own devices, the committee police divided the city into districts and set about the systematic inspection of suspicious premises. A water police was also formed, under Captain Wakeman, with responsibility for patrolling under the wharves and inspecting incoming vessels for Australian criminals. The regular city police continued patrols, trying not to notice that their efforts were paralleled by the agents of the committee.

One of the sentiments underlying the formation of the Vigilance Committee was the desire to economize in government. For all the feelings about crime, there was also the thought that the police department was too large and costly. Our nineteenth-century predecessors just were not in the habit of paying large numbers of people to perform public jobs. In June, at the height of the vigilance excitement, a measure was introduced in council to reduce the pay of officers to $5 a day. In July, after a spate of resignations, in part attributable to the lack of pay, the force was formally reduced to forty-six men, the three police districts were reduced to two, and the pay of officers was set at $7 a day.[13]

The effect of the new order was soon felt. Within a few days of Jenkins's hanging, the police reported that the Stockton and Sacramento steamers were daily carrying away a large number of notorious scoundrels.[14] Part of the migration and the corresponding drop in predatory crime, as pointed out by Mary Williams, was due to the regular summer movement of large numbers to the mines.[15] But there can be little doubt that the summary acts of the committee had an effect on those who contemplated causing trouble. The *Alta* at mid-month reported that the recorder's court had taken on a different appearance. Whereas in the past there had been a vast number of burglary and larceny cases brought each morning, now there were only a few drunks. While the court had previously been required to sit well into the afternoon, its business was now adjourned an hour after opening.[16] The *Picayune* announced that "a great number of the most notorious *cribs* [on Pacific Street] have been closed. Dens, around the doors of which, but a week or two ago, great hulks of fellows, with faces marked with traces of every species of desperate crime, might have been seen lounging; and from which at night, the murderer and burglar stole out upon a mission of crime, are now deserted; and on the closed doors may be seen notices that they are for rent, or sale."[17]

Not everyone took the hint right away. On June 15, a delegation of the committee visited James Hethcrington, reputed to be a Sydney immigrant and keeper of a resort for thieves in North Beach. Another delegation visited William Burns. Both were told that they were to be deported in five days. Hetherington balked at the order; a few days later, 100 members of the committee marched in military formation, seized him, and held him for deportation. Burns asked for and received an extension to put his affairs in order, but in the end both were deported to Australia.

One of the ostensible reasons for the formation of a Committee of Vigilance was to put an end to arson. If so, the effort failed. There was fear that a fire would break out on the anniversary of the June 14 fire of the year before, but the day came and went without one. On Sunday, June 22, at 10:30 A.M., however, the town's worst fears were realized when smoke was seen issuing from under the eaves of a house on Pacific and Powell streets, belonging to committee member Eugene Delesert. The town's gravity-flow reservoirs, most of which were empty anyway, were below the level of the fire. Fed by the prevailing winds, the fire spread quickly to nearby buildings; before being put out, it destroyed the previously untouched northwest quarter of the city, including the city hall. Earlier fires had burned out gamblers and merchants. The fire of June 22 victimized the less affluent members of the workingmen's district. Many were ruined financially and left the city for the mines to make another stake—which perhaps accounts in part for the reduction in crime. The less affluent tend to commit the kinds of crimes that bring them to the attention of police courts and arouse the interest of vigilance committees.

The fire resulted in several deaths. Three men were supposed to have burned, two were reported shot by the police, and two more were beaten to death by hysterical crowds. A French sailor, heading up Pacific Street to help a friend move some endangered goods, was observed to pick up a burning coal (to light his pipe). The cry of "incendiary" was raised and the luckless sailor was stomped by the crowd, with fatal results. Elsewhere, a Mexican carrying a bale of goods away from the fire scene was ordered to put his bundle down. When he refused to do so, he was also kicked to death by the crowd. A man arguing with another about the best way to put out a burning barrel of tar was accused of trying to spread the fire—had a Vigilance Committee patrol not intervened, he would probably have suffered the same fate.

Arson was immediately suspected. "The Sydney Ducks made their final defiant gesture," reports Herbert Asbury, "they . . . once more destroyed a large portion of the city."[18] According to the *Annals*, "there was no doubt that the fire was the work of an incendiary. No fire had

Contemporary lithographic cartoon showing the central characters of the vigilante drama: crooked police and politicians, Australian criminals, and determined vigilantes. Note the ingredients for arson in the foreground. (*California Historical Society*)

been used in the house in which it started for any purpose whatsoever. As it progressed, the flames would suddenly start up in advance, and in one or more instances persons were detected in applying fire."[19] The committee conducted an investigation that turned up several theories of arson and offered a $5,000 reward for the identity of the perpetrators, but no chargeable suspects were found. The main business district was spared in this fire, but enough was destroyed for merchants to bring goods previously sent upriver back to the city, according to contemporary observer Francis Marryat, in the hope of a rise in prices.[20]

The fire of June 22, 1851, was the last of the major fires to afflict Gold Rush San Francisco. As we have seen, the general judgment of history has been that most of them were set by Australian criminals. We now know that was probably not the case. Arson at any time is one of the most difficult crimes to prove. It is usually committed in secret and very often all evidence is consumed as a result of the crime. We can, however, at the remove of 150 years, make an attempt to reconstruct what we know of the early fires. The most common cause was probably accident.

The first of the great fires in December 1849 may have been set, if at all, not by Sydney criminals but by a black man seeking revenge for a racial attack. The second great fire, in May 1850, may have been set by an Australian, if the rumors that circulated in the Australian community at the time are to be believed. The third fire on June 14, 1850, started, according to contemporary press reports, in a faulty chimney in a bakery. Shortly after the fourth fire on September 17, 1850, an evening paper reported that most of the ruinous fires probably resulted from the careless placement of flues and stovepipes.

In the fifth great fire, arson was at first suspected; but upon calm reflection, it was decided that it was probably started by accident or carelessness. The sixth and last fire, though attributed to arson on sketchy evidence at best, was just as likely the result of accident. (Like the fifth great fire, it started in the upper story of a building. A careful arsonist could certainly have found a better opportunity for starting a fire without being discovered than in the upstairs of a usually inhabited dwelling in the full light of day.) That makes four of the six great fires that probably started by accident.

For those that may have been set, we must consider others than the Australian criminals usually charged with the offenses. There are a number of motives offered by Charles E. O'Hara to explain why people set arson fires.[21] There are those who set fires to conceal another crime, either to destroy evidence or "to divert attention in order to loot the burning premises or burglarize others" (the Australian criminal thesis). The arsonist may light a fire for revenge (the December 1849 fire seems to have been of this type).[22] The firebug may set a fire to intimidate an adversary (as with the recent killer hotel fire in Puerto Rico in which dozens died—the result of a labor dispute). Or arson may be the result of pyromania, either to gratify sexual impulses or to appear as the hero who turns in the alarm and helps extinguish the blaze.[23]

Of all the motives for arson identified by O'Hara, however, arson for economic gain was found more frequently than all the others combined. One of the ways in which a convenient fire can benefit a business enterprise is that "the stocks on hand may have lost value by reason of the seasonal nature of the business, [or] obsolescence. . . ." Property losses attributable to incendiary fires vary, he says, "from a low of 5 to 10 per cent to a high of 40 per cent, with 25 per cent being most commonly selected for 'normal' business conditions. When business is booming the lower figures obtain; while conditions are unsettled and the economic future appears dark the higher percentage is probably more accurate. . . ."[24]

Statistics are not evidence, and we are not in a position to charge members of the commercial establishment with any concerted plan to burn down the town to their own economic advantage. But, coupled with the charges made by Rosales and Wilkes, the frequency of economic motives in the crime of arson generally cannot be discounted in considering the possible motives for those arsons that did occur. We have traced the incidence of the fires against the fortunes of the economy—and there is a match. It would be ironic, if true, that some of the very people who hanged others for setting fires had a hand in them themselves.

Not surprisingly, jail escapes declined after the rise of the committee. With a determined group outside the walls waiting for any excuse to hang them without observing the niceties of the law, the inmates no doubt made the observation that they were safer in jail. And, for the first time, San Francisco finally had a secure jail. The prison brig had ended its term of service. In April, it had been sold; in May, its inmates were moved to the station house jail. (The brig was later reacquired by the city and in early June towed around to North Beach, where it was put to use as the town's first "lunatic asylum.")

After the county government had run out of funds in the spring to complete the county jail on Broadway, and attempts to complete the structure with convict labor had failed, Sheriff Hays set about raising private funds to finish it. In early June, the first twelve prisoners were delivered from the station house to the county jail—and just in time, because the old station house and the city hall that enclosed it burned down in the June 22 fire. Thereafter, the stone county jail on Broadway was the main prison facility in San Francisco. (By June, the complaint was made that the partially completed county jail, most of which was still unusable, was congested with 40 prisoners. In July, after a visit to the new facility, the Executive Committee of the Committee of Vigilance asked the general membership to subscribe money to finish the jail. By September, $15,000 was raised in this way and the jail was put in shape to hold 200 prisoners securely. With the coming of the winter rains, however, the press thought it might be a good idea to raise the money to put a roof over the courtyard.)

Statistically, as might be expected, crime did go down some, for a number of reasons. In truth, a summary hanging can have a salutary effect on the crime rate, albeit a short-lived one. There was the usual summer migration to the mines as Williams remarked, increased by those who lost their homes in the June fire, which no doubt drew many of the less affluent out of the city. Only the dullest of predators would have failed to notice that the rules of the game had changed. Doctor Johnson was right: "Depend on it, sir, when a man knows he is to be hanged in a fortnight, it concentrates his mind wonderfully."

As noted earlier, the figures of predatory crime for the first six months of 1851 leading up to the establishment of the committee differed little from the preceding period. In fact, robbery had gone down. Though the criminal elements had apparently left town after the formation of the committee, their departure does not seem to have had an effect on the incidence of reported robbery immediately after the Vigilance Committee took the law into its own hands. Shortly after Jenkins's hanging, a man was robbed of $500 on Cat Alley; later in the month, another attempted mugging occurred on Montgomery Street —about the same rate as before. It seems it was the burglars who left town. As previously discussed, after a high of seventeen in March, there were six burglaries reported in April, eight in May, and five in June, but the bare figures are misleading. All five of the June burglaries occurred in the first ten days, culminating in the one that led to Jenkins's downfall. Thereafter, there were to be none until well into July.

Criminal homicide of the sort that predominated in Gold Rush San Francisco is the one crime that least lends itself to control by enforcement measures. Still, as Brannan testified before the coroner's inquest and as the committee suggested in the proclamation establishing its existence, murder, along with arson and burglary, was one of the major reasons such extraordinary measures were taken. But, as noted, the usual average of about one criminal homicide a month continued for the period prior to and into the reign of the committee.

There simply were not any one hundred murders in the months leading up to the formation of the committee—there were not even ten. The figures given in chapter 16 are accurate and complete. The *Picayune*, true enough, in the excitement following the Jenkins hanging, reported without any supporting data that "it is known that within the past twelve months 54 murders have been committed in San Francisco. . . ."[25] But the official announcement proclaiming the establishment of the Vigilance Committee, published in the city's leading journals the same day, ended with a passage designed to explain why such extraordinary measures had been necessary. "Our fellow citizens," the announcement concluded, "remembering the escape of Withers, Daniels and Adams; of Stuart, Windred and Watkins, and the tardy manner in which the incendiary Lewis is being brought to justice, will see the necessity of the stringent measures we have adopted."[26]

One is forced to wonder at the examples selected by the committee to justify its existence. The choice of some of the names can easily be understood. Lewis of the quashed subpoena was very much in the public eye. Adams and Watkins were among the well-known burglars who had been using the city jails as a revolving door in the last few months. Windred also had recently escaped, and the committee doubtless considered "Stuart's" fourteen-year sentence and murder trial in Marysville tantamount to an escape.

But what of Withers and Daniels? This study cites every criminal homicide reported in the *Alta* from the start of American San Francisco to June of 1851—and it has been a long time since we have encountered the names of Withers and Daniels. The crime with which Withers had been charged occurred in December 1849; he was finally acquitted by a jury in San Jose in September 1850, almost a year before the establishment of the committee. The killing by Daniels had occurred in August 1849; it was in July 1850, also a year before the tenure of the committee, that the state supreme court ordered a new trial because of irregularities in the trial before Alcalde Geary. The cases cited may well have been miscarriages of justice, but one would think—had there been anything like the number of murders commonly referred to—that examples closer to hand would have been available to the committee for its proclamation.

CHAPTER 20

The Real James Stuart

THE INTEREST OF THE committee's members in its activities had begun to flag by the end of June. The Jenkins hanging had been exciting enough; in the days following the execution, the ranks of the committee swelled with recruits. The military parade through the streets to seize and expel Hetherington had been exciting too. But after that, committee activities settled into a boring routine. The Executive Committee met daily and the nightly patrols continued, but more absences were noted at meetings and it became more difficult to staff patrols. Early in July, Sam Brannan resigned as president of the committee after a disagreement with the sergeant-at-arms in the committee rooms, and he was replaced by Stephen Payran. Selim Woodworth replaced Brannan as president of the General Committee.

The committee remained convinced that there were members of a criminal gang about, but there was no way to get at the organization. Then, shortly before Brannan's resignation, there was a break in the form of an arrest that set in motion a series of events that breathed new life into the committee. On July 2, a man in the vicinity of California and Powell streets, then the thinly settled western outskirts of the city, discovered that he had been the victim of a theft and raised the alarm. His neighbors responded and began to search the tangle of scrub oak covering what was to become Nob Hill. In the nearby shrubbery they came upon a well-armed man who said his name was James Stephens and that he was on his way from the Mission to North Beach.

He was not the thief they were looking for, but the residents became suspicious of the route he had selected to get to his stated destination. By choosing to go from the Mission to North Beach by ascending the heights of Nob Hill rather than taking the much leveler route a few blocks to the east, he seemed to be avoiding the more inhabited parts of the city. The neighbors turned him over to the Vigilance Committee. When questioned, the man repeated that his name was Stephens, that he was a recent arrival in the city, having walked from Sonora in the southern mines, and that he had not yet established lodgings. His inquisitors were impressed by his seeming candor but wondered how, if he had walked all the way from Sonora, his clothing could be as clean as it was. They decided to hold him overnight. The next day, in the press of other business, the prisoner's presence was overlooked for a time and he sat quietly and uncomplainingly in his cell. At the change of the guard in the afternoon, John Sullivan, the very same boatman who had arrested Jenkins, was assigned to guard Stephens, whom he immediately recognized as James Stuart, the robber of Jansen and murderer from Yuba County who was thought by the committee to be awaiting sentencing in Marysville.[1]

The Vigilance Committee had finally caught a big fish. At first, the man denied that he was Stuart.[2] But in the end, after several days in the custody of the committee, he became convinced that the jig was up. In return for a promise from the committee that he would be turned over to the authorities in Yuba County if he named his confederates, Stuart agreed to confess. His attorney obtained a writ of habeas corpus from the state supreme court; while Sheriff Hays made halfhearted attempts to serve it on the committee, Stuart related a tale of evil long suspected but never told in its entirety by an insider. The prisoner said that he had been born in England and transported for forgery to the penal colonies in Australia at the age of sixteen. Six years later, he was paroled; five years after that, he went to Peru, where he spent a few years before joining the Gold Rush to California in 1849. He went directly to the mines, where he worked for a few months trying to run a store and boardinghouse. After he was cheated in a card game, he continued, he stole his money back, plus some more he found in the trunk of the man who had cheated him. He was arrested for the theft and was almost lynched by a mob before the authorities intervened.

While the sheriff was away, Stuart made his escape, stole a horse, and made his way to Sacramento, where he sold the horse and committed a burglary with some friends. He went to San Francisco, where he took part in the robbery of the brig *Caskie*, in the harbor off Clark's Point in October 1850. He then returned to Sacramento, where he worked with a gang of horse thieves and ran a fencing operation for stolen goods. He was arrested several times for burglary in Sacramento but was freed, he claimed, through perjured testimony, suborned by his attorney, Frank Pixley.

During one of his stays in the Sacramento prison brig, a police officer identified him as the accused murderer of a man named Charles Moore at Foster's Bar in Yuba County. While his attorney used legal tactics to delay his return to Yuba County, Stuart escaped from the brig and made his way again to San Francisco, arriving in December 1850. There he took part in several crimes, including the Jansen robbery.[3] Stuart and his gang next attempted several burglaries, some of which were successful and some not. After the gang lost its tools in one burglary arrest, Stuart went to Gold Bluff.[4]

In April 1851, he was in Monterey, where he testified under the name of Carlisle for some of his friends charged with the $14,000 burglary of the Customhouse. When the trial ended in a hung jury, Stuart, with the connivance of the sheriff of Monterey, he said, broke his friends out of jail and headed for the southern mines. In June, he ran into two men there who recognized him as Stuart; fearing exposure if he remained, he returned to San Francisco, where he was arrested, ironically, during the investigation of a crime he did not commit.

He began to talk on the evening of July 8 and completed his confession in the morning hours. In his statement he named more than twenty men as his close criminal confederates. There was Dab the Horse Thief, with whom he worked selling stolen horses, and James Burns (Jimmy from the Town) and others with whom he pulled the *Caskie* robbery. Other well-known and soon to be well-known thieves and robbers that he named were Samuel Whittaker, Robert McKenzie, George Adams (aka William Wilson), Jim Briggs, and Billy Hughes, who in various combinations participated with him in burglaries and robberies around the state, including that of Jansen. Stuart said that former port warden T. Belcher Kay cased and participated in some of the burglaries. Frank Pixley, his attorney and city attorney of San Francisco (elected as a Whig in the April election), suborned perjury to get criminals released. Sheriff Roach of Monterey County participated in the split of the proceeds of the Monterey burglary. San Francisco police captain Andrew McCarty and assistant captain Robert McIntire of the Third Police District had a long association with his gang, he said, and arranged for officers to be elsewhere when the gang wanted to commit a burglary.

It was later said that Stuart was hanged because he withheld information from the committee. If anything, it is more likely that he was hanged because he talked too much. Victims of many of the crimes he related sat on the Executive Committee, which examined him further after his confession. There before them sat the living incarnation of all that they had suffered in the preceding months. Notwithstanding the existence of any agreement to turn Stuart over to the sheriff of Yuba County, the Executive Committee recommended to the General Committee that he be hanged.

On the morning of July 11, 400 members of the General Committee convened in the committee rooms. Stuart's confession and a review of the evidence against him were read to them; when the question was put, they voted unanimously that the prisoner had not performed according to the terms of his contract and confirmed the verdict of hanging.[5] While the members of the General Committee were held in the committee rooms, Colonel Stevenson addressed the crowd gathered outside, informing its members of the verdict and sentence passed by the committee and asking for their approval. Almost to a man, the excited crowd shouted its endorsement.

That afternoon, after receiving the ministrations of an Episcopal clergyman, Stuart was taken from the committee rooms, placed in the middle of a formation much like the one that surrounded Jenkins, and marched to the Market Street Wharf at its junction with Battery Street. There he was hanged from a derrick in full view of thousands assembled on the shore. Coroner Gallagher was the only public official who tried to interfere, but he was easily brushed aside. The committee published Stuart's confession in the public press to explain the action it had taken and then set about running down those he had named as accomplices. Some of those it sought were never brought to book. Among this group were Edwards, Morgan, Briggs, and Hughes.[6] Those who had not already departed or gone into hiding before certainly did so when the confession was published.

The hanging of James Stuart from the end of Market Street Wharf. By using the wharf, the vigilantes assured a good audience for their efforts and eliminated lines of approach for any intended rescue by officials. (*Bancroft Library*)

Some were not so fortunate. Among those captured by the committee in July was James (Jimmy from the Town) Burns, a Sydney thief and ne'er-do-well, well known even before Stuart named him. He was picked up in Marysville on July 16 and returned to the Vigilance Committee in San Francisco. There he was examined by the committee; he gave a statement before it turned him over to the sheriff on July 24. The grand jury promptly indicted Burns the same day for the theft of a trunk in February, and his trial was set for the next day. The district attorney asked for the death penalty, according to the provisions of the recently enacted law that made grand theft a capital crime; but at his trial, completed before the month was out, Burns received a ten-year sentence.[7]

On July 17, the Sacramento marshal arrested James Welch, who had previously escaped from the San Francisco station house, where he had been serving a sentence for conviction of horse stealing. At first the marshal had not recognized Welch's companions, but he returned the next day and arrested George Adams and another Australian, Thomas Ainsworth, who were preparing to leave the country. They were also turned over to the San Francisco Vigilance Committee. Dab the Horse Thief, named by Stuart as one of his criminal confederates in Sacramento and Gold Bluff, was arrested in Marysville and returned to San Francisco, where he was imprisoned by the committee. Sam Brannan, still a member though no longer president, released him before the committee had an opportunity to examine him fully, for some reason that has never been explained.

Port warden T. Belcher Kay, another confederate named by Stuart, also came under the committee's scrutiny but somehow escaped its toils. He was arrested in Sacramento and allowed liberty on the promise that he would not try to escape. He returned to San Francisco instead by a circuitous route disguised as a woman and turned himself over to the regular authorities. There were no criminal charges against him, but he was permitted to remain in jail as a lodger for his own safety. When Kay later tried to depart from the jail, the Vigilance Committee asked Judge Campbell to order his retention. The judge did so, but released him on August 1 when "the Grand Jury [a majority of which were vigilantes] represented to the court that they had no presentation to make against the defendant."[8] Kay immediately took passage on a ship headed for the east coast.

Once in custody of the committee, those who were caught were examined to find out what they knew about others and a series of interlocking stories were extracted from them. Mrs. Hogan, the keeper of a house frequented by Stuart's gang, and the paramour of Sam Whittaker, another of those named by Stuart, was picked up in San Francisco and released, in the hope that Whittaker would try to contact her. At the end of July, Robert McKenzie, another of those named by Stuart as a member of the criminal gang, was also arrested in Sacramento and taken to San Francisco, where he was held in the committee rooms.

There is no doubt that the actions of the committee had some effect on crime, at least for a time.

Comparison of Reported Crime in San Francisco in 1851

	Jan	Feb	Mar	Apr	May	June	July
Criminal Homicide	2	0	2	1	2	2*	1*
Robbery	0	4	0	0	3	2	2
Burglary	10	7	17	6	8	5	3

The overall number of robberies really does not seem to have been overly influenced by the existence of the Vigilance Committee, and the two in July, about the same rate as during the preceding months, cannot be blamed on Stuart's men. They were all dispersed or under arrest by then. On July 26, a robbery was attempted at Lombard and Dupont streets, with "courage and coolness," the *Alta* declared, in the face of the committee, which would punish severely. On the last day of the month, a drunken miner was robbed by two men who identified themselves as police officers.[9]

The pattern of burglary during the early months of 1851 is in part explained by Stuart's confession. He departed for Gold Bluff after his confederates were arrested and lost their tools in the sand hill burglary. The arrest of a number of his other associates in the March burglary of Stevenson's house also put a crimp in their act. Burglary was under reasonable control, then, even before the Vigilance Committee took over and thereafter it was not totally eradicated. Someone removed a trunk at 2:00 A.M. on July 23 from a house within ten feet of the rear of the police station on Ohio Street. The same day, J. C. Pelton's house on Stockton Street was burglarized.

The usual one-a-month rate of criminal homicide continued without much attention to whether the committee was in force or not. Indeed,

---

*Does not include vigilante hangings or the men stomped to death at the June 1851 fire.

one murderer may have escaped any punishment at all through the offices of the committee. On July 12, Francisco Guerrero, a longtime *californio* settler (and public official) from before the coming of the Americans, died of head wounds he received on the plank road to the Mission. According to testimony given at the coroner's inquest that followed, Guerrero had agreed with a man named LeBras to race their horses along the plank road. One witness testified that she looked out the window of her house and observed two men on horseback. One struck the other on the head with an object, and the horse of the man who was struck bolted, running for a distance along the plank road before its rider, Guerrero, fell off. Two physicians testified at the coroner's inquest that Guerrero's head wounds were inconsistent with a fall from a horse and there was physical evidence of blood at the top of the hill from which the "race" commenced and on the planks of the road in advance of the spot where Guerrero fell off.

LeBras was seized when he tried to sell the horse he had been riding (which belonged to Guerrero) and turned over to the Vigilance Committee. LeBras (also called Baptiste) was known to the police as a feebleminded town character. He had been arrested a few months before for stealing the pall from a coffin in an undertaking parlor but released without trial. It was thought by many that he was physically incapable of harming anyone. The committee held him for five days but, apparently unable to come to a decision about his guilt, turned him over to the regular authorities. He was put on trial on a charge of murder before the regular courts. Without leaving the jury box, the jury voted an acquittal and he was released. Curiously, neither the woman who testified to the coroner's jury about the fight on horseback nor the two physicians who testified about Guererro's injuries were called to testify at the court trial. A taint has always hung over the case.

One of the central issues in San Francisco from the start, as has been mentioned, was the question of land titles. It was at the center of Hyde's problems as well as those of Leavenworth. The issue does not seem to have been much in the public eye when Brannan and his fellow monopolists were in control, but it never went away. In later years, much of the violence and murder in San Francisco was rooted in disputes over land ownership. To bring the matter to some kind of a resolution, the federal Congress had appointed a land commission in 1851 to decide on land titles and the merits of competing claims. At the time of Guererro's death, the commission was beginning to sit in San

Francisco in a series of sessions that would go on for decades before the title question was finally put to rest.

Guerrero, as a living embodiment of the land question before the coming of the Americans (he was subprefect at the time of the conquest and was again elected to the office by the Americans in 1849, stood in the way of powerful men, who, the theory goes, stood to profit if he did not testify. It would be impossible to reconstruct enough evidence at this late day to identify who was behind the killing, but Bancroft was convinced that his death was murder.[10] So was Zoeth Skinner Eldredge.[11] William Heath Davis, who was around before and during the conquest and knew Guerrero well, said that he had been murdered with a slung shot in broad daylight by men with an interest in the Santillán claim.[12] A. A. Green, a contemporary resident of the Mission, wrote in his memoirs that LeBras was the tool of the land schemers who wanted Guerrero out of the way.

There is evidence that LeBras did not get a full judicial hearing and there are charges by contemporaries that things were other than they seemed, but the complete facts of the case are lost in the dim mists of time. There is certainly no direct evidence linking Guerrero's killing to the vigilantes or even demonstrating that they took part in a cover-up; but something smells about the case, and we could have expected more from men who vowed to let "the heavens fall" to be assured that justice was done.

CHAPTER 21

A Double Standard

As A PRACTICAL MATTER, it is a fairly simple proposition to locate and punish criminal predators as long as a society has superior force and the will to use it. Our quintessentially practical predecessors knew how to do that. In September 1852, a known criminal was seen prowling a neighborhood near Gilroy; he was taken in due course before a magistrate but promptly released because there was really no legal reason to hold him. Immediately after his release, the people of the neighborhood seized the arrestee and "hung him up" three times. After he was hoisted with a noose around his neck for the third time, which, according to a contemporary account, "was rather severe," he admitted the theft of a horse and pointed to the thicket where it had been stashed.[1] Was it effective?—you bet.

There is an appealing simplicity to the sort of justice that cuts through the pettifogging inability of the regular institutions of justice to get at what is really going on in a society. It would be a difficult brand of justice to sell, however, to the innocent French sailor who was stomped to death at the June 22 fire, or to the man who was strung up three times in June 1852 before it was decided that he knew nothing of the crime of which he was accused, or, indeed to the "graybeard" in Stockton, who was hanged summarily and then, after his death, found to have been innocent. As things turned out, it was the man who led the lynching party who was responsible for the crime for which the old man was executed.[2] There are many examples of self-help justice at the time that went awry.

Our protections against such abuses, though sometimes observed in the breach, can be found in the Bill of Rights, the first ten amendments to the federal constitution, which protect the citizenry from the abuses of government officials. The Fourth Amendment, much in the public eye nowadays because of interpretations such as the Miranda decision (which is claimed in some quarters to "handcuff" the police), assures that persons and their houses are to be secure from unreasonable searches. The Fifth Amendment requires that no person can be held to answer for serious crimes except on the presentment or indictment of a grand jury. Under the Sixth Amendment, a defendant is entitled to a public trial, to be confronted with the witnesses against him, and to compel the attendance of witnesses in his behalf.

Though viewed by some as a sanctuary for criminals, and despite some grievous lapses and questionable interpretations that lend a measure of legitimacy to the arguments of its detractors, the law in the United States does a reasonably good job of protecting the citizenry from the abuses of power. The provisions of the Bill of Rights were not based on the fanciful imaginings of its framers, but on their experience with hard reality—they were well aware of the abuses of searches at the whim of agents of the crown and private star chamber trials, in which the accused had no means to offer a defense.

Gold Rush San Franciscans were very familiar with the law; if they were not, they were educated by the establishment press. In May 1851, as the city rushed headlong toward the establishment of the first Committee of Vigilance, the *Alta* lectured Marshal Crozier's new police about the laws of arrest and about citizens' protections under the Fourth Amendment, guaranteeing freedom from unwarranted searches. A few days later, the paper, which was soon to champion the vigilante cause and endorse the extralegal methods it employed, again cautioned the police about overstepping their authority. "Liberty is a dear thing," said the editor, "and officers should make distinctions."[3] On June 12, even as the committee was mobilizing itself to take over the administration of justice when city authorities expressed an intention to break up a meeting in Portsmouth Square on the grounds that the assemblage was riotous, the *Alta* was quick to remind it in some detail about the First Amendment right to public assembly.

But exacting standards of constitutional rectitude were reserved in the summer of 1851 only for the opponents of vigilance. The *Picayune*, it will be remembered, was satisfied in January to let members of the California Guard patrol the streets but only if "they be permitted to take their own way in the treatment of public offenders."[4] A few days after the *Alta* had last reminded the authorities about the constitutional protection of provigilante assemblies, however, when Broderick's Law and Order faction circulated a handbill calling for a meeting on June 22 that would have opposed the committee, the paper turned a neat 180 degrees and complimented the mayor for suppressing the handbill. The only object of such a meeting, said the editor, would be to agitate the committee and cause a riot.[5] The *Picayune* chimed in, offering the disorderly conduct of the meeting of June 12 as a reason.[6] On July 7, after some residents on the outskirts of town complained about being stopped by private police for no cause, the *Alta* reminded them that the town was infested with criminals bent on robbing them in the dark. When a citizen complained a few days later that his rights had been violated by a vigilante patrol, the paper assured him with mock seriousness that his rights would most certainly have been secured by vagabonds if they knocked him down and robbed him.[7]

During the June 22 fire, Felix Argenti, banker and prominent vigilante, hired a Sydney immigrant named Metcalf for $50 to move possessions belonging to his mistress from a location endangered by the fire. Metcalf hauled away four wagonloads of goods; when his mistress later notified Argenti that only three loads had been returned, the banker rounded up some of his vigilante friends and raided Metcalf's house in search of the goods.[8] Metcalf went to law—he sued Argenti in civil court for trespass and asked for an award of $25,000. Not everyone, either inside or outside of the committee, approved of unwarranted searches; but on July 5, after the issue had been raised by the Metcalf suit, the committee published a notice that it intended to enter any place where there was thought to be evidence of crime. Judge Campbell and even Mayor Brenham objected to this stance; but the *Alta*, which little more than a month before had explained the constitution to the police, criticized Metcalf's attorneys for filing the suit, saying they were going to force a confrontation between the committee and the regular authorities.[9]

Viewed this way, it was not the law as administered in San Francisco in 1851 that was found wanting, but the fundamental constitutional protections against governmental abuse. There was no expectation that the standards imposed on the regular authorities would be followed by the committee. (In a July 10 letter to the *Alta*, a member of the regular police force pointed out that he and his colleagues were policemen, not judges. Had they taken that authority, he said, they would have frightened the desperadoes out of town months before.)

While the committee took a strong stand against criminal violence, it seems to have excepted violence committed by its own members. Early in July, William H. Graham (#116), a member in good standing of the committee, started a gunfight in Portsmouth Square that resulted in the shooting of two innocent bystanders. George Lemon had been sharing the affections of Graham's intended wife; when the cuckold found out, he tried to draw his rival into a duel. When Lemon did not issue the expected challenge, Graham posted him as a coward in Portsmouth Square and in two newspapers, vowing to shoot him on sight. On July 1, they met in the town square; in the following exchange of gunfire, Graham, a sailor, and a young boy bystander were shot. There is no indication that Graham's violent proclivities damaged his standing with the committee.[10] The standard position on that issue, as expressed by Williams and others when the committee declined to involve itself in Gallagher's shooting of Pollack in June, was that "the Committee refused to assume jurisdiction over crimes of sudden passion."[11] In other words, the committee was concerned only with the criminal activities of organized gangs. In the proclamation announcing its establishment, the committee spoke sternly of the murderers present in the community. But as we have seen in the review of every press-reported criminal homicide in San Francisco to date, the vast majority of unlawful killings were more on the order of the Lemon and Graham shooting than the product of any criminal organization.

But there was an even more dangerous inconsistency in the way events were conducted in the summer of 1851. The reason for the constitutional right to a public trial is so that people can confront witnesses against them in open court. Who is to know what goes on in a private tribunal but its participants? If a defendant is not permitted to mount an independent defense, there is the obvious danger that his legal rights will not be observed. When the prosecutorial and judicial elements of the process are of one mind and their opposition ends up hanged, who is to say what went on behind closed doors? The record of a private tribunal is what the tribunal wants it to be. There are indications that the record of the Executive Committee of the Committee of Vigilance is somewhat different than it would have been if the activities had been carried out in the full light of day.

Most of what we know of the Vigilance Committee, the written record, comes from the committee's own files and from the pages of compliant newspapers. On one hand, the Vigilance Committee is to be commended for leaving a record at all on which its actions might be judged. (Records maintenance is not the strong suit of lynch mobs.)[12] On the other hand, it must be recognized that the retention of its records was a self-serving act to vindicate its members in the judgment of history. There are gaps and distortions.

First, there is the matter of Stuart's confession. On the basis of his statement as presented by the committee, reputations were smeared at the time and before the bar of history. There is the question of the agreement between Stuart and his captors, which both the Executive Committee and General Committee apparently believed Stuart failed to live up to. Mary Williams and George Stewart purport not to know what the agreement was. But there is a document in the committee papers—edited by Williams—signed by both Stuart (as Stephens, which may or may not have been his real name) and Stephen Payran, the president of the Executive Committee, to the effect that, if Stuart delivered up ten of his confederates to the committee, he would be turned over to the authorities in Yuba County to be tried for the murder he was accused of committing there.[13] In his confession, Stuart named twenty-six of his criminal colleagues, yet he was hanged anyway. Williams does not know why. No doubt, Stuart was every bit the criminal he is represented to be and very much deserved to hang. But the fact of the matter is that we shall never know for sure because the proceedings that led to his demise were conducted in the secrecy of the committee rooms.

In the Metcalf case, according to Executive Committee member John Spence, who testified at a later hearing in court, a faction of the committee tried to pass a resolution in executive session that would have sent a warning to Metcalf's lawyers to desist from pursuing their suit. The Executive Committee as a whole, to its credit, voted down the resolution. However, according to Spence, the minority faction reconvened after the Executive Committee had adjourned and passed the resolution, which was delivered to the attorneys. The fact was entered into the record book as though the entire Executive Committee had passed the motion.[14]

Dab the Horse Thief, named prominently in Stuart's confession, as already noted, was arrested in Marysville and transported by steamer to San Francisco, where he was jailed by the committee. By all indications, he was as bad as the rest who were tried and hanged; indeed, Stuart seems to have been in some fear of him. Yet Sam Brannan, for some reason that remains unknown to history, released him from the committee rooms—suggesting again that more was going on than was either seen by the contemporary eye or placed in the written record.

James Hetherington, when he went before Recorder Waller, claimed that he was not an Australian but a native of Virginia. The best the recorder could do was to suggest that he ought to leave town for a few days. Hetherington may have been lying about his place of birth; but if not, the committee banished to a foreign country an American citizen against whom, said Mary Williams, "There may have been unrecorded information that established [his] guilt. But the testimony in the documents [of the Vigilance Committee] proved little more than a close alliance with well known convicts and wouldn't have carried a conviction in any court of law." [15]

A small matter perhaps—but tarring someone falsely as an Australian in San Francisco in 1851 would help to cast him beyond the pale of community sympathy. There is also some question about the true nationality of port warden T. Belcher Kay. According to the committee's version of Stuart's confession, Kay was an Australian ex-convict; yet we know that when Kay was released from jail and left San Francisco, he took ship for the east coast of the United States. Police officer Phineas Blunt, who displayed a general sympathy for the committee in his memoirs, reported that Kay was from Boston, where he had run a boxing academy.[16] We are forced to wonder at the accuracy of Stuart's confession, upon which much of what passes for knowledge of the criminal business in 1850 and 1851 is based.

Could it be that discerning members of the committee realized that some aspects of Stuart's confession would perhaps not hold up under close scrutiny? Several public officials were named by Stuart as being in league with the criminal gang—surely a feather in the committee's cap, it would seem—but none of the officials whose names were published in the public press were ever called before the body to give evidence or to answer the allegations against them. Stuart charged that the Yuba County sheriff had stolen his money after his 1850 arrest. He also said that his personal attorney, San Francisco city attorney Frank Pixley, had kept his money and suborned perjury on his behalf. Sheriff Roach and Constable McCarthy of Monterey had shared in the proceeds of a theft there, he said, and San Francisco police captains McCarty and McIntire had helped his gang with several burglaries.

When Stuart's confession was published in the public press, city attorney Pixley immediately published a denial in the newspapers, refuting the allegations point by point.[17] Some of Sheriff Roach's friends leaped to his defense, arguing that the reputation of an honorable man should not be allowed to be besmirched by the uncorroborated testimony of a felon.[18] When Stuart had first been captured by the committee, captains McCarty and McIntire, as well as attorney Pixley, had refused to identify the prisoner to what they rightly considered an illegal body. When Stuart's accusations against them were published in public print, the officers asked for an opportunity to appear before the committee and give their side of events.[19] They were ignored. It would have been useful to our full understanding of the events of 1851 if they had been allowed to appear and have their version of events recorded.

One of the principal sources of information to the committee was Joseph Hetherington (no apparent relation to James), who was no doubt given immunity to testify against his former friends.[20] One of those against whom Hetherington gave evidence later published in the press was a man named J. J. Arentrue. In a letter of response to the committee, Arentrue pointed out that Hetherington was part of the criminal gang that hung out on Central Wharf and that he had recently been prosecuted for perjury. Arentrue said that he had tried to gain entrance to the committee twice to refute the charges against him but had been turned away. It is hard to believe, were he guilty, that Arentrue would have courted danger by meeting in private with a secret society already known to have summarily hanged two criminals who ran afoul of it. He was later arrested by the committee but turned over to the regular authorities; he was charged in court with a conspiracy "with unknown persons to kill an unknown man at an unknown place." Presumably, his accusers knew when the crime was going to occur. Not surprisingly, the case came to nothing.[21]

These examples of questionable veracity tend to show that perhaps all was not as it seemed—the victors might have been doing a bit of tampering with what came to be the historic record of the Committee of Vigilance.[22] This is not offered in defense of Stuart and his gang, who probably got only what they deserved; but if we are to understand the events of 1851, we should know them as they occurred. One nearly contemporary historian, and staunch defender of vigilance, did not think much of Stuart's confession. According to Theodore Hittell, "Stuart's confession endeavored to involve various other persons against whom he evidently held grudges. No one [at the time] put much faith in his statement on account of its source and its mean and treacherous spirit."[23]

The problem is that the accusations have been duly recorded, and the records of the secret tribunal have passed as just about all that remains to history. The story of Stuart's confession is an object lesson in the need for the protections found in the constitution against arbitrary governmental action. There is a very real appeal to the simplicity and seeming effectiveness of summary justice—but there is also the danger that great injustices can occur in the dark recesses of secret tribunals.

CHAPTER 22

Law and Order

LIMITED AS WE LARGELY ARE to the written records of the committee and its supporters, we are left with the impression that the vigilante movement had the overwhelming support of the citizens of the city. It is true enough that the committee could claim the support of a numerical majority. The leading merchants and businessmen supported it from the inside, of course, and their colleagues in the establishment press parroted their views. Denied an insider's view, and urged on by the promptings of the press, the general public—particularly the loungers around Portsmouth Square—seems to have heartily endorsed the idea of public hangings.

Some public officials were at best lukewarm. Mayor Brenham, noticeably absent during the events leading up to the Jenkins hanging, finally issued a mushily worded proclamation on the day Stuart was hanged containing a pro forma request for good citizens to dissociate themselves from the extralegal body.[1] Governor McDougal issued his first proclamation a week later, acknowledging the right of the citizens to organize, but only to assist the regular authorities.[2] As might be expected, Brenham's police were no threat to the committee. The department was reorganized in July, as previously noted, according to the terms of the new charter passed at the April election. But in the face of a seeming crime wave, the force of seventy-five was reduced to forty-six, the districts were reduced from three to two, and the pay of the officers was trimmed. The regular officers went about their patrols and tried to collect their reduced pay while the vigilantes ran the town. (It is useful to remember that in any age conservative interests who ask that we "support our local police" and complain that officers are handcuffed in the conduct of their duty are least willing to support law enforcement efforts with money. Liberals, on the other hand, who are often charged with being soft on crime, seem more willing to fund law enforcement programs and just about every other type as well.)

Some San Franciscans actively disapproved of the committee. The out-and-out criminal element, as might be expected, was opposed to its actions, but there were also more respectable opponents to the group that had taken over the town. Hall McAllister, remember, testified that a large part of the crowd on Portsmouth Square objected to Jenkins's hanging. But, while of spotless reputation himself, as a lawyer he was of the class that could be expected to object to the Vigilance Committee on two grounds. On the one hand, attorneys had a vested financial and professional interest in the justice process. On the other, the action of private citizens to wrest the governance of the city from the professionals was a living indictment of their inability to manage affairs. As a class, attorneys and professional politicians came down on the side opposing the committee.

Judge Campbell of the court of sessions, as a member of the legal profession, also opposed the committee. But there was more to his opposition than irritation caused by treading on his professional turf. The execution of Jenkins, for all the pretense of a trial, resembled nothing so much as a lynching: a spontaneous outburst of public indignation and altogether a good show. Stuart's case was different. He was hanged deliberately and with ceremony after more than a week of incarceration, examination, and trial. He was not hanged hastily in the dark of night by a group quickly thrown together; rather, he was marched through the streets in broad daylight then hanged from a public pier in full view of the assembled populace. If Jenkins's hanging was a mark of public frustration, Stuart's was a sign of open contempt for the constituted authorities.

Judge Campbell was outraged at the hanging of Stuart; in asking the grand jury to indict his executioners, the judge pointed out that, whatever the previous tardiness of the courts, they were now functioning efficiently and that the Stuart case could have been handled by the regular processes of justice in ten days. He was right about that. After Jimmy from the Town had been turned over to the regular authorities by the committee, he was indicted, tried, and convicted, all within ten days. (There was little chance, however, that the grand jury would follow the judge's instructions to indict Stuart's executioners, because eight of the twelve jury members were also members of the committee.)

One of the themes that has emerged so far suggests that the motives of the Vigilance Committee and its members were not always entirely altruistic. It would be convenient if we could show that its opponents were all men of high character. But life and history do not fit into neat little boxes. While it can be argued that the members of the committee were not above reproach, neither were their opponents. In fairness to the committee, we must also show the other side of the question.

From the first, it was state senator David Broderick who led the opposition to the committee. He tried to rally support on the night Jenkins was hanged in order to rescue the thief for the regular authorities. He spoke out against the extralegal tribunal at the coroner's inquest. He spoke out at the public meeting in Portsmouth Square following the Jenkins hanging and tried to organize his own meeting for June 22. On the day before Stuart was hanged, Broderick, along with a prominent fireman and political operative named Charles Duane, chaired a meeting of Law and Order forces at which resolutions were passed pledging help to the city officials in their efforts to prevent the infliction of punishment without due process.

On the face of it, Broderick's opposition can be viewed as reflecting the position of the class of politicians to which he belonged. Viewed another way, his opposition can be seen as a matter of principle. If he had been merely counting votes, he might well have sided with the numerically superior vigilantes; but almost until the end, he stood against what has been reported as an obvious tide of public approval. The Whigs, after all, controlled the city administration at the time and any embarrassment of them could have been turned to serve his interests.

According to one scenario, Broderick was, "for all practical purposes, in absolute control of San Francisco's political machinery"—a city boss in the classic nineteenth-century mold.[3] His political biographer, however, sees him as "an egalitarian democrat who put his faith, and would place ultimate political authority, in the hands of the general citizenry."[4] Far from being a creature of Tammany, he had come to California because he could not succeed politically in Tammany-controlled New York. But whatever his political orientation, he operated, as he had to, in the real world of mid-century urban politics.

The above-mentioned Charles P. (Dutch Charley) Duane was very much a part of that real world—his career personifies in bold relief much of what was wrong with the political/legal system in San Francisco in 1851, and his behavior lends support to the reasoning of those who thought that the only way to correct things was to take matters into their own hands. As already discussed, political practices in nineteenth-century urban America lagged behind the emerging social realities of the time. With no governmental controls yet devised to deal with the new problems facing the electoral process, elections had degenerated in many places into a contest to determine which faction could physically dominate the polling place. To do that, political leaders of all parties surrounded themselves with bodies of fighting men, "shoulder strikers," who saw to it that electoral matters were conducted the way intended. Charles Duane, one of the leading operatives in Broderick's camp, was the quintessential shoulder striker. Broderick was not alone in this. By employing men to "protect" the ballot box, he was merely subscribing to the practices then common in the reality of urban political life.

Duane was born in Tipperary, Ireland, in 1829 and came to Albany, New York, with his family as a young boy.[5] Even as a boy he was larger and stronger than most; when he was a young man, he went to New York City, where he apprenticed himself to a wagon maker. Soon he was "running with the engines," an essential precondition to a life in urban politics. With his superior physique, he excelled in athletics, earning the nickname "Dutch" Charley after a man he bested in an athletic contest. Duane's place in politics was to put his physical attributes to good use.

He arrived in California in January 1850 at the age of twenty-one; soon afterward, though nominally a Whig, he attached himself to Broderick's political camp. His life can be traced by his frequent outbursts of physical violence. Duane's name first appears in what remains of the public record the following July, when he came before the recorder on a charge that he beat a man described as a quiet citizen. In September, he was again before the recorder on a charge of battery and riotous conduct, but he was discharged after two police officers testified that he was a peaceable man.[6] Sufficient contemporary news accounts of his public disputes survive that we can still discern his fighting style at the remove of more than 130 years. Tough as he was, Duane was not one to give his opponent a chance to swing first. While his adversary was still talking, Duane would swing; once his opponent was on the ground, Duane would stomp him.

In December 1850, Duane was again before the court for choking and stomping a police officer named Gould.[7] The officer said that he was trying to cite Duane for shooting a dog when Dutch Charley attacked him. Duane said that he shot the dog because it bit him and that he did not know Gould was an officer. He said he thought the officer was the owner of the dog, trying to present him with a bill.

On February 18, 1851, Duane attended a ball given by the actors of the French Theater. One of the actors, Fayolle by name, accidentally stepped on Duane's foot while dancing. The actor tried to apologize, but Duane was not in a mood to accept and had to be restrained from beating the hapless Frenchman then and there. Shortly thereafter, however, he approached Fayolle from the rear on the dance floor and shot him in the back. He then calmly waited for the police to arrive.[8] Fayolle did not die from his wounds, and the matter was pushed to the rear of the public consciousness by the excitement that accompanied the Jansen affair the following day.

While out on bail, Duane was present and assisted in fighting off the crowd that wanted to hang Berdue the following Saturday;[9] in March, while still on bail, he was reported to have joined a police officer in beating a prisoner in the basement of the station house jail.[10] There was some question raised about what a private citizen facing charges himself was doing there in the first place, but the inquiry came to nothing. At his trial in late March for the assault on Fayolle, the jury could not agree on his guilt and he was released; in May, in accordance with the recent judiciary act, his retrial was transferred to the court of sessions.

Later that month, a battery warrant was issued for Duane and others after they were involved in some type of a fight over a land dispute. On July 21, in the midst of the vigilance uprising, Duane and another "shoulder striker" went to a masked ball, where he ran into Frank Ball. Ball was a member of the Vigilance Committee (#192) and was well known and liked as a singer in Clayton's Saloon. He had been on Duane's jury in the Fayolle trial and had voted for conviction. Duane, ostensibly objecting to Ball's humorous singing of a song about Jenkins, whom Duane claimed as a friend, assaulted the singer, knocking him down and stomping him severely.[11] Duane was tried quickly in the city courts; given his long history of violence, the proponents of the Vigilance Committee were outraged when he received only a one-year sentence. (On August 14, Duane's bail was vacated and on August 17 he was pardoned by Governor McDougal. When the Executive Committee found out about the pardon on September 4, it ordered his arrest, but he had already skipped to Panama.[12] By 1852, he was back in town, continuing his life of violence.)[13]

On the face of it, Duane was a bully who had to be stopped, though he was merely the most effective and most prominent of a type found among supporters of political factions at the time. When once questioned about his association with men like Duane, Broderick is supposed to have said that he was only doing the same as his opponents and that he was willing to dispense with his "poll watchers" when they were.[14] Whatever the case, apart from concern about substantive crime, it was in part fear of gratuitous violence—as personified in the behavior of Duane and others, who were with some justification seen as being of a piece with the regular criminals—that drove some people to support summary justice.

After the July 10 meeting of the Law and Order party at the Saint Francis Hook and Ladder Company, the day before Stuart was hanged, Broderick came to the realization that, notwithstanding any resolutions his group might make to support the regular authorities, those authorities were simply not interested in confronting the Committee of Vigilance. Broderick thereupon withdrew from formal active opposition to the committee—thereafter, the committee had the field virtually to itself.

CHAPTER 23

Whittaker and McKenzie

IN OUTWARD APPEARANCE, the city seemed to be prospering and crime conditions appeared pretty well under control by August. The burned district from the May fire had been completely rebuilt, and work on the damage from the June fire was well under way. The business section of the city was being rebuilt in fireproof brick. The message had finally sunk in. There would be more fires, some of them large ones, but not for another fifty years would San Francisco again be afflicted by a massive general fire disaster. At mid-month, the editor of the *Alta* recommended that numbers be placed on houses so that strangers could find their way about. San Francisco was taking on the attributes of a big city.

In fact, business was still sluggish as the summer ended, even though it was expected to improve in the fall. There were still few jobs and as many as twenty applicants might show up for a single job opening. Immigration was off, due to the business stagnation and concerns about the unsettled state of political affairs. With a nod toward potential immigrants and shippers, the *Alta* reported on July 28 that there was now peace and quiet in the state and that the constituted authorities were in full performance of their duties, aided by the Vigilance Committee, which was being maintained more as a "conservator" of the law than as its "executor."

Confidence had been restored in the court of sessions, and the July grand jury in its report published on August 3 stated that it had considered ninety cases in the twenty-four days it sat, returning forty-four true bills, ignoring thirty-three, and dismissing thirteen, mostly because of a lack of witnesses. The jury, eight of whom were members of the Vigilance Committee, also saw fit to approve of the actions of the committee and to criticize Judge Parsons of the district court.[1] On August 6, the Executive Committee, over the objections of the General Committee, decided to turn the well-known burglar George Adams over to the regular authorities and did so.[2]

The police were also back in favor. "The new police are now entered in the active discharge of their duties," reported the *Alta* and "were winning the opinion for the quiet orderly manner in which the city was kept." On August 8, the paper commented that there was not one case for the recorder, leading the editor to conclude that the state of morals of the town had much improved. (Such individual editorial reports must be taken with a grain of salt. On August 19, the same paper reported that on the previous Sunday "the whole rowdy world had let itself out," filling the recorder's court with business the next day. But that, as we shall see, was to be an exceptional weekend.) By the end of the month, the *Alta* was wishing editorially that "somebody would get up a fight or shooting match on the Plaza, so there would be some police news to report."[3] Jail escapes had come to an end. With a hempen rope awaiting them outside, perennial escapees like Adams and Burns welcomed the safety of prison walls; had they tried to escape, the solid walls of the new county jail would prove more formidable than the tissue-thin sides of its predecessors.

By actual count, there was not a lot of change in the incidence of reported predatory crime from month to month. Predatory crime was reduced about as much as would be expected by the elimination of Stuart and his cronies.

Comparison of Reported Crimes in 1851

	Jan	Feb	Mar	Apr	May	June	July	Aug
Criminal Homicide	2	0	2	1	2	2*	1*	1*
Robbery	0	4	0	0	4	2	2	0
Burglary	10	7	17	6	8	5	3	4

*Does not include those hanged by the Vigilance Committee or beaten to death in the June fire.

The usual monthly murder occurred on August 9 after 8 P.M. when a black man named Thomas Wheeler left his job at the Nightingale Saloon at the end of the plank road. He was not seen again; nine days later, his murdered body was found 100 yards off the road. Sam Brannan, who lived nearby, caused the arrest of two men found loitering around the location at the time the body was discovered. The Vigilance Committee held the men for ten days before releasing them without charge.[4]

There were no robberies reported in August, but burglary started to edge up again. On August 2, when a house was burglarized at Kearny and Broadway, the *Alta* wanted to know where the new police were. (The press attitude toward the incidence of a single residential burglary points up the mid-nineteenth-century belief, widely held, that the newly established "preventive" police departments should somehow be able to suppress virtually all criminal predation.) Another house in North Beach was reported burglarized on August 18, and an office on Front Street on August 25. The scoundrels were busy again, reported the *Alta*; on August 30, a black man named Jake Larkin was arrested for a residential burglary.

It was not the Australians who were committing the crimes. The members of Stuart's gang had been scattered or were in jail. Many of the rest of the Australian immigrants decided the time was ripe for them to leave. The fears of an Australian invasion in May were groundless, for gold had been discovered that summer in Australia and many Australians decided to return home.[5] To the extent that crime decreased at all, we can wonder how much is attributable to the efforts of the committee and how much to the natural departure of large numbers of adventurers. Nevertheless, crime seemed pretty well under control. The general perception was that crime was down, the police and courts were believed to be doing their jobs, and prisoners remained in jail. It would seem that it was time for the committee to relinquish its active participation in the administration of justice— time, as reported by the *Alta*, for the members of the committee to become the conservators, not the executors, of the law. But they were not through hanging yet.

After Adams had been turned over to the regular authorities over objections from the General Committee, Robert McKenzie was the only important criminal named by Stuart remaining in the committee's custody.[6] He was not as prominent a criminal as Adams, so the reason he was held while Adams was turned over to the regular authorities is not readily apparent.

The committee also kept after Samuel Whittaker.[7] A posse of vigilantes had been in pursuit of him but lost his trail on July 19 and returned to San Francisco. The committee released Mrs. Hogan and kept a watch on her in hopes that the two lovers would establish contact. Whittaker lay low in Sacramento for a time and then headed south toward San Diego, where he planned to meet Mrs. Hogan and take ship out of the country. While en route, he was recognized in Santa Barbara and taken into custody by the sheriff of that county. The sheriff escorted Whittaker to San Francisco, arriving on August 11; leaving Whittaker on the steamer, he set out to find a San Francisco official to whom he could turn over his prisoner. Members of the committee got wind of Whittaker's presence in the city and intercepted him. The prisoner was placed in custody in the vigilante rooms along with Robert McKenzie. There Whittaker gave his confession.

He said he had come to California from Australia in August 1849 and had worked for three months in a saloon on Broadway Street. He then bought a boat and a horse cart and had men working for him. He also worked as a butcher in Happy Valley, where his troubles began. When a horse he bought turned out to be stolen from Charles Duane, he was hailed before the district court. His case was never tried, he said, but his money taken in evidence disappeared. It was then that he returned to a life of crime. He admitted to being involved in the Jansen robbery, which, he said, started out to be a sneak theft that turned violent. He also implicated T. Belcher Kay in the Jansen robbery, admitted that he had helped Windred escape from the prison brig, and said that Stuart had admitted the Moore killing to him.

He also implicated public officials in corruption. In one case, he said, he avoided a ten-day sentence given to him in the recorder's court by the payment of $230.[8] He said that he had once given Captain McCarty three ounces in gold and that at the request of McCarty and McIntire he had gotten twelve foreigners to vote for Marshal Fallon.[9] (There was other more damaging evidence against the former marshal. Thomas Ainsworth, arrested along with Adams in July, stated that the marshal had arrested him repeatedly until he agreed to steal for him.[10] In late August, a man about to be hanged by a mob in Sacramento, with his neck literally in the noose, is said to have made "grave charges" against the mayor of Sacramento and Marshal Fallon of San Francisco.[11] By that time, the out-of-office marshal was running the Rip Van Winkle Saloon on Pacific Street and the committee never did call him to account. So we shall probably never know for sure whether there was anything to the allegations.)

On August 14, McKenzie also broke. He admitted only to two previous robberies and said that he knew police captain Ben Ray. The
committee believed he knew a lot more than he revealed. It really did
not matter too much whether the prisoners confessed like Whittaker
or held back like McKenzie; on August 15, President Payran recommended to the full committee that they both be hanged on Monday,
August 18.[12] The Executive Committee concurred; the execution was
scheduled to take place the following week. Over the weekend, rumors
abounded that a double hanging was to take place. On Monday, the
full texts of the statements made by Whittaker and McKenzie were
published in the local dailies. On August 19, the General Committee
met again and set the execution for the next day. The prisoners were
to.be hanged in the harbor in full view of any criminals remaining in
Sydneytown on the slopes of Telegraph Hill.

On August 19, having heard of the impending hanging, Governor
John McDougal decided that things had gone far enough and that he
should do something.[13] He left Sacramento by steamer that day and arrived, by himself, in San Francisco that night at 11 P.M. He went to the
Union Hotel Bar across from Portsmouth Square, where he was told by
an informant who had infiltrated the committee that the execution was
scheduled for the next morning. McDougal then located Mayor Brenham, who told the governor that it was his plan to show up at vigilante
headquarters at 8 o'clock the following morning with the entire police
department and seize the prisoners.[14] Unbeknownst to McDougal, one
of the men with Brenham was a member of the committee and reported
the mayor's plan back to committee headquarters.

McDougal and Brenham then sought out Sheriff Hays, who was at
first reluctant to assist them in rescuing the prisoners. But the governor prevailed upon him; the trio went to superior court judge Myron
Norton, who, at the request of the governor, issued an arrest warrant
for Whittaker and McKenzie. McDougal discarded Brenham's plan to
confront the committee in the morning as too likely to create a general
disorder and instead decided to make his move earlier and with only a
small force.

At vigilante headquarters, in the meantime, a fifteen-man death
watch had been established to see the prisoners through the night.
When news of Brenham's plan to seize the prisoners at 8 A.M. was
received, it was decided to move them before the police arrived. The
leg shackles were removed from the prisoners and they were taken to
a spot near the front door of the vigilante headquarters prior to being
moved from the building.

Shortly after 3 A.M., the governor, mayor, sheriff, and Deputy Sheriff Caperton arrived outside the committee rooms. The plan was simple. The mayor was to remain with the horses on the street. The governor positioned himself at an inside landing near the front door. The sheriff was posted at the front door to keep it ajar once it was opened. Deputy Sheriff Caperton was to rush into the detention area and seize the prisoners. The plan worked.

Once the front door was opened (presumably the rescuers had obtained the password), the sheriff loudly announced his presence and intentions. Members of the guard quickly slammed the door shut, but the governor broke it open again, and Deputy Sheriff Caperton rushed in to seize the prisoners. Thinking a large police force was attacking them, the vigilante guard was paralyzed into inactivity, and the prisoners were spirited down the stairs and away. The alarm was raised, and the outraged General Committee assembled in the committee rooms, sure that the prisoners had been released only through treachery. By then, the prisoners were safely ensconced in the county jail.

Committee members went home but returned again at 8 A.M. to decide what to do about this new turn of affairs. By that time, a measure of calm was restored. A resolution to storm the jail and retake the prisoners was tabled and the chief of the vigilance police was suspended pending the outcome of an investigation into his conduct; a subcommittee, which included Sam Brannan, was appointed to investigate and report on the reasons for the success of the escape. Later that day, the committee reconvened to hear the report of the investigative subcommittee. It was determined that there was no collusion on the part of members of the Executive Committee; while he was found guilty of gross neglect in allowing the escape, Van Bokkelen was reinstated as chief of police.[15] It was moved and carried that the death penalty was still in effect.

On August 20, Governor McDougal issued his second proclamation calling for cooperation with the forces of law and order.[16] The *Alta*, while still supporting the committee, suggested that it allow the authorities to keep the prisoners. The *Courier*, on the other hand, criticized the authorities for making the rescue as an "unnecessary attempt to produce a collision."[17] The *Herald* complimented the committee for its restraint in the face of official provocation.[18]

Within the committee, a small detachment of thirty men was designated to retake the prisoners; on the following Sunday, after Sheriff Hays had, wittingly or unwittingly, allowed himself to be drawn away from the jail to watch a bullfight at the Mission, members of the rescue party entered the county jail under the ruse that they wanted to attend the church services there. At 2 P.M., while services were under way, they let their fellows in. Whittaker and McKenzie were seized, hustled into a carriage, and whisked to vigilante headquarters, where, within a few minutes of their capture, they were hanged side by side in full view of 6,000 jeering onlookers hastily assembled by the tolling of the city's fire bells.

The press in general approved.[19] The *Alta* waffled. The paper that just a few days before had counseled the committee to leave the prisoners with the authorities lamely approved of the hanging in its Monday edition, saying that such incidents were to be expected under conditions of misrule. The Vigilance Committee decided that public welfare required the hangings, the editor said; while the authorities were correct in making a rescue, the Vigilance Committee was also right to retake the prisoners and hang them.

Not everyone approved.[20] There were a few impromptu fights in barrooms that Sunday between the forces for and against the hanging. Associate justice Harvey Brown of the court of sessions promptly tendered his resignation, saying that the criminal calendar had nearly been cleared, yet people persisted in hanging men on the grounds of weakness of the courts. Let the people appoint the one they wanted to be a judge, he said. The *Alta* commented that Brown had done his duty faithfully and regretted his resignation due to "an undue degree of sensitiveness."[21] The *Herald* said that it had neither praised nor damned him but recommended his course to Judge Parsons.[22] Judge Campbell announced that he had said all he had to say at the time of Stuart's hanging.

If conditions were improving, as by all accounts they seemed to be, why did Whittaker and McKenzie hang? One critic of the committee suggests that they knew too much about members of the committee. That theory is lent credibility by the fact that the last pages of Whittaker's confession turned up missing.[23] Some have implied that Whittaker and McKenzie knew something about the involvement of members of the committee in starting some of the fires and that they had to be silenced.[24] If so, we shall probably never know.

There are other possibilities, not dependent on speculative conspiracy theories, but first we must dispose of conventional wisdom on the matter. Mary Williams asserts that the committee held and punished those whose crimes were most heinous and released the rest to

The hanging of Whittaker and McKenzie. (*California State Library*)

the regular authorities. But if that is the case, why turn Adams over to the authorities and hang McKenzie? Adams was surely the more prominent criminal of the two. Williams suggests that the comparatively mild sentences given to Adams and Jimmy from the Town in the regular courts sealed the fate of McKenzie and Whittaker. But Jimmy from the Town was sentenced at the end of July, before the decision was made to turn Adams over to the regular authorities. And Adams was not sentenced until after Whittaker and McKenzie were hanged.

George Stewart thought that Whittaker and McKenzie hanged because cooperation between the committee and the authorities was not working.[25] T. Belcher Kay had escaped, he said, and justice was moving slowly against the others in official custody. But Jimmy from the Town was convicted within ten days of being turned over to the authorities, and T. Belcher Kay "escaped" only after a grand jury, the majority of whom were members of the Vigilance Committee, failed to indict him. Therein lies a clue to why Whittaker and McKenzie had to hang.

Bancroft lets the cat out of the bag. They were hanged, he says, because the "people" feared they would be acquitted in a regular court of law. Even in the face of overwhelming evidence, he continues, it would have been hard for a grand jury to find a true bill or a court to convict.[26] One is compelled to wonder, if the evidence was so overwhelming, why it would be so difficult to convict. The simple fact of the matter was that there was very little usable evidence against Whittaker and McKenzie except what came out of their own mouths; those who might have been expected to give evidence against them had already been hanged or driven off. There is no real reason to believe that the two hanged men were other than the Vigilance Committee said they were. But, as always with justice administered in privacy, the question remains.

It may seem to some like a trivial matter, but it is one of the central underpinnings of our system of law and the basis for our national civility that a person under our legal system can be convicted only for what he does, not for what he is. There are safeguards to assure this in the justice system as regularly administered. With vigilante justice, those safeguards are ignored so there is no way to establish guilt with sufficient certainty. If, as all indicators suggest, conditions leading to the putative need for a committee were improving, the executions of Whittaker and McKenzie were not acts of outraged justice but acts of vengeance carried out to feed the mob's appetite for blood.

Part V AFTERMATH

CHAPTER 24

Vigilance Triumphant

IN CURRENT CONVENTIONAL press imagery there are a number of recurring illustrations familiar to all, such as the panoramic shot of a crowded beach on the first day of a summer heat wave or the picture of a lost child, surrounded by friendly police officers, wearing an officer's hat and eating an ice cream cone. Another is the image of a group of earnest-looking people captioned "Neighborhood Vigilantes." In the accompanying story, a group of householders assert that they are fed up with crime in their neighborhood and that they are going to patrol the streets themselves to identify criminals and notify the authorities. There is usually a comment from the police chief, who agrees that crime conditions are bad, but cautions them not to take the law into their own hands.

If one did a follow-up a few weeks or months later, one would probably find that the members of the patrol had quietly gone on to other things. All organisms, social and biological, have a finite life span, a beginning and an end, but the lives of volunteer police organizations are shorter than most. Community involvement of some sort in police affairs is a positive thing. Indeed, it is probably the only way a real dent will ever be made in urban crime in a free society. But members of hastily put together volunteer patrols quickly find out, in a paraphrase of the words of Gilbert and Sullivan, one of the little-known realities about life on most police beats: "When constabulary's duty's to be done," the policeman's lot is not only not a "happy one" but usually downright boring as well. On all but the most active beats, particularly in the late-night hours, very little happens. After volunteer neighborhood vigilante patrols spend a number of long, cold, lonely nights during which nothing occurs, the attractions of a warm hearth, favorite television show, or a friendly tavern take on a new appeal. One by one, group members find other things to do and the group fades quietly into oblivion.[1] Voluntary police patrols are difficult to sustain, and the simple fact is that people will not do patrol work without being paid in one way or another.

Thus it was with a note of genuine relief that William Heath Davis welcomed the establishment of a regular police after the trial of the Hounds in 1849, allowing the suspension of the temporarily established volunteer patrols. The interest in the volunteer anticrime patrols formed in the spring of 1851 had begun to flag before the Vigilance Committee rose to the fore.[2] In September, the Vigilance Committee suspended active operations. On the one hand, it had begun to become apparent that the people had experienced enough reform for a while and it did not look as though there was to be much more hanging. Within the committee itself, dissension flourished. Factions vied for power and charges and countercharges flew.[3] Moreover, it was time for the fall business season to commence, and members began to look to their own affairs. Key members began to resign. There were some, however, who did not wish to see the power of the committee decline. Even before the hanging of Whittaker and McKenzie, there was a group of fourteen members who selected a slate of candidates for county and state offices in the September election.[4] The Executive Committee of the supposedly nonpolitical committee formally disavowed the ticket when it was published on August 28, but it was well understood by all that the ticket was sponsored by leading members of the committee.[5]

One of the provisions of the 1851 charter passed in the April election was that elections to city offices would henceforth be held on the same day as elections to county and state offices. The Whig city government, elected in April, chose to interpret the charter to mean that the first such election should be held after it had served an entire year (i.e., in September 1852). The out-of-office Democrats, not surprisingly, chose to interpret the charter to mean the election should be in September 1851. If that was the case, said the Whigs, their terms would be shortened to four months. So, while the Whig-dominated council did not schedule a city election for September 1851, the Democrats advertised a slate of candidates for all city offices. The Vigilance Committee stood aloof.

On September 3, 1851, 6,000 San Franciscans went to the polls and voted for state and county officers and the slate put forth by the Democrats. No Independent party candidate without regular party support won on his own, but regular party candidates who also had Independent endorsements all won. Committee endorsement by itself was not enough to ensure election, but it was enough to swing a vote one way or the other. Among those elected with Independent party endorsements was county judge William Campbell.[6] Of the total of 6,000 voters in the election, 1,000 cast ballots for the Democratic candidates for city offices. The Whigs refused to retire from office, however, and the Democrats went to court.

Business seemed to be picking up with the usual fall increase.[7] On September 14, the *Alta* reported that the markets were the best of the season. The fact that Marysville and its stock of goods had burned to the ground a week before made things look encouraging. By September 17, the paper reported prices were up.

The police department was now comprised of officers of high moral worth, said the *Alta,* "eager to do their duty because suspicion and blame had attached to them." They should be paid in cash to forestall the temptation to take bribes, thought the editor. There were officers, he said, who had served for a year without receiving their first dollar in cash.[8] But when things got down to specifics, the paper changed its tune. On September 16, the paper said that the payment to the officers should be postponed because it would cause the city to exceed its legal debt limit.

As for the courts, things remained calm. It seemed for a time that the old problems persisted, but nobody got particularly excited about it. The justices of the peace elected in September could not decide among themselves which two of their number should serve with the county judge on the court of sessions, so Judge Campbell appointed two. One of the appointees declined to serve, saying that Campbell had no legal power of appointment, so the county judge appointed another in his place. A few months before, such a situation would have been added to the reasons to throw out the court; but by September, there were other fish to fry. In October, Levi Parsons resigned from the district court to the delight of his detractors; in November, he was replaced by Delos Lake. There were no jail escapes right away. The new county jail was holding the inmates securely; in December, the pressure of overcrowding in the jail was reduced when state prisoners were removed from the county jail and placed on the brig *Waban*, which was towed to Angel Island as the first state prison facility.

People were starting to feel good about the incidence of crime, even though, when all is said and done, there was not a great deal of change in the reported statistics. When all the rhetoric is stripped from the issue, there was little difference in most types of reported crime for the periods before, during, and after the activities of the extraordinary crime-fighting group.

Comparison of Reported Monthly Crime in 1851

	Jan	Feb	Mar	Apr	May	June	July	Aug	Sep	Oct	Nov	Dec
Criminal Homicide	2	0	2	1	2	2	1	1	0	1	2	1
Robbery	0	4	0	0	4	2	2	0	0	1	2	2
Burglary	10	7	17	6	8	5	3	4	0	4	2	2

September was the one month in the period in which no serious crime was reported in the *Alta*, so any claimed respite from crime attributable to the actions of the committee can be said to have lasted for little more than a month. On September 1, the *Alta* reported that crime was down and that anyone who took the trouble to compare the statistics would see that it was down a great deal from six months before. On October 3, the paper again said that crime was down in the last four months; but by mid-month, it seemed to the editor to be on the increase again.[9] The *Times and Transcript* hoped that the town would not go through another crime wave like that of the preceding winter and spring but thought it looked as though it was going to.[10] On October 20, the *Alta* reported the arrival in town of a gang of thieves and scoundrels and hoped that the police would be alert so that the Vigilance Committee would not be needed. On November 15, the paper reported that five stabbings had occurred in the last few days, four of them by Mexicans. (Mexican miners were making their seasonal migration home from the southern mines through San Francisco. No doubt some were lured by the bright lights of the city.)

There were no robberies reported in August and September, but then they increased to about the same rate as before. On October 31, the *Alta* reported the mugging of a new arrival in town; on November 1, Patrick Kelly lost $750 to a bludgeon-wielding mugger. A few days later, a man was arrested for an attempted street robbery; on December 13, the *Alta* reported on the "gross outrage" when the ex-sheriff of Santa Cruz was mugged for $500: "It proves the scoundrels are again among us." On December 20, according to the paper, a man was mugged leaving a grogshop on Pacific Street.

There were no burglaries in September, four in October, and two in November; on the occasion of one, the *Alta* said that, if the police were half as vigilant as the committee, the robbers could not get a foothold. In reply, a police officer wrote to the editor pointing out that the force was too small to be at every back door. One burglary was reported in December.

The usual monthly criminal homicide did not occur in September, but in October things picked up again. The homicides were of the same sort as before, during, and after the active period of the committee. In October, the body of a man named San Miguel was found with multiple stab wounds on Leavenworth Street at North Beach. A man named Marcelino was arrested, but the case came to nothing. On November 9, a man named Greenfield chided a merchant from Stockton named Charles Brown for insulting the Irish in a saloon on Pacific Street. Brown stabbed him to death and was found guilty of manslaughter, but was later pardoned by the governor.[11]

On November 11, several Chileans went ashore from a storeship. During a squabble on their return in the early morning hours of the next day, one fatally stabbed another. The assailant was arrested, tried, and convicted, and received a three-year sentence for manslaughter. On December 30, Alfred A. Green killed Adrian A. Bartolf in a bar in the Mission in a personal dispute. He was indicted and tried, but the jury found him not guilty.[12]

It was in this context that a subcommittee of the Executive Committee was appointed on September 9 to draft a plan of reorganization for the Committee of Vigilance; on September 17, the Executive Committee adopted it. Active operations such as police and tribunals were to be suspended, but a 45-member executive committee was designated to keep an eye on things. The water police did find themselves in action one more time, however. On October 15, the committee heard that one of the uncaught criminals named by Stuart, Jim Briggs—believing the heat was off—had come to San Francisco, still in possession of the fruits of earlier crimes, to embark for Sydney. Members of the committee chartered a steam tug and put to sea after him. They boarded two vessels but found nothing and, since the fuel bunkers of the pursuit ship were running low, returned to port.[13]

There was one more event, in the closing months of 1851, that caused a full mobilization of the Committee of Vigilance and sheds some light on what it was all about. In late 1851, the committee mobilized one more time, to defend against an attack on one of its own. From the beginning of American San Francisco, as we have seen, merchant shipmasters were very much a part of the commercial establishment. It was in their interest that the first ordinance was enacted to prohibit runaway seamen (so that the masters would not take their business elsewhere). It was also in their interest that the body that evolved into the Hounds was formed. It was a merchant captain, remember, William Howard, who gave direction to the first judicial effort of the Vigilance Committee and another, Ned Wakeman, who placed the rope around the first victim's neck.

It was a member of that class, Robert (Bully) Waterman, who set sail from New York City on the newly launched clipper ship *Challenge* on July 13, 1851, headed around Cape Horn for San Francisco in what he and the owners hoped would be a record passage.[14] The clipper *Flying Cloud*, which had left just before, had depleted the pool of trained sailors willing to make the dangerous voyage around the Horn. The *Challenge* had to take what was left. Half its crew were seamen; the rest were the scourings of New York jails and wastrels looking for a free trip to California. Serving under Waterman as first mate to keep control of an unruly crew was "Black" Douglas, a 200-pound Scotsman who had joined the ship directly from another in New York Harbor to avoid having to go ashore, where he would have had to answer to the authorities for his conduct on his last berth.

The story of the voyage of the *Challenge* is a tale that reveals much of what was wrong with nineteenth-century shipping. Waterman, unquestioned master of both the ship and the fate of its crew, drove the men mercilessly in his attempt to set a record for the trip. Five men were thrown from the yards and died on the voyage. When sullen, mutinous crew members revolted and attacked the bully mate, Waterman joined the fray with a belaying pin and laid out three crew members, two of whom later died. The *Challenge* arrived in San Francisco in good but not record time on October 29; when Waterman promised to prosecute the mutineers, the entire crew jumped ship. The next day, as the ship docked at Pacific Wharf, hundreds of angry boatmen, sailors, and dock wallopers were on hand to greet the skipper. When, two days later, sailors maimed on the voyage were taken from the ship to the marine hospital, 200 men marched on the office to the ship's agent on California Street, looking for the captain and mate with the avowed intention of hanging them. A delegation searched the agent's offices, but the quarry had already fled.

It is one thing to hang a burglar or a thief, but it is quite another to hang a member of the establishment, no matter how many men he has killed. Mayor Brenham—most notable for his absence during the Jenkins trial and hanging, and remembered during the hanging of Whittaker and McKenzie for calmly sitting across the street on a pile of lumber while the culprits were illegally hanged—rose to the moment. The mayor ordered that the Monumental Fire Company's firebell be tapped with the familiar vigilante call to arms. Within minutes, 600 members of the committee gathered at his back. Brenham gave the crowd ten minutes to disperse. It did so, drifted away, and re-formed on Pacific Wharf, where there was some talk of burning the *Challenger*, but in the end it dispersed at the direction of the U.S. marshal.

"Where are they now who called the Vigilance Committee a mob?" asked the *Alta*, of another paper (the *Post*) that wondered at the seeming inconsistency between its desire to hang one month and an equal desire to stop a hanging two months later. The *Alta* would rather be right than be consistent, said its editor. The paper had always been in favor of law and order—the only question was whether the circumstances under which the Vigilance Committee acted were such as to justify its proceedings. Based on the results, said the *Alta*, it was.[15] The paper missed the point. Mary Williams calls it "a curious reversal of the usual relations between the Committee of Vigilance and the authorities of San Francisco. . . ."[16] She also misses the point.

A round of trials followed over the next few months, which, in their halting procedures, are reminiscent of the pace set by Parsons. But there were no mobs outside the courtroom shouting for instant justice; in the end, interest in the trials dribbled away to nothing. It was the merchant/shipmaster establishment that prevailed again—the establishment that founded San Francisco, that framed its first laws, that abandoned the law and imposed summary rule when its interests seemed in danger, and, in the case of Waterman, that mobilized to support the agents of the law again when it suited the welfare of its own adherents. In the words of historian Roger Lotchin, "the community [establishment] protected a ship captain, later convicted in court of having brutally mistreated his men, from a gang of sailors. Vigilante defenders saw this incident as an example of their fairness, but the failure even to investigate the charges is better proof of a double standard."[17]

One is confirmed in the revised historical judgment that the degree of outrage at crime and the need for summary punishment in Gold Rush San Francisco very much depended on whose ox was being gored. By the end of the year, the commercial establishment must have felt securely in control of the city—enough so that Sam Brannan and a group of his friends felt comfortable in chartering a sailing vessel, stocking it with provisions, and taking off on a pleasure cruise to the Sandwich Islands.[18]

It was asserted at the outset that this book would demonstrate that the hundreds of murders mentioned in the legend never occurred—that has been done. But for those who remain unconvinced—who believe that the murders occurred and that the press merely failed to report them—I shall make one more effort. Phineas Blunt, already referred to, was an overland immigrant from New York who arrived in California in 1850. On his journey across the plains, like many of his fellows, Blunt kept a journal of his daily adventures and ideas.[19] After his arrival, he did not have much luck at the mines; but late in the year, though a Whig, he was appointed as a member of Fallon's police department. In his thirteen months in the police department, Blunt continued to maintain his journal, setting down items of interest that occurred on the job. He describes from his point of view the excitement of the Jansen affair and the formation of the Committee of Vigilance. He also notes, from day to day, criminal homicides as they came to his attention.

What follows is a comparison of the homicides mentioned by Blunt and those reported in the daily issues of the *Alta* for the thirteen months Blunt maintained his diary as a police officer, showing where the two sources agree and where they diverge. Between the two sources, there were twenty-one reported homicides in the period in question. In twelve of those cases, the killings appear in both sources: November 26, 1850 (McMahan); December 1, 1850 (Lewis); December 30, 1850 (Foy); January 22, 1851 (a Frenchman); January 28, 1851 (Bartley); March 26, 1851 (Jarvis); May 4, 1851 (Lawley); June 22, 1851 (Gallagher); November 3, 1851 (McCabe); November 9, 1851 (Greenfield); November 11, 1851 (Sequel); December 30, 1851 (Bartolf).

Blunt lists two killings not reported in the *Alta*. On January 18, 1851, he mentions the body of a murder victim found near the cemetery (which was then located at the current site of the Main Library) and on March 26, 1851, another at the Mission. This variance from the newspaper record can perhaps be explained by the fact that Blunt was assigned to the First Police District, which included the entire area of the city south of California Street. Both of the murders he mentions that are not mentioned in the *Alta* occurred in the "sticks" of the First District, well south of the main settled portion of the city. It is very likely that a local police officer might know about a couple of low-grade homicides that escaped the attention of a downtown newspaper.

Seven of the killings are reported in the *Alta* but not mentioned by Blunt: December 27, 1850 (McMillan); April 12, 1851 (Burns); May 21, 1851 (Foster); June 1, 1851 (Brewer); July 12, 1851 (Guerrero); August 9, 1851 (Wheeler); October 9, 1851 (San Miguel). Three of Blunt's omissions (Burns, Foster, Guerrero) can be explained by the fact that no final judicial determination was ever made that the deaths were in fact caused by criminal agency.

In sum, this comparison shows a high degree of congruence between the criminal homicides mentioned in Blunt's diary and the incidents reported in the daily press. Yet there is enough difference between the two sources to demonstrate that Officer Blunt did not obtain his diary entries from a reading of the daily papers. In neither of the sources is there anything even distantly approaching the figures contained in the legend.

CHAPTER 25

The Year After

AS HAS ALREADY been pointed out, accounts dealing with criminal justice matters in Gold Rush San Francisco customarily skip over the period between the Hounds affair in 1849 and the Jansen robbery in early 1851. Similarly, the same accounts usually end with the reorganization of the Executive Committee in September 1851. There might be a mention of the Waterman case, by way of showing that the Vigilance Committee was not really a mob, or a brief discussion of some of the later rumblings of the committee in reaction to sudden increases in reported crime statistics. But we are left with the general impression that, after the reorganization of the committee, crime remained pretty well under control for several years until the period leading up to the second and greater Vigilance Committee of 1856.[1]

It was rampant crime that had supposedly called the committee into existence; once crime was brought under control, we are led to believe, the members of the extralegal organization retired gracefully to their own affairs. In fact, there was about as much predatory crime in the year following the year of vigilance, yet for some reason the citizenry did not rise again in righteous wrath. "Crime, during 1852, was perhaps not sensibly diminished," reported the *Annals*, always a supporter of the committee, "but in the increasing importance of other matters of public discussion, lower class criminals were tolerated, or less pursued."[2] Indeed! We are compelled to wonder, if that was the case, what all the excitement the year before had been about.

By early 1852, prosperity for most had returned to San Francisco. There would continue to be business fluctuations as cargoes landed to find glutted or empty markets, driving prices up and down. But in 1852, business practices began to take on a more regular aspect. Increased warehouse space allowed for the storage of more goods. Eastern shippers had begun to exhibit better business sense—no longer did they send stores of goods willy-nilly into an unknown market. The population increased—with 67,000 arriving by sea against 23,000 departures—providing customers to relieve the pressure of the glut of merchandise. By year's end, the permanent population of San Francisco was more than 40,000. Physically, the town took on a more permanent look. Having finally learned their lesson in the rash of disastrous fires, and having decided to make their home in San Francisco, builders more and more chose brick over highly flammable wood.

Municipal political conditions remained unsettled. By the end of 1851, the state supreme court decided that the Democratic candidates chosen at the September election were entitled to the city offices; in early 1852, the incumbent Whigs resigned and the Democrats took over. For all the excitement that had occurred during their tenure in office, members of the Whig city government have come through unscathed by history. Not surprisingly perhaps, the Democrats who replaced them were not so fortunate.

One of the important "other matters of public discussion" that occupied the citizenry in 1852 was the council's purchase of the Jenny Lind Theater to serve as a city hall. After the city hall purchased by the *ayuntamiento* in 1850 burned in the June 1851 fire, city offices were spread around the town at a yearly rental cost of $27,000. By year's end, the combined rental cost of city and county offices was $40,000; the new council decided to spend $200,000 to buy the Parker House and the adjoining Jenny Lind Theater on the east side of Portsmouth Square to serve as a city hall.[3] Charges were made, true, that the Jenny Lind's owner, Tom Maguire, was a good friend of David Broderick and that a more suitable building could have been built for less money.

The issue of the purchase of the theater remained in the public eye

Bird's-eye view of San Francisco in 1852 showing the great growth following the start of the Gold Rush and the clutter of ships both north and south of Market Street. Market Street Wharf is in the foreground. (*San Francisco Public Library*)

for months on end. There was the usual mass indignation meeting in Portsmouth Square protesting the purchase; in the excited disagreement that accompanied the matter, the editor of the *Herald* was shot in the arm in a duel with a member of the council. But in the end, the council approved the purchase of the Jenny Lind over a mayoral veto. For all the public discord that attended the acquisition of the building, it turned out in the end to have served its intended purpose well.[4]

Another of the "matters of public discussion" that so occupied the public interest in 1852 was actually one of the *ayuntamiento*'s chickens coming home to roost. During the tenure of Geary and Brannan's *ayuntamiento* in 1849–50, it will be remembered, the stated purpose of the January 1850 lot sale was to provide a city hall, a hospital, wharves, and other public improvements. The sale yielded $635,000 to be paid in quarterly increments; $300,000 was immediately appropriated to build wharves (to the financial benefit of Brannan and his friends). Another $150,000 was spent to buy a building from a member of the *ayuntamiento* to serve as a city hall. The idea of building a public hospital went begging; instead, the *ayuntamiento* government entered into a contract in February with Doctor Peter Smith to care for indigent patients on a per diem basis.[5]

As with everything else, Gold Rush San Francisco had more than its share of illness during its first few years. (It has been estimated that one in twenty gold seekers died, usually from illness, within six months of arrival in California.) Medical costs for indigent patients mounted as the impecunious city government paid Doctor Smith in depreciated scrip. When he eventually demanded that the scrip be redeemed for cash, the city could not pay, so he went to court and obtained a judgment ordering the city to sell its property to pay him. The funded debt commissioners, John Geary among them, tried to pay Smith what was owed, but he refused to accept it; he wanted the court sale to proceed. Then, on the advice of their attorney, Solomon Heydenfelt, the funded debt commissioners discouraged the public from taking part in the sale, saying it was sure to be overturned by the courts. In the end, the sale was upheld and the city was done out of most of its property.[6]

While the Vigilance Committee marched through the streets in July 1851 and hanged a few predatory criminals, the sheriff was selling off the city's property for a pittance to the highest bidder. (The city hall lot and the Pacific and Broadway wharves were sold in this way. The brig *Euphemia* was sold to settle the claim of another creditor.) The sale did not begin to settle the judgment, and later sales were conducted. At one, on January 30, 1852, 2,000 acres of city-owned land were disposed of. The whole matter might have been avoided or at least moderated if the *ayuntamiento* government, Brannan in the fore, had restrained its selfish interests in 1849 and established a city hospital instead of building commercial wharves to its own benefit.

But what of predatory crime? The *Annals* was right. Crime seems to have occurred as frequently as the year before, but the city, which had been thrown into paroxysms of retributive justice just a few months before, supposedly over unchecked crime, did nothing. If anything, burglary was up. On January 3, two "old offenders" were arrested for breaking into the cabin of a boat in the harbor but were released a few days later when a witness failed to show up in court. A week or so later, the *Alta* expressed outrage when three men were arrested trying to break into the rear of a jewelry store. They also were discharged a few months later because there was no one to testify against them. Before the month was out, a series of hot prowl burglaries began that went on for two months.[7] There was one on January 24 and another the next day. There were two more on January 26, at which time the *Alta* began to voice some excitement about crime conditions.

In February, twenty-four burglaries were reported, the highest of any month in Gold Rush San Francisco. It was evident that some professional criminals were at work. Their method of operation was to enter a house or hotel where there were a number of people sleeping. They would collect the trousers of the sleeping men and take them to another room, where they would remove any valuables. Often, on departing, they would lock the sleeping residents in from the outside. There were burglaries on February 1, 3, and 4. There were others on February 6, 7, 12, 13, 15 (two), 16 (four), 17, 19, and 21. A man was arrested on February 22, but there was no evidence against him and he was released. The burglaries continued on February 23 (two) and 25. The next day, it appeared that the police had struck paydirt. A black man named John Hawkins was discovered hiding under the bed in a room in the Bella Union Hotel. In his pocket they found a key to the room and an $8,000 certificate of deposit. Hawkins was held, indicted, and later convicted of burglary, but still the crimes went on.

Not all the Australians had gone back home. On February 26, Richard Hall and George Spiers, the same men who had been accused of the murder of Brewer on June 1, 1851, were arrested in the commission of a burglary on Broadway near Stockton. They too were held and later convicted, but still the crimes continued unabated. More hot prowl burglaries were reported on February 27 and 28. On March 1, with a tip of its hat to the professionalism of the thieves, the *Picayune* remarked on the seeming crime wave, "The skill with which their burglaries are effected and the success which almost universally attends their effort, denotes quite satisfactorily that they are villains above the common herd—those of the polished broadcloth tribe." The burglaries continued. On March 2, a man arrived home to find his room barricaded from the inside. He raised a cry and the thief fled. On March 3, the *Alta* reported the burglary a few nights before of an office next to the police station, as well as the attempted burglary of a residence near Stockton and Clay streets in which the thief had been frightened off by a bulldog. On March 7, a residence on Pacific Street was burglarized; on March 11, another on Stockton at Vallejo was the victim of a hot prowl burglary. The same day, burglars tried unsuccessfully to break into Colonel Stevenson's residence on Stockton Street, where, it was reported, an armed party awaited them inside. On March 12, jewelry and a pistol were taken from the residence of a police officer on Pike Street, and the same day residences on Green Street and Dupont Street were also burglarized. On March 13, there was another break-in at Sacramento and Dupont.

At 4 A.M. on March 14, two police officers were on their rounds on Jackson between Powell and Mason when they heard a suspicious whistle. They followed the sound and came upon a black man with burglar tools and a revolver in his possession, along with jewelry taken from one officer's nearby house on Virginia Street. The officers started off to the station house with their prisoner, one of them holding him by the coat. The prisoner broke away and bolted. One officer fired four shots after him in the pitch darkness, but the prisoner escaped.[8] The *Alta*, commenting that he was probably part of a regular organized band of black thieves responsible for most of the recent "robberies," was confident that he would soon be brought to book. Indeed, the arrest made by the officers on the morning of March 14 seems to have ended the crime wave—after the suspect escaped into the darkness, burglary assumed a more usual rate.[9]

On March 18, someone stole $800 from Tong Woo and Company on Sacramento Street. On March 19, an attempted burglary was thwarted at Battery and Sacramento; on March 29, a woman reported the burglary of a neighbor's residence at Vallejo and Mason. In April, there were three more burglaries; in May, there were four. The crime wave was clearly over. As shown in the following tabulation, there were no burglaries reported in June and few in the remaining months of the year.

Comparison of Reported Incidents of Burglary in 1850, 1851, and 1852

	Jan	Feb	Mar	Apr	May	June	July	Aug	Sep	Oct	Nov	Dec
1850	0	0	0	3	0	0	6	6	12	7	9	9
1851	10	7	17	6	8	5	3	4	0	4	2	2
1852	6	23	14	3	4	0	1	4	2	1	8	3

The slight upward surge in November 1852 is no doubt attributable to the usual winter return of miners to the city, some of whom were broke, occasioning press reports that the city was again "infested with a horde of scoundrels determined on plunder."[10]

Looking back to the litany of crimes offered as the reason for the establishment of the Committee of Vigilance in 1851, the burglary statistics of 1852 do not seem a great deal different. They were not. On March 17, 1852, before the realization had time to sink in that the spate of burglaries had been brought to a halt, the General Committee of the Committee of Vigilance was called to a meeting in the old committee rooms on Battery Street to select new Executive Committee members, the terms of the incumbents having expired. They met because of the recent increase in crime, thought the press.[11] Bancroft concludes the same thing: "But as crime crawled forth again," he says of the early months of 1852, "the Committee found it necessary to hold a general meeting . . . [and] again there was a visible and sudden falling-off in the number of burglaries and murders committed."[12] The fact of the matter was, as noted, that the General Committee met to select replacements. If there was any real concern about the state of crime in the city, it was certainly not translated into any meaningful activity on the part of the committee.

Only a few months before, the entire mercantile establishment had mobilized itself and taken the unprecedented step of displacing the justice establishment, ostensibly because of unchecked crime; now, when burglary was measurably more frequent, the same leading citizens seem to have almost ignored the fact that it was even taking place. It appears that their appetite for amateur crime fighting had been sated. Also, by early 1852, the economy had again turned around. The committee had been established in 1851 in the traditionally slow months of a slow business year when there was little else to do. By 1852, however, business had picked up and the mundane concerns of commerce occupied the attention of the business community. Further to the point of how much crime there actually was in Gold Rush San Francisco, it seems that in 1852 a few Australian and black burglars were able, on their own, to create what passed for a crime wave. Overall, the reported robbery rate did decline for the year, but that was not evident in the first few months.

Comparison of Reported Incidents of Robbery in 1850, 1851, and 1852

	Jan	Feb	Mar	Apr	May	June	July	Aug	Sep	Oct	Nov	Dec
1850	1	0	1	0	0	0	1	0	3	4	3	7
1851	0	4	0	0	4	2	2	0	0	1	2	2
1852	2	0	1	0	2	1	1	0	1	0	0	0

Criminal homicide, despite Bancroft's allusion to a decrease after the meeting of the General Committee in 1852, remained at about the same rate as before, during, and after the heyday of the committee. Early in January, José Feliz, suspected of being the real killer of Captain Jarvis in 1851, was killed in a fight at the Sanchez rancho. On January 22, the body of a man, the victim of murder or suicide, was found at the foot of a cliff under Telegraph Hill. James Edgerton, a police officer, was arrested, tried, and eventually found guilty of manslaughter for killing a prisoner who had struck him at the booking counter of the station house. The body of a man with his throat cut was found in the bay on February 2. On February 23, a former police officer, an out-of-office Whig, stabbed a man to death in a dispute in a brothel on Dupont Street.

In April, Captain Ritchie died of injuries he received when he was mugged by unidentified assailants. The same month, a Spaniard named Joaquín was killed in a fight with some of his fellows. In July, a Chinese prostitute was examined by the recorder after the body of her infant child was found in a dump at the end of Stockton Street. On July 11, the Irish keeper of the tollhouse at the county line was killed in an apparent robbery attempt; a German vegetable seller was arrested but eventually released. Later that month, another man was found floating in the bay with his throat cut.

On September 2, Dolores Martinez was arrested for killing another woman living in a "dance house" on Kearny Street and was eventually convicted of manslaughter. On September 13, José Forni (or Forner) was arrested for the murder, during a robbery, of José Rodriguez.

On November 3, Abellardo Torres killed John Chapel in a "house" on Murderer's Alley. Torres was arrested but released when it was shown that he had acted in self-defense. An inquest the same day found that C. H. Gridley had died from poison, probably administered in a brothel belonging to Mary Washington. Also on November 3, one special police officer killed another, resulting in a charge of manslaughter. On December 24, a man was killed in a dispute over the right to inhabit a residence on Bush Street. Eventually, a woman named Quigley, an Australian, was found guilty of manslaughter.

Comparison of Reported Incidents of Criminal Homicide in 1850, 1851, and 1852

	Jan	Feb	Mar	Apr	May	June	July	Aug	Sep	Oct	Nov	Dec
1850	0	0	1	0	1	1	1	1	2	2	4	3
1851	2	0	2	1	2	2	1	1	0	1	2	1
1852	2	2	0	2	0	0	3	0	2	0	1	1

So homicide continued at about the same rate as before—yet the committee manifested no alarm in 1852. Mary Williams concludes that the quiescence of the committee in the winter of 1851–52 "may have arisen from the fact that most of the tragedies in the city and in the state at large were attributed to sudden passion rather than to such deliberate intention as had signalized the operations of James Stuart and his confederates."[13] But we have reviewed the "tragedies" up through 1852 (and those beyond summarized in the appendix), and "sudden passion" can be seen as the precipitating impulse in almost all of them. Stuart and his colleagues were deliberate enough burglars, just as were those who followed them in 1852.

But if the committee did not rouse itself about other types of predatory crime, no matter how frequent, it was not so sanguine about arson. The press continued to report occasional attempts to burn down the town; on the anniversary of the May fires of the two previous years, rumors of an impending great fire spread. The Executive Committee, in a card published in the *Herald*, called upon the general members to meet in their wards and to form night patrols because, "from information received by the Executive, they have every reason to believe that there yet exists within the limits of our city an organized band of thieves and incendiaries, who have within a few days past made several ineffectual attempts to fire the city, and . . . our strict observance of vigilance may prevent the evil by an early detection of fire, should it be the result of *accident* or design" (emphasis added). There was no fire on the anniversary, and we may assume that the persons who had predicted disaster attributed its absence to their own vigilance.

The *Alta* was able to report on May 3 that, though there was a great deal of talk about fire, "There is no danger of San Francisco ever being reduced to ashes again." The three elements that would prevent it were now in place: the fire companies were well manned, much of the new construction was brick, and there was finally an adequate water supply. As 1852 neared its end, though, fire again struck the state. Early in November, Sacramento virtually burned to the ground; a few days later, a square block in Marysville burned. Fire also hit San Francisco. Toward the end of October, there were several reports of attempted arson; at 8:30 P.M. on November 9, a fire broke out at Merchant and Kearny streets that was not extinguished until thirty-two buildings had burned. Unlike its larger predecessors, however, this fire did not spread beyond the block. It was stopped by the nonflammable city hall on Kearny Street on one side, by the California Exchange on the other, and by the brick buildings facing Montgomery on the east. Had the brick buildings been in place earlier, the city's history of fire would doubtless have been different. As usual, the various fires were attributed to arson, by a rear guard of Australian criminals in one account, taking revenge on the Committee of Vigilance. In San Francisco, one man was arrested by the Executive Committee but apparently turned loose in the end.

It is part of the legend of multiple unpunished murders in San Francisco that in all the period of carnage there was but one legal hanging, that of a "friendless Spaniard." It was indeed a Spaniard, José Forni, who earned the distinction of being the first legally executed man in San Francisco, for the murder during a robbery of a Mexican named José Rodriguez, but the implication in the legend that he hanged because he was Hispanic simply is not true. The crime occurred, as mentioned above, on September 13, 1852, in Pleasant Valley near Second and Howard streets. In the words of Edward Townsend, who was present:

A savage murder was committed within thirty yards of our house in broad daylight today. . . . At about half past three in the afternoon, I was awakened from a nap by the screams of a woman and immediately jumped up and looked out the window. I saw a man lying on his back, and another running up the hill pursued by a third with a large stick in his hand. The murderer, for so he proved, was brought to bay at the top of the hill. . . . He was a Spaniard named José Forni. As soon as I saw the murderer stopped, I ran out to the victim, he was just breathing his last, and expired in two minutes. A purse of gold containing about $300 was found on Forni, who said that the other had tried to rob him and had stabbed him in the leg, when he wrenched the knife from him and killed him in self defense. I consented to sit on the Coroner's Jury. The evidence of four persons who witnessed the deed, showed that Forni was first seen pursuing the other down the hill, that both fell to the ground near the foot of the hill, the other about ten feet in advance, that Forni recovered himself first and bounding upon his victim stabbed him repeatedly as he was in the act of rising and again as he fell. We found eleven horrible wounds in his back, breast and head.[14]

On September 17, Forni was sent to district court; on September 22, he was indicted by the grand jury. On October 15, a jury found him guilty; on October 19, he was sentenced to hang. At first, it was proposed that he be hanged in front of the county jail on Broadway Street, but then it was decided that he should be hanged on the top of Russian Hill as an example to all. Finally, squeamish souls prevailed and the gallows was moved 100 yards down the other side of the hill. On December 10, still protesting that he had acted in self-defense, Forni was hanged in front of a crowd of up to 10,000 spectators. "It was a proud day for the law," says Bancroft. "True it was only a Spaniard who was hanged, José Forin [sic] for the murder of a Spaniard, but then it was the first legal execution San Francisco had ever seen, and the young metropolis was very proud of it."

> About half the town turned out; so new a thing it was for the law to punish a murderer. The poor prisoner thought it unfair to begin with him; the law had liberated so many hundreds of worse men . . . though he protested his innocence to the last, the law was brave and hanged him right manfully. True, the poor fellow was a stranger, without money, friendless, and unable to speak the English language. I did not say that for these he was hanged; true, hundreds more deserving of his fate stood gaping by, thinking how awful it was, how righteous the law that punished him who sinned—and was caught at it. It was a happy sight, I say, this hanging of the moneyless, friendless Spanish stranger. . . . The streets were lined with carriages; husbands brought thither their wives, and mothers their children, to witness the rare entertainment. . . . Finally, with arms pinioned, legs bound, and black cap drawn over the face, a blow from a hatchet cut the rope that held in place the platform, and the friendless unfortunate dropped into eternity.[15]

Bancroft is one of those who seems to have been unable to accept that the regular authorities can do anything right. He originated the idea of the "friendless Spaniard," which became part of the legend. More recently, this interpretation turns up as "José Forner was apprehended and executed for a crime that probably would have gone unnoticed had he come from Pike County rather than Valencia in old Spain."[16]

There is a current school of revisionist history that casts Hispanics as the hapless victims of the American interlopers. There is much for Anglos to apologize for in their treatment of the native peoples they found on their way west, but hanging Forni is not one of them. Forni was not hanged because he was a Spaniard, but because his was the only solid provable murder case up to that time. Murder, as has already been defined, is the unlawful killing of a human being with malice aforethought. Everything else is manslaughter or noncriminal homicide. A review of the killings listed in the appendix shows that most of them before that of Rodriguez by Forni—many of Hispanics by other Hispanics—must be classified as manslaughters. The *Alta* on October 15, 1852, remarked that there had been only two previous convictions for murder before that of Forni. Hall had been convicted of the Brewer murder, the paper said, but the evidence tended to prove him innocent of that crime. In the fall of 1849, Daniels had been convicted of murdering a Frenchman, but the case had been over-turned by the supreme court for irregularities. Both were killings for the purpose of robbery. If we examine the remaining homicides sum-marized in the appendix, it soon becomes clear that the majority of them cannot be classified as murders. Most occurred during some kind of spontaneous fight—hence, by definition, they must be categorized as manslaughters.

Forni's crime, homicide during the commission of a robbery, clearly came within the statutory definition of murder. Furthermore, unique among the cases we have reviewed, there were disinterested witnesses who saw the killing and were willing to testify. In his statement, Forni said that he had gone to the top of the hill to relieve himself when he was attacked with his own knife by the deceased, who dropped the knife as he ran away. It was then that Forni picked it up, he said, and chased the other man. Good try—the problem is that there was physical evidence showing that the victim had received his first cuts at the top of the hill. To continue with Townsend's contemporary account: "The hat of the murdered man was found on the top of the hill with two cuts and marks of blood showing he had received the wounds on his head before he was seen running down the hill." [17]

No, Forni was not hanged for being a Mexican. He was hanged because he was the first defendant in San Francisco against whom there was a provable case with independent witnesses that came within the statute defining murder. Let us hope that the remainder of the legend of rampant unpunished murder in Gold Rush San Francisco is finally put to rest.

CHAPTER 26

Some Observations

IN THE END, THE VIGILANTES had it their way. For many years, they were remembered as a group of public-spirited citizens who came together in the face of intolerable conditions of predatory crime and a paralyzed justice system. In recent years, the altruism of the 1851 committee—and particularly the 1856 reincarnation—has increasingly been called into question. But it is only now that we have any clear idea about how much crime there actually was in Gold Rush San Francisco. On balance, it would seem that crime was not prevalent enough to justify the extraordinary measures taken. There was certainly not as much as we have been led to believe.

A number of interacting variables dictate the amount of predatory crime and criminal homicide at any given time and place. There are economic factors, such as poverty, particularly in the midst of plenty; cultural traditions like the comparative value placed on property and life in a society; and social factors such as the relative social homogeneity or diversity of a community. There is also the degree to which the society is willing or able to use police force to bring about the type of community it desires.

In some societies, such as Japan and Great Britain, crime and violence are traditionally low compared to the United States. (It was not always so, and things are changing.) There are places in emerging Third World countries where crime is much on the rise. For example, middle-class residents in parts of postcolonial Africa sequester themselves in concrete blockhouses at night to avoid being murdered in their homes by gangs of panga-wielding youths who invade suburban dwellings and escape before the police arrive. It was recently reported in the press that predatory crime and criminal homicide are increasing exponentially in Mexico City, which is fast becoming the world's most populous city.[1] And, as has been mentioned, rising crime in Brazil has occasioned the reinstitution of death squads that select and summarily execute troublesome criminals who seem to be beyond the reach of the law.[2] So it is a difficult proposition to try to draw meaningful comparisons between crime rates in different places at different times and the legitimacy of measures used to bring it under control.

In 1987, Detroit, which William Rasberry compares to the savage society in William Golding's *Lord of the Flies*, had four times the rate of criminal homicide of San Francisco. Oakland, just across the bay from the Gold Rush city, had twice as much.[3] As has been discussed at some length, San Francisco in the 1850s was certainly a different kind of place than it is today. But these variations aside, the murder rate in the Gold Rush boomtown was not a great deal different from that of many American cities today.[4] Certainly, the murder rate did not begin to approach the figures set out in the legend.

But if all the murders did not occur, where did the stories come from? The earliest account of the version of 100 murders in the few months preceding the formation of the Vigilance Committee appears in the *Annals of San Francisco*, written in 1854 by men who were present at the time the events in the legend supposedly took place.[5] The comment appears in a hyperbolic section devoted to the establishment of the Vigilance Committee in San Francisco in 1851. The thrust is to defend the actions of the committee, so perhaps the authors failed to scrutinize reality too closely. The section is chiefly devoted to events occurring in San Francisco, but it also includes comments about conditions in California generally. Addressing the disruption caused by the great Gold Rush migration, the authors write, "Over all California it was the same." In discussing the fires that plagued the city, they comment that Stockton and Nevada City also burned. In light of the facts, we can in charity only conclude that in their assertion about 100 murders they were referring loosely to conditions in the entire state, though the number seems high even for that larger area.[6]

The version that there were 1,200 unpunished murders between 1850 and 1853—from which the other accounts citing 1,000 or more criminal homicides evidently originate—first appeared in the *California Chronicle* in December 1853, in a statement attributed to San Francisco district attorney Henry H. Byrne.[7] Writing in 1858, Democratic wheelhorse Ned McGowan, associate justice of the court of sessions during the period of the first committee and arch foe of the second Committee of Vigilance in 1856, said, "The ridiculous story . . . originated in this way about three years ago. H. H. Byrne, esq., the District Attorney for San Francisco, in making a speech in a case of capital punishment, told the jury there had been 200 murders in that city in the past five years, with but few convictions and less executions. The next day it found its way into the newspapers with a mistake of 1000, making it 1200, instead of 200. This piece of information was ridiculed at the time."[8]

Mary Williams was willing to accept the high figures. Writing in the main text of her *History*, she remarks, after mentioning various versions of the legend, "The acceptance and repetition by contemporary writers of the current summaries of crime is *conclusive* evidence that the estimates were not at variance with the facts as to the existing conditions" (emphasis added).[9] In a footnote a page earlier, however, she is less certain. Citing McGowan's above-quoted statement, she says, "The *Phoenix* [McGowan's newspaper] was too scurrilous to deserve credence on any subject," but, she adds, "this paragraph may or may not contain a hint of truth."[10]

Not only did she accept the fact that crime had indeed occurred in the amounts suggested by the legend, but she also subscribed to the notion that the Vigilance Committee had a beneficial effect on the incidence of predatory crime. Summing up her thoughts on crime, she says:

> In the dearth of official summaries [of predatory crime] the following paragraph published in the *Herald*, April 14, 1852, becomes a matter of interest: "The idea is very generally entertained that the number of sudden deaths by accidents or violence is very great in this city.

This, however, is incorrect, as the records show that but twenty-eight inquests have been held during the past eight months. For a city so large this is quite a small number." [11]

From this she concludes that the committee had reduced the rate of violent death from some previous astronomical high:

This brief report of the coroner covered the period from August, 1851, to March, 1852, during which the influence exerted by the Committee of Vigilance was a most stern reality. It showed an average of less than four deaths a month from accident and violence combined. If any reliance whatever can be placed on the figures quoted from other sources [she was too good a historian to swallow the legend whole], it also indicated that the immediate result of the rule of the Vigilantes was a diminution of crime that deserves our respectful attention. [12]

We have painstakingly worked our way through the existing press reports and tabulations of crime and criminal homicide in Gold Rush San Francisco, and we know that the rate of violent death cited by the *Herald* in 1852 applies not just to the period following the rule of the committee but indeed is representative of the entire Gold Rush period —before, during, and after some citizens of San Francisco decided to take the law into their own hands. The fact of the matter was, as already noted, that "the quiet citizen the ruffian seldom molested, except in cases of robbery. At no time in the history of the country need any well-behaved man, minding his own business and avoiding drinking saloons, have greatly feared for his life." [13]

Others have claimed it; this book has demonstrated it. Predatory crime, specifically criminal homicide, at least according to present-day standards, was not out of proportion—and, we might add, the actions of the Vigilance Committee did little to bring an end to what crime there was.

What of fire? Revenge, as a motive for arson fires, seems to have played a larger part than at present in the criminal lexicon of nineteenth-century America. Arson for profit, at a time and place where fire insurance was in its infancy, seems to have tended more toward reducing undesirable stocks of goods held on consignment. Roger Lotchin suggests that, in the absence of evidence to the contrary, we must accept contemporary accounts of arson as having their basis in fact. [14] Perhaps so; we have no real evidence that the press was cooking up stories of arson.

But in truth, as we have seen, most of the fires—at least the major ones that devastated the town—were probably not set by any criminal agency but started instead by accident. Once they began, in the absence of an adequate fire service, water supply, or building restrictions, they spread wildly through the tinderlike structures of the town. If we are looking for the perpetrators of fires that might have been set, we must not only look among the Sydney criminals who have traditionally been held responsible, but also consider those who stood to gain the most.

What of the criminal justice system? The police, like urban police elsewhere in nineteenth-century America, were feeling their way in a new and alien institutional environment. Coming out of a tradition where policing was a self-help, pay-as-you-go proposition, confronted by an establishment unwilling to accept the fact that one must pay for city services, and paid, when at all, in depreciated scrip, some members of the police department no doubt resorted to various forms of corruption to pad their salary. But, on the whole, they did their job well under extremely adverse conditions. The existing arrest figures attest to the fact that, as crime went up, so did police activity. It cannot be laid at the feet of the police that the jail and court system were unable to handle the work they brought in.

The courts were also puzzled. Trying, as they were, to employ the judicial practices of earlier, simpler times, they were soon confronted with a serious backlog, and cases began to slip through the cracks. As we have seen, reforms were enacted that brought case loads up to date; but before the changes had time to take effect, the vigilantes were at work. Leaving aside instances of individual corruption, which merely reflected the state of municipal ethics at the time, the courts were probably as efficient as one could have expected them to be.

When the cases backed up in court, the jails, neglected from the first, overflowed with prisoners awaiting trial. Even the Whig police, presumably in sympathy with the ends of the committee, were unable to prevent escapes until the new county jail was placed in service. Credit for completing the construction has gone to the Vigilance Committee; but, as with the judicial reforms that speeded up the court procedures, reform was already under way by the time the committee took it upon itself to intervene. The new secure jail, thanks to funds that Sheriff Hays had been raising by subscription with council approval since May, was ready to receive its first prisoners just as the committee was establishing itself. What the committee actually did was to raise the funds that paid for putting the finishing touches on a jail already substantially completed.

When the situation is viewed dispassionately and from the remove of more than a hundred years, it can be discerned that the necessary reforms were well under way at the time the committee erupted into existence—had its members waited a few short months, the changes would have taken hold, making the committee unnecessary. There is a strong impulse to sympathize with the committee, whose members, after all, had no better insight than the regular authorities into the implications of the process of urbanization they were suffering through. They asked, understandably enough: how does a society deal with the likes of James Stuart or Charles Duane, who seem to have been impervious to the regular workings of the law? Cast in current terms, the question is: what can we do about the mindless urban violence in New York subways and vicious murderers who congest the courts with interminable appeals? From behind the ornamental grillwork securing our residences, we can argue that there really was not as much crime as is generally believed. We can even show that some of those who in the end took matters into their own hands not only tolerated but actually created the conditions that made their actions inevitable. And we can demonstrate that the institutions of justice were already coming to grips with the problems. But the men of 1851 did not have our benefit of hindsight and would not be impressed with our arguments. Coming as they did out of a national tradition of self-reliance, hardened by the frontier experience, they took matters into their own hands and made no apologies about it.

What happened in early American San Francisco is that trade, in effect, preceded the flag; even before the success of the conquest, members of the commercial establishment put their stamp on the town. From the first, they opposed governmental controls of any type, and damn the public weal. Cost-conscious businessmen, they looked to the cheapest way to run public affairs. With the rush that followed the discovery of gold, the problems multiplied. In the fierce competition for profits in boomtown San Francisco, public affairs were neglected and public disorders grew until it was thought necessary to convene the first of a number of public tribunals to deal with the criminal Hounds. But even after a municipal government was formed, and while it was trying to catch its breath, the city—no different in this sense than urban America generally—was visited with a puzzling rise in crime, though nothing like the level propounded in its lore.

While regular institutions of justice felt their way to a solution to the problem of predatory crime, the members of the business elite, who had alternately stood aloof or profited from the confused state of affairs, took matters in hand. In their own cost-effective but extralegal way, they set forth on a campaign to cleanse the town of criminal predators. Some objected to the methods they used or took the position that there was no need for the Committee of Vigilance in the first place. The general judgment of history, with a few exceptions, has been that the first committee was needed and that it fulfilled the purpose for which it was intended.

So what if it summarily hanged a few criminals who needed hanging? (Though Slater, wrongly accused of the murder of Jarvis and almost hanged by the men of the Mission, might interject a caution here.) Nineteenth-century criminals of the type who ran afoul of the first Committee of Vigilance expected to end their days at the end of a rope—and by accounts that survive, they do not seem to have minded much that the rope was in the hands of private citizens rather than public officials.

But there is a legacy to be regretted. Curiously enough, the Vigilance Committee of 1851, by the very restraint it apparently showed as compared to classic lynch mobs, contributed to the legitimization of an attitude that afflicts American society to this day. Several years after the committee of 1851 was effectively adjourned, the "leading citizens" of San Francisco saw fit to reactivate it. In 1856, again charging that crime was rampant and that politicians were doing nothing about it, members of the former committee—Sam Brannan, of course, among them—organized the greatest of all the committees of vigilance in San Francisco or anywhere.

They hanged four men that time and banished a number more before they adjourned at the end of the summer. Ample recent scholarship has shown that the roots of the second Committee of Vigilance lay in the desire of merchant leaders—not to put an end to predatory crime, for there was little to speak of—to effect what they saw as needed political and fiscal reform.[15] Citing the precedents of 1851 on rampant crime and disorder, they wrested the city government from duly elected officials and set about imposing their own type of law and order. For more than a decade, the People's party, the political arm of the Committee of Vigilance, dominated political life in San Francisco. It was during this period that the legend of widespread murder took root. The men who seized the reins of government from the lawful authorities in the 1850s and who governed for a decade after were not any group of drink-maddened miners in an isolated camp hanging a thief in the absence of any established legal authority. They were the leading citizens of a modern city that had a fully articulated, functioning criminal justice system. It was in their interest that San Francisco be remembered as a crime-ridden frontier boomtown.

Throughout the rest of the nineteenth century and even into the twentieth, other bands of vigilantes, neo-vigilantism in Richard Maxwell Brown's definition, which "found its chief victims among Catholics, Jews, immigrants, Negroes, laboring men and labor leaders, political radicals, and proponents of civil liberties,"[16] pointed to San Francisco as an example to be emulated. The men of San Francisco had demonstrated, it was thought, through admirable self-restraint, that citizens could take the law into their own hands without degenerating into a lynch mob. That impulse is still very much alive today.

There is an undoubted popular appeal to the exercise of summary justice, as is evident in the outpouring of public approval of the acts of such men as the "subway vigilante," who was recently acquitted by a multiracial jury of all but a technical charge of illegally carrying a gun. Similarly, Jack Spiegelman, who carried a pistol in a hollowed-out book into a San Francisco courtroom to shoot his daughter's killer, was sentenced by the court to a term of probation. Perhaps, like Thomas Jefferson's occasional revolutionary blood on the tree of liberty, a smattering of self-help justice does stimulate the regular system. Court matters did move somewhat faster in the summer of 1851, and it does seem that the case of the killer of Spiegelman's daughter started moving more quickly through the system after the aggrieved father shot him.

But the question is whether we want to pay the full cost that tolerating criminal justice self-help implies. The impulse to private vengeance runs deep; once it is set loose, the critical faculty is suspended and injustices are done. In Saxon England, when the "hue and cry" was raised, the object was to "catch and kill." No one asked if the person who raised the cry might have personal reasons for doing so. ("In most instances," says Charles Rembar, "probably there was guilt, but there must have been a few mistakes, and likely now and then a frameup. It would take no great imagination for the miscreant to start a hue and cry against an innocent bystander.")[17] The Mafia, for whatever reason it was formed, turned into a criminal gang oppressing the people it purported to protect. The Regulators of South Carolina did rid their county of crime, but in their victory they were so brutal and vindictive that a counterorganization calling itself the "Moderators" was called into existence; according to Richard Maxwell Brown, "it can be argued that they [the Regulators] introduced the strain of violence and extremism that was to be the curse of that Up Country. . . ."[18]

The same thing is happening today in Brazil. Law-abiding residents there have come to accept extralegal death squads as a natural component of the justice system. They do not see a lot of difference between the death squads and the regular police. But, warns the local police commander, "Those groups are uncontrollable."[19] He might as well have been speaking of the Hounds who afflicted Gold Rush San Francisco. Family feuds in which entire families were virtually wiped out in the Kentucky hills went on for generations, long after the reasons for their origins were forgotten.

There is something base and dehumanizing in the phenomenon of self-help justice that appeals to the darker side of the human psyche. Death squad killings in the suburbs of Rio de Janeiro have become so common that their victims' remains are sometimes left lying "like dead animals," unnoticed and unremarked in the city streets.[20] Doctor Henry Gray, who was present at the hanging of Whittaker and McKenzie, recollected in his *Judges and Criminals* that "the jeers and imprecations which were heard on every side, the loud laugh and the obscene jokes which were cracked in the crowd below; with the evident glee and humor with which the members of the Committee carried out their bloody purpose, will long remain vivid in the minds of those who witnessed this occurrence of blood, this violation to law, this violent outburst of popular passion."[21] (Actually, the behavior of the crowd at the vigilante hangings was little different from that reported of crowds at legal executions of the time.) The hue and cry, Rembar reminds us, was more than an instrument of government: "it was also a sport, and there was probably never a more popular one. Here was homicide without risk—either from its victim, he being so outnumbered, or from the law, which did not scold, but instead approved, indeed demanded, so that conscience could not spoil the fun."[22] It was a response to a form of the same impulse that for decades resulted in public hangings of blacks, sometimes on little or no evidence, which remain a blot on the American record. We like to think that we have advanced beyond our predecessors in our social thinking; perhaps we have, but to the extent that we condone the behavior of the vigilantes of 1851 —or applaud that of their linear successors—we are regressing to the attitudes of a time in which most of us probably really would not want to live—especially the Berdues and Slaters of the world.

Appendix

Homicides Reported in the Alta California from January 1, 1850, through December 15, 1853

This appendix contains summary accounts of every homicide reported in the establishment press as having occurred in San Francisco during the period in which, according to the most common version of the legend of widespread murder, there were supposed to have been 1,200 criminal homicides. In law, homicide is the killing of another human being. It can be noncriminal (accidental or justified) or criminal (manslaughter or murder). Murder is the unlawful killing of a human being with "malice aforethought." Manslaughter, simply stated, is an unlawful killing without previous malicious intent. In the following listing, these distinctions are assigned to each case, so that a determination can be made as to the legitimacy of the charge that the justice system in Gold Rush San Francisco was incapable of punishing offenders appropriately.

1850

On March 3, two Frenchmen leaving a brothel on Pacific Street between Dupont (Grant) and Stockton were accosted by three men identified as Chileans. After an exchange of angry words, one of the

Frenchmen, Plantier, was stabbed mortally by one of the Chileans. The primary assailant, identified as Braelo, escaped, but his two companions were arrested; at a trial ending on April 4, one of them, Francisco Ramirez, was convicted of manslaughter for having aided and abetted Braelo. On April 5, he requested a new trial. [Manslaughter]

The proprietor of the Eagle Saloon became engaged in a dispute with a customer on April 23. Robert Harris, a seventeen-year-old employee of the saloon, was killed accidentally when the pistol he was handing his employer discharged. [Noncriminal]

The *Alta* reported on May 15 that two friends were roughhousing in a brothel at Kearny and Jackson streets. One of them, Shelton Dennis, was killed when he was thrown to the floor. A coroner's jury ruled that the death was accidental. [Noncriminal]

On May 19, Daniel Matthews was arrested by Officer Casserly on Pacific Street for the stabbing death of a French sailor, Joseph Blancoe, resulting from a quarrel. When the case was called in district court in late July, Matthews, who had been freed on $4,000 bail, did not appear. [Manslaughter]

In early June, Domingo Basquez (*sic*), identified as a fourteen-year-old Chilean, stabbed a man named Labi (or Labrie) who had slapped his face during a quarrel over a cigar. Basquez was tried, convicted, and sentenced to three months in jail for the cutting before Labi died of his wounds. In August, Basquez was indicted for murder and claimed that the previous conviction for assault was a bar to further prosecution. [Manslaughter]

On July 6, Louis Bernal, a native of Mazatlán who spoke no English, shot Carmelita Bertrand fatally in the head in a drinking and gambling house, frequented mainly by blacks and Mexicans and situated on Stockton Street at the alley near Broadway. At his examination before the recorder and at the trial that followed in August, there was conflicting testimony as to whether Bernal had discharged the pistol intentionally or whether it had gone off by accident. The jury found him guilty with a recommendation for mercy. His attorney moved for a new trial, and the motion was granted on the ground that the jury had failed to fix a sentence, as was then required by law. Bernal was acquitted by the jury at his second trial; the *Alta* commented magnanimously that in a case in which a human life is at stake, none of the forms prescribed as proper by the people should be dispensed with, even if the guilty should go free. [Noncriminal]

On August 2, two men identified as Indians, José Miguel and Pedro

Loqui (or Nolasco), beat a fellow Indian named Aurichi to death with clubs in a drunken row at the Mission. Aurichi died a few hours later, and the killers were arraigned on a charge of manslaughter. In early September, they were found guilty and sentenced to serve six months for their offense. [Manslaughter]

An Indian named Damasques was found September 9, lying in a street in the Mission with his arm almost severed. He was taken to a hospital, where he died before he could name his assailant, but Philip Santiago and Rito Carlan, who had been seen previously in his company, were arrested. [Murder, possible]

On Friday, September 20, an unnamed Mexican who had been stabbed in an affray on September 19 died at the marine hospital. [Manslaughter]

Captain Briet of the French brig *Gruges*, anchored in the harbor, awoke at 1:00 A.M. on Monday, September 23, to see some luggage going over the side of his ship. He armed himself with a pistol and fired at the men retreating in a small boat, who refused to heed his order to stop. He struck and mortally wounded Captain Pierre Delion, who had been in the act of luring sailors from Briet's ship. After a determination by the recorder that his act had been justified, Briet was released. [Noncriminal]

On October 16, a Chilean woman, familiarly called Big Mouth Mary, quarreled with a Sydney woman named Louise Taylor about their respective lovers, in the same saloon in which Carmelita Bertrand had been killed in July. Big Mouth Mary stabbed Taylor fatally in the groin and fled. The victim's lover ended up in jail when he went to the house and assaulted Mary's boyfriend. [Manslaughter]

On October 20, the *Alta* reported that an unnamed black man had been found dead of multiple stab wounds at the Mission and that an arrest warrant had been issued for an Indian. The killer was arrested and brought to justice almost two years later, when he killed another man in a dispute at Martinez in June 1852. [Murder, possible]

On November 4, Jack Smith was shot by (Judge) J. H. Jones in what the *Alta* the next day called a murderous affray at the Verandah Saloon. It seems that Smith, who died a month later of his wounds, started the trouble (like Landers in 1847) by claiming that he could whip any man in the house. Testimony at the recorder's examination developed the fact that he had brought the trouble on himself. The recorder ruled on December 14 that the killing was justified. [Noncriminal]

On Saturday night, November 24, (Doctor) Fish was accused by a

man named Cook of stealing money in a faro game at the El Dorado
Saloon. The ensuing fight ended when Fish said that he had had
enough. Testimony was later given that, as he rose from the floor, Fish
drew his pistol, which discharged when a bystander tried to pin his
arms behind his back. As was common with saloon shootings, most bystanders did not remember having seen anything. Fish was taken to his
home, where he died twelve hours later, claiming that the man who
fought with him had fired the fatal shot. A postmortem examination
bore him out by showing that he had been shot in the hip, from back
to front, and that the ball that killed him was rifled and too large to fit
his smooth-bore Allen revolver. Cook was unavailable to give his side
of the story, having sailed on the steamer to Oregon the night of the
shooting. [Manslaughter]

On November 26, Michael McMahan, a twenty-one-year-old recent
arrival from Sydney, Australia, became involved in an oral dispute with
a man named Arthur O'Connor at a gambling table in the Rendezvous
Saloon at Kearny and Washington streets. As usual, no one saw much
except that there was an exchange of harsh words; O'Connor stabbed
McMahan in the left breast, mortally wounding him, and escaped.
The *Alta* was confident that he would soon be caught since he was
well known to the police and editorialized that such incidents were
becoming so common that an ordinance should be passed requiring
each gambling house to maintain one or more policemen at its own
expense—not so much to stop the assaults but to arrest the offenders.
[Manslaughter]

Also on November 26, Thomas James, employed as a watchman by
the store of Fox and O'Connor on Pacific Street, shot Charles Beckett,
a Sydney man he caught burglarizing the store. Beckett, who ran a
cabaret on Stockton near Pacific, was stealing a cask of ale when he
was shot. The shot severed an artery, and he died on November 28.
[Noncriminal]

A coroner's inquest on November 27 determined that John Toby had
come to his death by a blow from a sharp instrument in the hands of
John Bolton a few days before on the bark *Salvador*. [Murder, possible]

On December 1, Charles Boyle, ten years old, was brought before the recorder for shooting a seven-year-old named T. J. Lewis to
death on the Mission Road the previous Sunday. Boyle was discharged
according to the statute barring prosecution on the grounds that "an
infant under the age of 14 years shall not be found guilty of any crime."
[Manslaughter]

The December 27 edition of the *Alta* reported on the inquest of J. McMillan, who had been found dead in the bay at the foot of Washington Street. Because of the nature of the wounds to his head and face, the jury decided he had come to his death by violence "at the hands of another." [Murder, possible]

James Foy, sixty years old, left his wife and son at home on the evening of December 29 to go drinking at the Limerick Lass on Pine Street. Later that night, he was known to have been playing cards with James Davis and another young man at the Broadway House. The three left together; at 4:00 A.M. on December 30, Foy's murdered body was found on California Street. Davis was brought before the recorder but discharged because there was not enough evidence to sustain a criminal charge. [Murder, possible]

1851

On January 15, the *Alta* reported the accidental shooting death of a seaman on a British ship in the harbor by a mate. [Noncriminal]

An unnamed Frenchman was killed in a dancing and drinking saloon on Pacific Street between Dupont and Kearny on January 21. Shortly thereafter, Officer Coffin arrested Hosea (*sic*) Fernandez as the supposed murderer. [Murder, possible]

Charles Bartley was harassing Charles Barnett in a drinking saloon on January 28, according to one witness. Another testified that what started as playful roughhousing turned serious and ended in a duel with pistols at five paces. Barnett shot and killed Bartley. After hearing testimony, the recorder dismissed the charge of murder against Barnett and placed him on bail on a charge of manslaughter. [Manslaughter]

In its March 16 edition, the *Alta* reported that days, even weeks, could go by without recording a sudden or violent death. Of the three deaths reported in that edition, one might have been a criminal homicide. The headless body of a man identified as a Mexican or Kanaka was found floating near Central Wharf. [Murder, possible]

On Saturday, March 22, a man named Warnecher picked up a revolver from the counter in the store of a friend named Cramer. The weapon discharged accidentally, killing Cramer. [Noncriminal]

On March 26, (Captain) Elijah M. Jarvis was stabbed to death on his doorstep in the Mission in the presence of his wife and infant child. A young man named William Slater was arrested for the crime. The previous Sunday, Jarvis had silenced Slater with a piece of wood when the young man had drunkenly challenged the patrons of the Mansion

House barroom to a fight. Slater had supposedly vowed vengeance. At Slater's examination before the recorder, testimony was given both that he was seen near the Mission and that he was home in bed at the time of the killing. A group of men visited Marshal Fallon on March 28 and asked that the prisoner be taken back to the Mission for a "trial." On March 31, while the marshal was escorting Slater under a heavy police guard from the courtroom along Kearny Street to the police station, a group of horsemen from the Mission tried unsuccessfully to ride down the police guard and seize the prisoner. At the conclusion of testimony in the preliminary hearing, when Slater's defense attorney made a motion that the prisoner be discharged, the examining justice agreed that there was no case against him, but said that if he were discharged he would not last twenty-four hours. The defense attorney withdrew his motion. Slater was eventually released; the *Alta* commented that there had been no basis for a trial against him. It was a good thing for Slater that the "people" did not get their hands on him. In one court hearing, Slater's defense attorney as much as charged that the young widow Jarvis had a hand in her own husband's death. Almost a year later, in January 1852, it was bruited about that another murder victim, José Feliz, a known outlaw, had somehow been involved in the murder of Jarvis. [Murder, possible]

On April 12, the bound body of a man named Callaghan was found floating at the foot of Sacramento Street. James Burns was arrested and examined but released. [Murder, possible]

In the midst of the madness of the great fire of May 4, William Lawley, a translator and interpreter, shot and killed Carmelita Castillo on Jackson Street near Kearny, before turning the pistol on himself. Lawley died a week later in the city hospital of the self-inflicted wound without giving any explanation for his actions. It was later revealed that the two had previously lived together. [Murder, possible]

An account of an inquest reported in the May 21 edition of the *Alta* described a man found floating off Rincon Point with a stake tied around his neck, whose skull and jaw had been broken, presumably with a slung shot. He was believed to be a recently escaped prisoner from the jail named Foster, but his face was beaten past the point of recognition. The jury's verdict was that he had been beaten to death. [Murder, possible]

Frank Brewer, a thirty-year-old Native American who had come to California from the eastern states, made it big at the mines and headed to San Francisco to celebrate. He fell in with some newfound friends with whom he went drinking; late Sunday night, June 1, his dead body was found in the street at Pacific and Montgomery. The coroner's jury first decided that the victim had died of unknown causes. After the corpse was disinterred and a postmortem examination was conducted, it was determined that he had died by ingesting a mixture of morphine and arsenic. Three Sydney men, William Hall, George Spiers, and Joseph Turner, were arrested for the crime. Turner was released and Hall was convicted of the murder after a protracted trial that ended in July. Hall's defense attorney filed an appeal; after Spiers was acquitted on the same conflicting testimony that had convicted Hall, the district attorney declined to retry Hall. A year later, commenting on another murder case, the *Alta* mentioned that disclosures had been made that tended to prove Hall innocent. [Murder]

The coroner's jury that considered the death of John Jenkins in June concluded that he had come to his death "at the hands of and in the pursuance of a preconcerted action on the part of an association of citizens, styling themselves a Committee of Vigilance" (see chapter 18). [Murder]

Accounts of the June 22 fire frequently refer to looters shot by the police while the fire raged. The June 26 edition of the *Alta* wondered at the whereabouts of the bodies of the men, "said to have been shot by the police." The paper believed that at least the one shot on Bush Street, outside the limits of the fire, should have turned up. The shootings probably did not occur; but, as with other matters, rumor has turned into legend that in the retelling has turned into a form of historic fact. [Two doubtful noncriminal]

The *Alta* in its June 24 edition reported that, during the fire, the owner of a bale of goods ordered a Mexican who was carrying it away from Washington Street to put it down. When the man refused to do so, the crowd knocked him to the ground and stomped him to death. The same edition reported on the inquest on John Baptiste Durand, off the French ship *Monte Lambert*. It seems that Durand went to Pacific Street during the fire to help a friend remove some endangered goods. When he stooped over to pick up a coal to light his pipe, he was seized by the crowd as an arsonist and stomped. He died of his injuries a few hours later in the county jail. The verdict of the coroner's jury was that he "died from an inflammation of the brain caused by injuries received during the fire." [Two manslaughter]

During the same fire on June 22, a gambler named Lewis Pollack had a disagreement with Samuel Gallagher, whom he called a coward.

That night, while Pollack was bedded down with Gallagher's woman, Jane Hurley, in a brothel on Merchant Street, Gallagher entered and confronted him. Gallagher was ejected from the room; but when the partially clothed Pollack followed him into the hallway, Gallagher shot his tormentor fatally in the head. The Vigilance Committee arrested Gallagher but turned him over to the regular authorities for trial. His first trial ended in a hung jury; at another trial ending in November, Gallagher was found guilty of manslaughter and sentenced to a term in prison. As one of his final acts in office, Governor McDougal pardoned the killer. [Manslaughter]

On July 11, the Committee of Vigilance hanged James Stuart from a derrick on Market Street Wharf (see chapter 20). [Murder]

On Saturday, July 12, Francisco Guerrero fell from his horse and died on the plank road to the Mission. The coroner's inquest developed the information that Guerrero's injuries were too severe to have been caused by a fall from a horse, that he had been seen in a scuffle with another horseman just before his horse bolted, and that there was blood on the plank road before the location where he had fallen off. The verdict of the jury was that Guerrero had died from blows on the head received from the other man on horseback. François LeBras was arrested as he tried to sell the horse he was riding, which belonged to Guerrero. LeBras was held by the Vigilance Committee for several days and then turned over to the regular authorities for trial, at which he was acquitted (see chapter 20). [Noncriminal]

At 8 P.M. on Saturday, August 9, Thomas Wheeler, a black man, left his job in a public house named the Nightingale at the end of the plank road to the Mission and was not seen again; on August 18, his body was found with a severely crushed skull about 100 yards off the road. Two men, John Ollingen and W. L. Harding, were arrested by the Vigilance Committee on the grounds that they were unsavory characters and had been found loitering around the neighborhood ten days after the killing. After an examination by the committee, they were released on August 30. [Murder, possible]

On August 24, two Australian criminals, Samuel Whittaker and Robert McKenzie, were hanged by the Committee of Vigilance (see chapter 23). [Two murders]

The *Alta* reported on August 25 that a man named John R. Lowe, also known as Red Dick, had refused to leave a ship in the harbor when ordered to do so by the captain. It was said that Lowe was in the business of assisting seamen to desert. The captain hit Lowe in the head with a pump handle and he fell into the bay and drowned. [Noncriminal]

The body of a Mexican named San Miguel who had recently escaped from a Sacramento jail was found with twenty stab wounds on Leavenworth Street at North Beach on October 9. There was some speculation that his death was the result of an "affair of honor." On October 14, Officers Blunt and Duffie arrested a man named Marcelino and two others who were supposed to have been involved in the killing. They were found hiding under a house on Broadway Street almost opposite the county jail. The suspects were later released because there was not enough evidence to hold them. [Murder, possible]

The November 3 edition of the *Alta* reported an altercation between two stall keepers at Central Wharf in which a drunken Edward McCabe threatened John Wilson with a pistol. Wilson laid his head open with a cleaver as he walked away. McCabe died a few days later; the official ruling was that Wilson had acted in self-defense. [Noncriminal]

On November 9, in a house called the Repose on Pacific Street, George Greenfield accused Charles Brown of insulting the Irish people. In the fight that followed, Brown, identified as a visiting merchant from Stockton, first cut Greenfield on the hand. The combatants were separated, but Brown returned and cut his victim in the abdomen. The assailant ran but was captured by the police. Greenfield died of his wounds; at a trial in late December, a jury found Brown guilty of manslaughter, with a recommendation for clemency. In the end, Brown was pardoned by the outgoing Governor McDougal on the grounds that he had demonstrated the character of a good and peaceable citizen and that the act had been committed under many mitigating circumstances. [Manslaughter]

Two friends, José Contreras and Clemente Sequel, went ashore together from the storeship *Edwin* moored at the foot of Jackson Street. A little drunk, on their return in the early morning hours of November 11, they got in a fight in which Contreras fatally stabbed his friend. His first trial ended in a mistrial because of a technical error; at a second trial in late December, he was found guilty of manslaughter and sentenced to three years' imprisonment. [Manslaughter]

Adrian A. Bartolf, who rented the premises from Alfred A. Green where he ran a public house, the Pavilion, could not pay his rent.

So Green obtained a judgment to sell Bartolf's personal property. Moreover, it seems that Green had called Bartolf's live-in friend from Sydney a low prostitute. At the same time, Bartolf was spreading the story that Green was a cuckold and that he knew the men who had had "improper connection" with the wife. They ran into each other on the afternoon of December 30 at the Milk Punch House near the plank road, where Bartolf was tending bar. According to testimony given at his trial for murder in January 1852, Green had entered the bar and accused the deceased of calling him a cuckold, which charge was admitted by Bartolf. After Bartolf made, or did not make, a furtive move, Green shot him dead. The jury promptly acquitted the defendant. [Noncriminal]

1852

Early in January, the mutilated body of a reputed outlaw called José Feliz (the one implicated in Jarvis's killing) was found in the southern part of San Francisco County (later to be part of San Mateo County). Feliz had died during a fight at a drinking party at the Sanchez rancho. Several men were arrested and examined; in the end, one was found not guilty by a jury, the district attorney declined to prosecute another, and the others were discharged. [Murder, possible]

On Thursday, January 22, the body of a dead Frenchman named Louis Caurad was found at the foot of Telegraph Hill, from which he had fallen (or been thrown) to Battery Street below. A pistol with one round discharged was found on the heights above. The coroner was unable to determine whether Caurad's death was murder or suicide. [Murder, possible]

On Saturday night, January 24, James Edgerton was among the officers who arrested a violently drunk Warren C. Norris for fighting with a Frenchman on Commercial Street. Norris, one of the proprietors of the Mansion House in the Mission, resisted arrest and was about to shoot Officer Treanor when members of the crowd that gathered disarmed him. While Officer Edgerton was giving the charges against the arrestee at the booking counter at the station house, Norris struck him in the head with his fist. According to Marshal David Thompson, who was assisting with the booking process, he tried to separate the officer from his assailant; but before he could do so, Norris struck Edgerton in the mouth. Saying he would not stand to be beaten to death in a police station, Edgerton pulled a bowie knife and stabbed Norris in the abdomen. Protracted hearings and trials followed at which extensive testimony was given by police officers and some of the twenty citizens who had been present in the station house at the time of the killing. In the end, Edgerton was convicted of manslaughter and received a sentence of four months in jail. A few days later, he resigned from the police department. [Manslaughter]

The *Alta* of Monday, February 2, reported that the body of a man who had apparently had his throat cut was found floating at the foot of Washington Street. At the inquest conducted the same day, testimony was given that he might be a man named Davis who had recently come down from the mines and had been staying at the Steamboat Hotel on Pacific Wharf. He had last been seen the previous Friday when he set out to visit a house out beyond the Mission. Evidence about his identity was inconclusive; the jury could only conclude that the deceased was an unknown man, "found floating in the water with his throat cut." [Murder, possible]

In the early morning hours of February 23, according to the proprietess of a "house" at Washington and Dupont streets, James McDonald was drunk and disorderly. McDonald, who had been on the Whig police department replaced by Democrats the previous January, stabbed John Carroll and escaped to Angel Island, where he was later found hiding in the state prison brig (this caused the *Alta* to wonder at the propriety of a public official—the prison keeper—hiding a man wanted by the law). At the judicial proceedings that followed, depending on which version one wants to believe, either Carroll intervened after McDonald abused a woman and was stabbed for his trouble or McDonald was merely defending himself after being struck by Carroll. McDonald said he could not shed much light on the matter because he had been drunk and confused at the time. Eventually, the case petered out; the following fall, when the Whigs regained control of the city government, McDonald was appointed a captain in the department. [Manslaughter]

On April 26, the *Alta* reported the death of Captain David Ritchie from injuries received as the victim of a mugging on April 15, complicated by "excitement of the brain caused by too much free living." Late at night, Captain Ritchie had been returning to his ship when he was set upon, knocked down, and robbed of a ring by two men he was unable to identify. He died on April 20. [Murder]

A Spaniard named Joaquín was found dead of sixteen knife wounds on Davis Street between Commercial and Clay at 3:00 A.M. on April 29. At the inquest, his partner, Blas Rivas, a Mexican who worked with the victim on a boat bringing meat from Contra Costa, threw the blame on a man named Louis who was supposed to have had a fight with the victim about money. Others testified it was Rivas himself who had been drinking with the victim and had fought with him. On April 30, a warrant was issued for Louis. [Manslaughter]

Diego Sandoval, recently discharged from jail, to which he had been sentenced for stabbing another man, took to terrorizing a little tailor named Alamoz every time he saw him. Alamoz asked the marshal for permission to carry a pistol to protect himself. At midnight on June 22, Alamoz and a friend were walking up Washington Street to Kearny when they were accosted by Sandoval and a number of his friends near the Customhouse on Kearny. According to the *Alta*, Sandoval demanded $3 of Alamoz, "if he did not want to die." The tailor backed fifteen feet out into the street with Sandoval after him, carrying an 18-inch double-edged bowie knife. Alamoz shot his aggressor. [Noncriminal]

The body of the infant child of a recent female Chinese immigrant was found at the foot of Stockton Street. It appeared that the body had been thrown there to be devoured by the pigs and rats. The mother was arrested and examined before the recorder on July 2. The story was brought out that the child had sickened and died and that the mother had given an Irishman and the Chinese cook at a brothel $27 to bury it. Instead, according to the account, they pocketed the money and threw the child's body away. Because of the absence of a witness for the prosecution, the case was continued. [Murder, possible]

William Ravenhill, a fifty-year-old Irishman and keeper of the tollbridge at the county line over San Francisquito Creek, was shot in the head on the morning of July 11 and had his house ransacked. "Dutch John" (Thomas Follmer), a German vegetable vendor supposed to have had a "weak mind," was known to have stopped there overnight. When Follmer was overtaken in the Mission, he gave conflicting stories as to his whereabouts at the time of the crime and was unable to account for bloodstains found on his shirt. He was arrested by a police officer on that evidence and bound over by the recorder for trial in the district court on a charge of murder. Later in the month, the grand jury ignored the bill against him and he was released. [Murder, possible]

The body of a respectably dressed man was found in the water between the Commercial and Sacramento Street wharves on the evening of July 24. He had a deep knife wound on his cheek running down to his throat, suggesting that he had been cut from behind. The body, which had no identification or money, also had a broken jaw. [Murder, possible]

Dolores Martinez and Serolla Olle, identified as two Mexican women living in a dance house on Kearny Street, got into a dispute at noon on September 2. According to the *Alta*, it was a matter of jealousy. Olle was fatally stabbed during a scuffle. Martinez was indicted for murder but found guilty of manslaughter at her trial and sentenced to one year's imprisonment. [Manslaughter]

When José Forni (or Forner) was hanged on Russian Hill on December 10 for the murder of José Rodriguez, he earned the distinction of being the first man legally executed in San Francisco since its acquisition by the Americans in 1846. At 4 P.M. on September 13, a number of disinterested witnesses saw Forni chase Rodriguez down a hill in Pleasant Valley and stab him repeatedly in the back. Testimony at later proceedings showed that Forni knew that Rodriguez had recently received wages of $280. On his arrest, $312 was found in Forni's possession. Forni's story was that it was Rodriguez who was trying to rob him and that what the witnesses saw was his reaction to that crime. The jury did not believe him; he was found guilty of murder, for which the only penalty was death. Forni went to his death claiming his innocence —in Spanish, for he spoke no English (see chapter 25). [One murder, one noncriminal]

On October 23, the *Alta* carried the report of an inquest on the body of George Le Marter, who was accidentally shot and killed by a firearm in the hands of his friend Thomas Folley. [Noncriminal]

On November 3, the *Alta* reported that John Chapel (Johnny Cab), a boatman from New York, was cut and killed by a Mexican in a brothel on the corner of Murderer's Alley (between Dupont and Stockton). A couple of days later, Officer Kelly of the police department arrested Abellardo Torres from under a bed on Jackson Street. At his examination before the recorder, Torres was able to show that Chapel had a bad reputation, that he had come into the house spoiling for trouble, and that he had abused Torres's wife and fired on Torres with a pistol. Only then did Torres cut him. The killing was judged to be self-defense. [Noncriminal]

On November 3, the *Alta* also reported on the inquest of C. H. Gridley of 220 Dupont Street, who was determined to have died from the effects of poison administered by some person unknown. There was testimony to the effect that he had been ill since he had drunk at the "house" of a woman named Mary Washington. [Murder, possible]

Special police officer R. W. Lane entered a Chinese brothel on Dupont Street on Wednesday night, November 3, to find a man named Murphy, also a recently appointed special officer, in a dispute with the barman, who demanded that Murphy pay for damage he had caused. Lane told Murphy that he should pay. Murphy refused; when Lane tried to walk him to the station house, he bolted and ran down Dupont Street to Commercial with Lane in pursuit. Lane later testified that he had fired two warning shots but that Murphy turned and threatened to shoot him. Officer Lane felled Murphy with one shot, killing him instantly. Murphy was found to have a slung shot in his hand. Lane was held for trial on a charge of manslaughter. [Manslaughter]

On December 24, a Mr. and Mrs. Quigley, with some friends and some of their eleven children, returned to a house on Bush Street from which they had recently been evicted. There they became involved in a fracas with John Kennedy, the new resident, who was fatally stabbed with a pair of sheep shears. Mr. Quigley left town and Mrs. Quigley admitted doing the cutting at the recorder's examination that followed. The victim asserted, before he died, however, that it was Mr. Quigley who did the stabbing. In January of the following year, Marshal Crozier tracked down Mr. Quigley to Benicia and returned him for trial. In the end, Mr. Quigley was acquitted and his wife was found guilty of manslaughter. [Manslaughter]

1853

On February 19, the *Alta* reported that Coroner Nathaniel Gray had disinterred the body of a man who died in a "sink of iniquity" on Pacific Wharf and that he had conducted a postmortem examination that led to the suspicion that the man had met his death by foul means. [Murder, possible]

On Monday night, February 21, special police officer Cornelius Stag saw the window to his room on Pike Street (Waverly Place) rise slowly and watched as a man tried to climb in. Stag arose, pursued the burglar down the street, and shot him fatally. A coroner's jury determined that the killing was justifiable. [Noncriminal]

Two of his friends testified that, in February, James Hardy, who had just returned from the mines and was known to have several hundred dollars on his person, was supposed to have left town on a salvage job with two men he met on Pacific Wharf. In mid-June, the body of the nineteen-year-old Scot was found several miles west of the Mission.

He had apparently been lured there and murdered for his money. [Murder, possible]

On March 4, James Moore, an escaped convict who had been re-arrested and was being escorted back to jail by Captain McKenzie of the police department, tried to escape by swiping at the officer with a bowie knife. The captain shot him dead. [Noncriminal]

The police found a man lying in the street, presumably drunk, on Kearny Street between Pine and Bush streets on Sunday night, March 20, and bundled him into a hand barrow for transport to the station house. When the man was checked later, he was found to be dead from five stab wounds in the back. When Otto Linden, a young German, read of the incident in the newspapers, he came forward and admitted that he had killed the man. The story told to the recorder was that Linden and a group of friends were accosted by the deceased, who insisted that they drink with him. When they declined, he assaulted them, knocking two of them down before pulling a dagger. Testimony was given that Linden took the dagger away from the man and stabbed him with it. The court decided that Linden had acted in self-defense. [Noncriminal]

On March 26, the *Alta* reported the arrest for murder of a man named Haywood for allegedly knocking John Gibbs from a ship at the foot of Spear Street, causing him to drown. [Manslaughter]

On May 9, Thomas Skelly, a twenty-four-year-old man from Liverpool, was seen very drunk on Pacific Wharf. He was later found drowned. The jury at his inquest "supposed that [the] liquor was drugged." [Murder, possible]

On June 13, the *Alta* reported the death of a man named Crane in a duel and editorialized at length on the evils of dueling. [Duel]

On July 5, Joseph West (or Wise) and Ben Young (or Johnson) had a drunken dispute over a card game on Davis Street. Testimony was given at West's inquest that he had punched Young in the face twice before Young fatally stabbed him. The *Alta* reported on July 9 that Young was sentenced to three months' imprisonment. [Manslaughter]

A Doctor Baldwin had bought a lot on Greenwich Street near Kearny in 1850; when he later took a trip east, he deeded a portion to his housekeeper in return for her taking care of the rest. The housekeeper sold the lot to Joseph Hetherington (the same man who informed on some of his associates to the 1851 Vigilance Committee and would earn a measure of fame when he was hanged himself by the 1856 Vigilance Committee). Hetherington held possession of the lot until August 1853, when Doctor Baldwin showed up armed with a shotgun and proceeded to erect a structure. Hetherington came on the scene and ordered Baldwin off the property. When Baldwin refused, Hetherington seized the shotgun and tried to shoot the doctor, but the weapon misfired. Both adversaries pulled pistols and Hetherington won the draw, shooting Baldwin in the arm. As Baldwin tried to escape, Hetherington came up behind him and shot him in the head. Hetherington was found not guilty of murder in a trial before the district court in October. [Noncriminal]

Peter Smith and a Lieutenant Scott, who had soldiered together in Jefferson Davis's Mississippi regiment during the Mexican War, met in an affair of honor at the Pioneer Racetrack in the Mission on August 3. Scott proved to be the better shot; Smith fell, mortally wounded. The verdict of the coroner's jury was that Smith had died of a gunshot wound inflicted by someone "to them unknown." [Duel]

Toward the middle of August, Martine Gonzales got himself killed in a drunken brawl in the southern part of the county. Three men were brought before the recorder, but charges against them were dismissed. [Manslaughter]

Charles Drew walked up behind (Doctor) Gillis on Clay near Montgomery Street on the evening of September 12 and shot him in the head. It developed that a divorce was pending between Drew and his wife and Drew suspected an "improper intimacy" between the victim and his spouse. Drew was eventually convicted of manslaughter. [Manslaughter]

On the night of September 18, a Mr. McKenzie, one of the parties to a dispute over the title to a storeship at Vallejo and Front streets, learned that a large party of men were on their way to dispossess him. He went to the police station but was told that there was no one to send, so he returned to the site of the ship, where his adversaries assaulted him. He armed himself with a shotgun; in the general shootout that followed, he fatally shot one of the other party. At the hearing, charges of "discharging a firearm" were dismissed. [Noncriminal]

John Williams, a black man fresh from the mines with a roll, went out to Pacific Street to celebrate his good luck on Sunday night, September 19. He was fatally stabbed in a fight with a man named José Maria, who was arrested by Officer McKenzie. [Manslaughter]

The October 5 edition of the *Alta* reported on the inquest of a man who had been lassoed around the neck and dragged to his death in a rural section of the county. [Murder, possible]

On the evening of October 10, two Americans entered a Chinese washhouse on the Jackson Street Wharf. When told that they could not have their laundry without a ticket, one of the Americans shot a laundryman through the heart with his pistol. A man was arrested but released when his pregnant wife testified before the recorder that he had been with her the whole time. [Murder]

Francisco, a Chilean, was seen to leave a "house" on Pacific Street on the evening of November 3 with two men, one named Polonio and the other William Mickle (aka Coyote Charlie). A few minutes later, a dying Francisco pounded on the door of a man on Vallejo Street and said that he had been stabbed by his friend Polonio. In the proceedings that followed before the recorder, Polonio was discharged and Mickle, whose frequent appearances in court dated back to his membership in the Hounds in 1849, was committed for trial on a charge of murder. Both were later indicted on a charge of murder by the grand jury, but eventually they were discharged. [Murder, possible]

On November 17, the *Alta* reported the discovery of the body of a man with a severely crushed skull floating near the dock at Jackson and Drumm streets. A man named Hyatt who lived in the vicinity said that about two weeks earlier he had heard a cry of "murder" preceding the sound of a splash at that location, but the coroner's jury concluded that the man had died from a cause unknown. [Murder, possible]

The November 29 edition of the *Alta* contained a report of the indictment of Thomas Hayes for the murder of an unknown man in an unincorporated portion of the county. At his trial in the court of sessions in late December, the jury acquitted him without leaving the box. [Murder, possible]

Benjamin Twitchell and Samuel Gilmore, agents for parties contending for the same piece of land in the Potrero district, ran afoul of each other on December 2. As Gilmore attempted to put up a fence at what he thought was the boundary, Twitchell tried to cross the line to make a survey. Gilmore shot him in the groin, and he died twenty minutes later. Gilmore was indicted for murder but acquitted at his trial. [Noncriminal]

At this point, district attorney Byrne made the comment ascribed to him about the amount of murder in Gold Rush San Francisco.

Notes

INTRODUCTION

1. In the absence of an English equivalent for the Spanish *norteamericano*, and with full knowledge that the other residents of the hemisphere are every bit as much entitled to the use of the title, I use the term "American" in this book to mean the Anglo settlers in California who originated in the eastern United States.

2. Roger Lotchin, *San Francisco, 1846–1856, from Hamlet to City*, p. 201.

3. Albert Benard de Russailh, *Last Adventure*, p. 41.

4. Frank Soulé, John H. Gihon, and James Nisbet, *The Annals of San Francisco*, p. 324.

5. Mary Floyd Williams, ed., *Papers of the San Francisco Vigilance Committee of 1851*, p. 1.

6. Soulé, Gihon, and Nisbet, *Annals*, p. 567.

7. Paul Drexler, "The Bad Old Days," *San Francisco Examiner*, August 4, 1985, California Living section.

8. Richard Maxwell Brown, *Strain of Violence*, p. 124.

9. Ibid., p. 358 note: "In San Francisco in the 1850s the contrast between the old and the new vigilantism is graphically revealed. The San Francisco vigilance committee of 1851 arose mainly in response to an orthodox crime problem stemming from Australian ex-convicts and other ne'er do wells. The vigilante movement of 1856 was in its objectives much

more typical of the new vigilantism." See also David A. Williams, *David C. Broderick, A Political Portrait*, p. 128.

10. Robert M. Senkewicz, *Vigilantes in Gold Rush San Francisco*, p. 75.

11. One exception is *We Were 49ers!*, translated and edited by Edwin A. Beilharz and Carlos U. López, containing (among others) the journal of Vincent Perez Rosales, a Peruvian merchant in Gold Rush San Francisco. Rosales illuminates the character of alcalde Thaddeus Leavenworth, a key figure in the events of that time.

12. Other newspapers, voicing all shades of editorial opinion, came and went during the early years of San Francisco. The *Alta California*, however, with its usually moderate stance, can be said to have been the closest thing to a newspaper of record at the time. It was the paper that most reflected the mainstream values of the day.

13. Mary Floyd Williams, *History of the San Francisco Committee of Vigilance of 1851*, p. 388.

CHAPTER 1: HISPANIC ARCADIA

1. It was in the early 1930s that the Federal Bureau of Investigation (FBI) began collecting crime data from local police departments according to standardized categories that allowed meaningful analyses of criminal experience. More recently, some analysts have questioned the accuracy and completeness of FBI figures (see discussion below).

2. Hubert Howe Bancroft, *Popular Tribunals*, 1:62. Much of Bancroft's work was actually written by a number of different employees in his famed history factory, who brought their own perceptions and beliefs to their work. Thus, support for just about every position on a subject can be found somewhere in his massive effort. Still, Bancroft's mammoth history of California (albeit taken with a small grain of salt) cannot be overlooked by anyone seriously trying to understand the subject.

3. Technically, *cholo* means the child of a Spanish father and Indian mother, but it is used in California as an offensive term to describe a person of low character. *Californios* were Hispanic natives of California, who saw themselves as descendants of pure Spanish stock and thus socially superior to the mixed-breed leaders of the government in Mexico City.

4. Department State Papers, Benicia Military, ms. at Bancroft Library.

5. George L. Harding, *Don Agustin V. Zamarano*, p. 47.

6. Hubert Howe Bancroft, *History of California*, 3:192.

7. Ibid., 3:190. The law does not seem to have been enforced in any other case. Governor Luis Antonio Arguello, second governor in the Mexican era and first native-born Californian, an otherwise moderate official, had enacted the draconian penalty a few years before in the belief that it

would bring thefts by *cholo* soldiers to a halt. Saying his predecessors had been too lenient and that crime had gotten out of hand, Arguello issued an edict calling for capital punishment on a conviction for housebreaking and thefts of over $25. (If force or false keys were used in the theft, the body of the executed thief was to be quartered.) For thefts of less than $25, the penalty was to be ten years in prison after the defendant was made to run a gauntlet.

8. Ibid., 3:193.

9. In this San Francisco wasn't much different from other American cities (see Frederick M. Wirt, *Power in the City*, pp. 161, 167). However, participation by commercial interests in public affairs was decidedly more prominent in Hispanic San Francisco than in other Mexican towns.

CHAPTER 2: CONQUEST

1. There was a legal process by means of which each party to a legal dispute would bring an *hombre bueno* (good man) of his own choosing to an informal hearing before a justice of the peace. If the justice could not bring about an agreement after hearing a presentation by both the plaintiff and defendant, he and the *hombres buenos* would meet out of the hearing of the parties and arrive at a decision. In the few cases in which the parties might not agree with the outcome, appeal could be made to other authorities. See David J. Langum, "Mexican California's Legal System," *Californians* (May/June 1987): 46, and Theodore Grivas, *Military Governments in California 1846–1850*, p. 159.

2. Walter Colton, *The California Diary*, pp. 3, 24.

3. John W. Dwinnelle, *The Colonial History of San Francisco*, addendum no. lxix.

4. Bancroft, *History*, 4:666.

5. Edwin Bryant, *What I Saw in California*, p. 321.

6. Zoeth Skinner Eldredge, *The Beginnings of San Francisco*, p. 544.

CHAPTER 3: THE POLITICS OF CRIME

1. Lincoln Steffens, *The Autobiography of Lincoln Steffens*, p. 285.

2. Edward Kemble, *A Kemble Reader*, p. 114.

3. Edward Kemble, *A History of California Newspapers 1846–1858*, p. 72. Brannan's reasons for opposing the established government might also have had a radical revolutionary dimension. Leidesdorff, early on, informed Governor Mason that the opposition to Hyde came from "the friends of California independence from the United States, supported by the Mormons" (Bancroft, *History*, 5:649 note). According to Grivas, *Military Governments*, p. 197, on this point, "Some people were convinced

that the threat of an independent California was largely imaginary." Still, just after Hyde's resignation from the office of alcalde the next year, Sam Brannan wrote to Brigham Young saying, "The tide of opposition that has heretofore existed against us [Mormons] under the recent control of the Alcalde here has received a successful defeat . . ." (Paul Bailey, *Sam Brannan and the California Mormons*, p. 118).

4. *California Star*, June 26, 1847.

5. Oscar Lewis, *This Was San Francisco*, p. 58.

6. *Californian*, September 15, 1847.

7. Lewis, *San Francisco*, p. 58.

8. *Star*, October 2, 1847.

9. Speaking of the period before the 1830s, James F. Richardson (*Urban Police in the United States*, p. 19) reports that "serious crimes, by the standards of subsequent decades at any rate, were infrequent." He cites the fact that Boston had one reported murder for the years between 1822 and 1834.

10. David R. Johnson, *Policing the Urban Underworld*, p. 7.

11. Ibid., p. 9.

12. *Star*, December 25, 1847.

13. Lewis, *San Francisco*, p. 58.

14. *The Laws of the Town of San Francisco 1847*, p. 3.

15. Ibid., p. 5.

16. Bancroft, *History*, 5:650 note.

17. *Californian*, December 1, 1847.

18. *Star*, December 11 and 25, 1847.

19. *Star*, November 6, 1847: "We are told that a case of this kind actually occurred. . . ."

20. That much of the criminality in Gold Rush San Francisco was rowdy against rowdy is borne out by the statement of John Hittell as cited by Mary Williams in her *History* (p. 351 note): "Even when homicides were most frequent the great majority of people were secure in their lives and property; but the percentage of deaths was large among gamblers, drunkards, holders of disputed land claims, thieves and borderers."

21. Bancroft, *History*, 5:650.

22. Kemble, *Reader*, p. 129.

CHAPTER 4: THE VICTORS WRITE THE HISTORY

1. Soulé, Gihon, and Nisbet, *Annals*, p. 567; Charles Keeler, *San Francisco and Thereabout*, p. 18; Bailey, *Brannan*, p. 185; Alan Valentine, *Vigilante Justice*, p. 137.

2. Gertrude Atherton, *Golden Gate Country*, p. 142; James A. B. Scherer, *The Lion of the Vigilantes*, p. 152; John Hittell, *The History of San Francisco and Incidentally of California*, p. 243; Theodore Hittell,

History of California, 3:462; William Martin Camp, *San Francisco Port of Gold*, p. 111; Andrew F. Rolle, *California: A History*, p. 253. All refer to the story of 1,000 criminal homicides in a few Gold Rush years in San Francisco. Bancroft, whose efforts were so diffused that he can often be found on the opposite sides of the same question, mentions the incidence of 1,200 murders in San Francisco in a few years in his *Popular Tribunals*, 1:131, but hastens to add that he does not vouch for the correctness of the statement. In his *History*, 7:215, he states flatly that the murders occurred. Frank Marryat in *Mountains and Molehills*, p. 389, Hinton Helper in *Dreadful California*, p. 159, Stanton A. Coblentz in *Villains and Vigilantes*, p. 48, John Bruce in *Gaudy Century*, p. 37, Joseph Henry Jackson in *San Francisco Murders*, p. 1, Oscar Lewis in *This Was San Francisco*, p. 140, and Mary Williams in her *History*, pp. 389–90, all seem to agree. Bancroft, in his *Popular Tribunals*, 1:748, quotes a contemporary newspaper as saying there were 1,400 murders in San Francisco by 1856. In 1948, Robert O'Brien, in *This Is San Francisco*, p. 119, picked up the tale and passed it on. This version is also cited by Richard Dillon in *The Hatchet Men*, p. 43.

3. Herbert Asbury, *The Barbary Coast*, p. 55.

4. Theodore Hittell, *History*, 3:462.

5. Comparisons of crime rates between different cities and widely separated periods of time are a chancy business, a fact we should keep in mind later when we compare the murder rate in Gold Rush San Francisco and contemporary urban experience. There are a number of variables that stand in the way of making such comparisons. One constant about predatory crime in any age, however, is that most of it is committed by young males in their late teens and early twenties. (Currently, the large majority of serious predatory crimes are committed by males between fifteen and twenty, a group comprising less than 10% of the population.) That profile just about matches the demographic makeup of Gold Rush San Francisco. Thus, we can expect that the crime rate would be skewed higher than in another city of like size.

6. See note 2 above and notes 8 through 13 below. It is not to fault the historians that their names are listed here but rather to show the degree to which the legend has insinuated itself into the history of the city. Most of them, after all, were not writing strictly criminal justice histories—and the legend of rampant murder is just too good a historical tidbit to pass up.

7. John Myers Myers, though he goes too far in characterizing the vigilantes as prototypical fascists in his *San Francisco's Reign of Terror*, does correctly state that the legend is incorrect, pp. 50, 279. More recently, Roger Lotchin, *San Francisco, 1846–1856*, p. 205, also questions the veracity of the legend, as does Senkewicz, *Vigilantes*, pp. 75–76, who summarily dismisses the legend of daily criminal homicides.

8. Herbert Phillips, *Big Wayward Girl*, p. 17; Adair Heig, *History of*

Petaluma, p. 37; and Curt Gentry and Tom Horton, *The Dolphin Guide to San Francisco and the Bay Area*, p. 50.

9. Kevin Starr, *Americans and the California Dream*, p. 81.

10. Arthur Chandler, *Old Tales of San Francisco*, p. 73.

11. *San Francisco Chronicle*, January 12, 1986.

12. Alistair Cooke, *The Americans*, p. 31.

13. Frederick M. Wirt, *Power in the City*, p. 110; John Bernard McGloin, *San Francisco: The Story of a City*, p. 58; Charles Wollenberg, *Golden Gate Metropolis*, p. 80.

14. Williams, *History*, p. 388.

15. John P. Young, *Journalism in California*, p. 13.

16. Jackson, *Murders*, p. 3.

17. *Star*, February 12, 1848.

18. At one point, Hyde felt compelled to disavow ownership of the *Californian* (Bancroft, *History*, 5:651 note).

19. Bancroft, *History*, 5:656.

20. *Californian*, March 8, 1848. In this Leidesdorff, though he would not live to see it, prefigured the solutions of a later time. Club law (see Daniel J. Boorstin, *The Americans: The National Experience*, p. 77) refers to one form of vigilantism practiced in middle America in the middle decades of the nineteenth century.

21. Bancroft, *History*, 5:651 note (Fourgeaud, E. P. Jones, J. C. Ward, Sam Brannan, William D. M. Howard, William Heath Davis, E. H. Harrison, William Leidesdorff, C. L. Ross, and Henry Mellus among them). It is worthy of note that all of these men owned land in the portion of the town fronting on Montgomery Street. William S. Clark, and others who supported Hyde, owned land at Clark's Point near Broadway and Battery streets.

22. Press reporters, then and even now, often incorrectly use the term "robbery" to describe what are really burglaries. The distinction, the importance of which will become evident as we analyze the crime occurring during the Gold Rush years, is that robbery requires the use of force or fear. It is a crime of immediate violence visited proximately by the criminal on the victim. Burglary, on the other hand, is usually a crime of stealth in which the culprit tries to avoid contact with the victim. Many of the "robberies" encountered in the pages of the press were really burglaries.

23. Bancroft, *History*, 5:651.

24. Hubert Howe Bancroft, *California Inter Pocula*, p. 590. Current judges, even surrounded as they are by armed bailiffs and sequestered behind metal detectors and bullet-proof glass, would sympathize with the judge. On October 22, 1986, the *San Francisco Chronicle* reported that four of the eleven concealed gun permits in San Francisco were held by judges who had been threatened. Every judge's secret fear, not realized

by those whose only role is to criticize, is that some party to an action might well take personal steps to deal with an unpopular decision. By the time the judicial process is complete, it is evident that all other hopes for a different disposition have been exhausted. Only the judge remains as a visible physical symbol of the wrong that has been done to the loser.

25. Soulé, Gihon, and Nisbet, *Annals*, p. 201. T. A. Barry and B. A. Patten in *San Francisco 1850*, p. 110, make a cryptic comment on this point, suggesting that all might not have been as it seemed: "The 'Annals of San Francisco' makes no honorable mention of his [Hyde's] name; but 'thereby hangs a tale.'"

26. Bancroft, *History*, 5:650 note.

27. William Heath Davis, *Seventy-five Years in California*, pp. 232–33. In his appendix (pp. 298ff.) Davis includes a statement by Hyde on the point and letters he solicited from others that tend to exonerate him of wrongdoing. Among them are letters from William D. M. Howard and Robert A. Parker, who were earlier induced by Leidesdorff and Jones to join in accusations against the alcalde.

28. *San Francisco Town Journal 1847–1848*.

29. Bancroft, *History*, 5:651. Actually, the footnotes in Bancroft's history at this location contain a rich lode of detailed information about what was going on at the time.

30. Elbert P. Jones became the owner of many city lots and returned to his childhood home a millionaire a few years later. At the time of his death in May 1848, William Leidesdorff was also the owner of many lots that, after the discovery of gold, became very valuable and eventually came into the possession of Joseph Folsom. Sam Brannan went on to become one of the wealthiest businessmen and property owners in San Francisco.

CHAPTER 5: THE 48ERS

1. Bancroft, *History*, 6:56.

2. Theodore Hittell, *History*, 2:689.

3. E. Gould Buffum, *Six Months in the Gold Mines*, p. 51. Still, according to John Henry Brown, *Early Days in San Francisco*, there were enough miners in town on Independence Day to stage a two-day blowout. Buffum was in Los Angeles until September and then went to the mines, so this is not a firsthand account. There must have been a certain amount of coming and going during the summer.

4. Eldredge, *Beginnings*, p. 449.

5. Milo Milton Quaife, ed., *Pictures of Gold Rush California*, p. 122.

6. *Star*, June 3, 1848.

7. Gentry and Horton, *Dolphin Guide*, p. 28.

8. Donald Dale Jackson, *Gold Dust*, p. 41.

9. Ibid., p. 54.

10. Bancroft, *History*, 6:269.

11. Jackson, *Gold Dust*, p. 67.

12. *California Star and Californian*, December 9, 1848.

13. *California Star and Californian*, December 23, 1848.

14. Biggs, *Conquer*, p. 200.

15. The story is told of how the alcalde at Santa Cruz, when a case was brought before him involving a vaquero sued by a woman whose miscarriage he caused while saving her from a rampaging bull, ordered that the vaquero should put her back in the same condition he found her. The judge ruled that her husband should pay the costs of the trial. On a more serious note, Stephen Field—who went on to become a justice of the United States Supreme Court—once, as an alcalde in a California mining town in the early days, ordered an unwarranted whipping, fearing that if he did not the crowd would have hanged the man.

16. Theodore Hittell, *History* 3:280.

17. Soulé, Gihon, and Nisbet, *Annals*, p. 208.

18. Oddly enough, it seems as though one stood a better chance of being murdered in rural California than in an urban setting, not just during the Gold Rush but during all of the frontier era. One recent study cited by Richard W. Crawford and Clare V. McKanna, Jr. ("Crime in California: Using State and Local Archives for Crime Research," *Pacific Historical Review*, 55 [May 1986]: 295) suggests that the rate of murder in San Diego County in the 1870s (79% of which occurred in rural areas) was 117 per 100,000 population. As a point of comparison, the current rate of criminal homicide in the same county is 5 per 100,000 (9.73 within the city limits of San Diego). The rate in Detroit, the "murder capital of the nation," is 49.11 per 100,000.

19. Eldredge, *Beginnings*, p. 450.

20. Biggs, *Conquer*, pp. 159–61.

21. *California Star and Californian*, November 25, 1848.

22. *Alta California*, January 4, 1849.

CHAPTER 6: THE RUSH

1. Soulé, Gihon, and Nisbet, *Annals*, pp. 243–44. According to Curt Gentry, *The Madames of San Francisco*, p. 6, "The twentieth century would arrive before there was a balance between the sexes in California—something to keep in mind when considering why certain 'peculiar habits' were of such long duration."

2. Bancroft, *Popular Tribunals*, 1:68.

3. Soulé, Gihon, and Nisbet, *Annals*, p. 206. When the square-rigged brig *Belfast* from New York docked at Broadway Street in September 1848, prices, which had risen in the conditions of scarcity, dropped 25% in the

first of a number of wild fluctuations that would characterize the economic life of the Gold Rush town.

4. Sam Brannan prominently among them, along with others who had opposed Hyde: Mellus, Howard, Jas. C. Ward, Harrison, and others.

5. *Alta*, January 25, 1849.

6. Theodore Hittell, *History*, 2:709.

7. Bancroft, *History*, 6:210.

8. The idea of postsentencing incarceration was still new even in the United States, dating as a reform since only about 1790. Before that time, corporal or capital punishment was used as a penalty for more serious crimes. Fines were imposed as penalties for less serious crimes for those who could pay them and public ridicule (such as ducking stools and stocks) was widely used for others (see Roger T. Pray, "How Did Our Prisons Get That Way?" *American Heritage* [July/August 1987]).

9. Dwinnelle, *Colonial History*, p. 65: "Happy was San Francisco, to whom the 'fact' criminal had not yet suggested the word 'jail': less happy, but more wise San Jose, whose experience had already advanced to the word and fact of 'prison.'" The mission settlements had been secularized by the time of Galindo's problem; a population shift had occurred from pueblo and presidial settlements to outlying ranchos and the military garrison had been moved to Sonoma. There were not enough permanent residents remaining in town to guard him.

10. Bancroft, *History*, 5:682.

11. Brown, *Early Days*, p. 35.

12. *Star*, March 18, 1848.

13. *Californian*, March 15, 1848.

14. *Alta*, February 9, 15, 1849.

15. Buffum, *Six Months*, p. 93.

16. See note 1 above.

17. *Alta*, April 14, 1849; June 7, 28, 1849.

CHAPTER 7: THE HOUNDS

1. The body conducting the quasipopular tribunal in July 1849 that brought the Hounds to book cannot properly be called a Committee of Vigilance, which, by definition, bypasses the regular institutions of government. The 1849 tribunal acted in cooperation with the existing civil authority, such as it was—Alcalde Leavenworth.

2. Brown, *Early Days*, p. 102. "Edward Harrison, W.D.M. Howard, James Layton, Captain Folsom, Robert A. Parker, and many others."

3. The term "bo hoys" or "b'hoys" or "boys" had a special meaning to New Yorkers and San Franciscans in mid-nineteenth-century America. It described groups of young barroom loafers, ready to fight at the drop of a hat and always on the lookout for an easy dollar to be made at the expense

of someone else. They were to be found among members of the New York regiment of volunteers and other early Gold Rush arrivals from New York City. The Bowery B'Hoys was a prominent nativist gang in mid-century New York City. As used, the term fits the Hounds perfectly.

4. *Alta*, August 2, 1849.

5. Beilharz and López, *We Were 49ers!*, p. 31.

6. Soule, Gihon, and Nisbet, *Annals*, p. 554.

7. Ibid., p. 555. A more balanced view is given by Carlos U. López. (See "The Chilenos in the California Gold Rush" in *The Californians* magazine, March/April 1988.) First to leave Chile for California were the American and English merchants of Valparaiso who took with them their stores of goods and set up shop immediately. Next to go were professional miners, experienced tunnel and shaft diggers. "A second group," reports López, "was composed of adventurers. . . . Among them were the prostitutes from Valparaiso and Talcahuano, most of whom would eventually marry and start long and respected family dynasties in California."

8. Ibid., p. 556.

9. Cornelius R. V. Lee was elected president, W. Anderson vice-president, J. A. Patterson treasurer, and Joseph T. Downey secretary. (Downey came to San Francisco in 1846 as an enlisted man on the *Portsmouth*. In his *Filings from an Old Saw*, he wrote humorously and fluently of the American flag raising at Yerba Buena. He supposedly was thwarted in an attempt to stuff the ballot box in the first alcalde election held in 1846 and was bundled drunk back aboard his ship. In 1849, he tended bar in the Tammany Hall drinking tent on Kearny Street frequented by the Hounds.) J. C. Pulis, who chaired the meeting, was made steward. "During the nineteenth century," Brown points out in his *Strain of Violence*, "the original terms *regulator* and *vigilante* were synonyms for Americans who took the law into their own hands by participating in an organized movement; by the late nineteenth century *regulator* had faded from general use." There are indications that the term fell into disuse, at least in the West, after it was contaminated in the public mind when adopted by the Hounds in 1849. Moreover, its widespread use before that time shows that in some perverted way the Hounds viewed themselves as part of the vigilante tradition.

10. Williams, *History*, p. 107.

11. Bancroft, *Popular Tribunals*, 1:100.

12. Woodrow James Hansen, *The Search for Authority in California*, p. 104.

CHAPTER 8: THE UNSEEN HAND

1. Bancroft, *Popular Tribunals*, 1:90.

2. Eldredge, *Beginnings*, p. 600 note.

3. James D. Hart, *A Companion to California*, p. 234.

4. The August 2, 1849, edition of the *Alta California* contains a good abstract account of the testimony given during the trial of the Hounds. Yet most historians writing about the Hounds have been satisfied with secondary sources that do not always reflect events as they occurred. There are clues in the testimony abstracted in the paper pointing to someone other than Alcalde Leavenworth as the main supporter of the Hounds.

5. *Alta*, August 2, 1849.

6. Soulé, Gihon, and Nisbet, *Annals*, p. 561.

7. Williams, *History*, p. 100 note.

8. Bancroft, *History*, 6:210.

9. *Alta*, August 2, 1849.

10. Ibid.

11. Ibid.

12. Beilharz and López, *We Were 49ers!*, p. 31.

13. Brown, *Early Days*, p. 104.

14. Ibid., p. 103.

15. *Minutes of the Proceedings of the Legislative Assembly of the District of San Francisco from March 12, 1849 to June 4, 1849.*

16. Ibid.

17. Kemble, *History of California Newspapers*, p. 90.

18. *Minutes of the Proceedings of the Legislative Assembly.*

19. Bancroft, *Popular Tribunals*, 1:92.

20. *Alta*, August 2, 1849.

21. Ibid.

22. Ibid.

23. Williams, *History*, p. 100.

24. Beilharz and López, *We Were 49ers!*, p. 31.

25. *Alta*, June 28, 1849.

26. Soulé, Gihon, and Nisbet, *Annals*, p. 556: "A young man by the name of Beatty, not properly one of themselves, but who happened to be among or near the band at the time, received a fatal shot from one of the attacked foreigners."

27. *Alta*, August 2, 1849.

28. The *Alta* on November 18, 1850, reported the discovery, on the "Pacific Beach" eight miles from town, of the dead body of a man with a receipt in his pocket made out to Samuel Roberts (perhaps?).

CHAPTER 9: A REAL POLICE

1. Bayard Taylor, *Eldorado*, 1:52.

2. Bancroft, *History*, 6:168.

3. Taylor, *Eldorado*, 1:55.

4. Soulé, Gihon, and Nisbet, *Annals*, p. 228.

5. Ibid., p. 230.

6. The presence of six constables in San Francisco in the first half of 1849 is commonly referred to, though I have been unable to find any more concrete evidence of their existence than the statement that they were there. I suspect the story came from the authorization given by the legislative assembly to Myron Norton to appoint two or more constables to carry out his orders. (Two constables times three justices equals six constables.) If the constables were appointed, they did not play any official part in the affairs of the town. Bodies taking enforcement action at the time, with or without official sanction, are invariably referred to as groups of private citizens.

7. Lewis Mumford, *The City in History*, p. 447, likens the destruction and disorder of the great cities between 1820 and 1900 to a battlefield: "Industrialism, the main creative force of the nineteenth century, produced the most degraded urban environment the world had yet seen. . . ."

8. Bancroft, *Popular Tribunals*, 1:62.

9. Roger Lane, "Urbanization and Criminal Violence in the 19th Century: Massachusetts as a Test Case," in Hugh Davis Graham and Ted Robert Gurr, eds., *Violence in America, Historical and Comparative Perspectives*, 2:362.

10. Johnson, *Policing the Urban Underworld*, p. 69.

11. Ibid., p. 78.

12. Gustavus Myers, *The History of Bigotry in the United States*, pp. 119–23, and W. Eugene Hollon, *Frontier Violence, Another Look*, p. 25.

13. Eric H. Monkkonen, *The Dangerous Class: Crime and Poverty in Columbus, Ohio 1860–1885*, p. 5 and passim, has shown that an increasing crime rate is not a necessary concomitant of the process of urbanization; but whatever the actual rate of predatory crime was in the various cities of the mid-nineteenth century, it is certain that public perceptions were that it was definitely on the rise. David Johnson points out (*Policing the Urban Underworld*, pp. 15–16) that "no reliable statistics survive in sufficient quantities to verify these charges [that crime was increasing greatly by 1830] and the picture of a crime ridden society was probably exaggerated. But the rhetoric indicates a widespread belief that crime had become a major problem and in the absence of any contrary evidence, that attitude became an important justification for changing the existing law enforcement machinery."

14. According to Cecil Woodham-Smith, *The Great Hunger*, p. 251, "A return from the Clerk of the Boston Police Court for 1848 demonstrates the effect of the recent immigration, three-quarters of it Irish, on behaviour in the city. During the previous five years complaints for capital offenses had increased 266 per cent, attempts to kill 1,700 per cent, assaults on police officers 400 per cent, aggravated assaults committed with knives,

dirks, pistols, slingshots, razors, pokers, hot irons, clubs, iron weights, flat irons, bricks and stones, 465 per cent"—100% of nothing is still nothing, perhaps, but 1,700% of anything is something.

15. Hollon, *Frontier Violence*, p. 24 and passim. John C. Schneider, *Detroit and the Problem of Order, 1830–1880*, p. 3, informs us that "as the city expanded in the late nineteenth century, however and as income began to replace occupation and ethnicity as the basis for residential clustering, potentially hostile groups rubbed shoulders less often, and neighborhood disorder all but disappeared." By the 1960s, conditions seemed to have come full turn.

16. Roger Lane, "Urbanization," p. 363.

17. James F. Richardson, *Urban Police in the United States*, pp. 3–19.

18. Richard Maxwell Brown, "Historical Patterns of Violence in America," in Graham and Gurr, *Violence in America*, 1:45.

19. Johnson, *Policing the Urban Underworld*, p. 16.

20. Ibid., p. 26.

21. Wilbur R. Miller, *Cops and Bobbies*, pp. ix–x.

22. Fallon to his family, August 30, 1849 (held by John B. McGloin, S.J.).

23. Quaife, *Pictures*, p. xxxi. See also Bancroft, *Popular Tribunals*, 1:29.

24. Williams, *History*, p. 86.

25. Doyce B. Nunis, ed., *The San Francisco Vigilance Committee of 1856: Three Views*, p. 28.

26. Bancroft, *Popular Tribunals*, 1:68.

27. Taylor, *Eldorado*, 2:33.

28. Mary Jane Megquier, *Apron Full of Gold*, p. 34.

29. *Alta*, July 8, 1850.

30. *Alta*, October 11, 1849; November 15, 1849; December 15, 31, 1849; Reynolds was probably black, though he is not specifically identified as such. His nickname was "Bones," given to him because he played in a black band.

31. Soulé, Gihon, and Nisbet, *Annals*, p. 730.

CHAPTER 10: CUI BONO

1. Soulé, Gihon, and Nisbet, *Annals*, p. 566.

2. Williams, *Papers*, p. 1.

3. *San Francisco Examiner*, June 3, 1986. The tradition of the responsibility of Australian criminals for the great fires has become so encrusted with respectability in numerous retellings that it has evolved into received wisdom on the subject. Over the years, it has been repeated in almost every account of the fires. Recently, John Burks in *Working Fire*, p. 19,

quotes historian Tom Cole, *A Short History of San Francisco*, p. 52, who in a section titled "Fire and Vigilantism" attributes the origin of the fires to Australian criminals, punishing those who would not pay them protection money.

4. The use of fire-resistant construction materials, mandatory sprinkler systems, and smoke alarms has served to reduce the cataclysmic effects of modern urban fires, as have improved water delivery systems and professionalized fire fighting services.

5. Daniel Wadsworth Coit, *Digging for Gold without a Shovel*, p. 81.

6. Burks, *Working Fire*, p. 55, quoting *Firehouse* magazine.

7. Asbury, *Barbary Coast*, p. 55.

8. "Emperor" Joshua Norton, eccentric character of a few decades later, is said to have gone mad after his attempt to corner the rice market went awry in the 1850s when a shipload of rice arrived unexpectedly and drove the price down. See Peter R. Decker, *Fortunes and Failures: White-Collar Mobility in Nineteenth-Century San Francisco*, p. 34: "By 1858 San Francisco had experienced four major business cycles, all quite independent of the national economy: June 1848–January 1850—boom; February 1850–April 1852—recession; May 1852–December 1853—boom; January 1854–January 1858—depression."

9. Beilharz and López, *We Were 49ers!*, p. 67 (Rosales was finally burned out in a fire and returned to Chile). Decker, *Fortunes and Failures*, pp. 44–45, points out that much of the property destroyed in the conflagrations was not held on consignment but was owned by merchants in their own right. Those whose goods were not destroyed made fantastic profits after the fires, but others were ruined financially.

10. Myers Myers, *Reign of Terror*, p. 53.

11. Theodore Hittell, *History*, 3:350.

12. Kathleen Ainsworth, "A Defense of Historic Trivia," *Californians* (November/December 1984): 22. The provision seems to have been placed there more because of fear that southern slaveholders would bring in gangs of black slaves and compete unfairly with individual white miners than from any sentiments of racial altruism.

13. Brown, *Early Days*, pp. 124–25.

CHAPTER 11: AYUNTAMIENTO

1. Soulé, Gihon, and Nisbet, *Annals*, p. 730.

2. In the imbroglio that followed, Prefect Hawes was charged with complicity with Colton in his scheme; but since Hawes plays no further role in this part of the history of the time, we shall not pursue his guilt or innocence. The conflict is of interest to us only because it caused the publication of evidence of scandalous conduct by others who are important to our story.

3. Theodore Hittell, *History*, 3:389.

4. Soulé, Gihon, and Nisbet, *Annals*, p. 230.

5. Eldredge, *Beginnings*, p. 607.

6. *Record of the Proceedings of the Town Council*, meeting of October 8, 1849. This perhaps gave a new meaning to the word "brig." Ships had long been used to hold prisoners (as we have seen, the ports of England were filled with prison hulks in the late nineteenth century until Australia was settled as a penal colony), but it was not until the mid-nineteenth century that the expression came into use among American seamen to mean a portion of a ship reserved to hold prisoners. During the Gold Rush years (mid-nineteenth century), the shipping of the world arrived in San Francisco; true to the way of sailors on shore leave, many no doubt found themselves lodged in the town "brig."

7. Bancroft, *History*, 6:217 note.

8. Ibid.

9. *Alta*, April 3, 1850.

10. Bancroft, *History*, 6:215 and note.

CHAPTER 12: HERE COME THE DEMOCRATS

1. Theodore Hittell, *History*, 4:451.

2. Mass public meetings, organized ad hoc around emerging public issues, had been a prominent feature of American life since prerevolutionary times. It was at such a meeting in 1847 that residents of San Francisco tried to form a town government until stopped by the military authorities. The same method was used again in late 1848 in an attempt to found a territorial government. That is how the legislative assembly organized itself in 1849, and the public measures taken to address the problem of the Hounds represent a good example of how the process worked. In San Francisco, as we shall see, public meetings as a way of conducting public business were to remain a feature of public life long after the establishment of regularly organized representative government should have made them obsolete. Though no longer used as a means actually to organize a government, public meetings still serve the function of influencing regular officeholders.

3. Nineteenth-century urban politics, not just in San Francisco but in most large American cities, consisted of what were essentially private associations, political parties, running ahead of governmental willingness or ability to regulate them. In the absence of any central register of voters, voter fraud was rife. In older, settled towns, neighbors all knew each other. In the anonymity of the growing cities, however, voters could go from poll to poll, voting names from the graveyard if they wished unless challenged. A challenge often had to be backed up by a strong fist if it was to prevail. Each slate printed its own ballots, often in different colors

so that strong-arm poll watchers could determine how people voted. The schemes to subvert the process by fraud and violence were endless. (At one mayoral election between the tenure of the vigilance committees in San Francisco, a candidate is supposed to have rolled a cannon up to the First Ward polls to assure that the vote went as he thought it should.) Vestigial remains of the excitement that attended nineteenth-century polling can be found in recently repealed laws against selling liquor on election day (to keep candidates from buying votes with liquor) and the laws still in effect against electioneering within 100 feet of a polling place (to keep bullies from browbeating voters at the box).

4. Broderick had a hand in preparing the San Francisco charter. Often characterized as a Tammany-type boss who ruled San Francisco with strict party discipline, Broderick, according to his political biographer David A. Williams, *David C. Broderick, A Political Portrait*, p. 260, was rather an egalitarian in the Jacksonian mold who put his faith ultimately in the hands of the people. The form of government devised by the legislature in 1850 bears out that estimate. Authority, and derivatively control of the police, was vested in a common council elected by wards of equal population. Appointments to the police were made directly by members of the common council. The marshal (chief of police) was elected by popular vote. Proponents of a centralized police management and hiring on a basis of professional competence might argue against such a potentially corruptive system, but it was certainly democratic in its conception.

5. *Alta*, May 6, 1850.

6. Marryat, *Mountains and Molehills*, p. 23.

7. *Alta*, June 22, 1850. In the aftermath of the June 14, 1850, fire, Commercial Street, previously nonexistent, was opened from the end of Central Wharf at Leidesdorff Street to Kearny, to the great financial benefit of property owners along the new street line. (Now the city is trying to deed a portion of the street to Rockefeller interests.)

8. *Alta*, June 15, 1850.

9. Pacific Street played a significant part in the annals of crime in San Francisco. The first murder in American San Francisco occurred there, as we have already seen; during the period covered by our story, it will recur as the location of a number of crimes. A decade or so later, the street would gain worldwide fame as the center of the notorious Barbary Coast; and in living memory, it had a reputation in the police department as one of the toughest beats in town.

10. *Alta*, May 20, 1850; June 13, 1850.

11. See Robert M. Fogelson, *Big City Police*, pp. 119, 277; also, Silberman, *Criminal Violence*, p. 204. As few as 11% of petty thefts from households are reported to the police (*Criminal Victimization Surveys in San Francisco*, National Crime Survey Report, 1977). But for crimes of

burglary and robbery, such as we are tracking, the reporting percentage increases: 72% of commercial burglaries and 77% of commercial robberies are reported. The victimization survey quoted did not consider the crime of homicide on the grounds that there would be little difference between the actual incidence and the number that came to the attention of the police.

12. *Alta*, May 17, 1851.

13. *Alta*, April 27, 1850.

CHAPTER 13: CRIME WAVE

1. *Alta*, July 8, 1850; August 5, 1850; September 11, 21, 1850; October 17, 20, 1850. I wonder if Carmelita Bertrand was any relation to the Bertrand found dead in December 1848. If so, that family had a way of picking the wrong friends.

2. *Alta*, November 5, 24, 26, 1850.

3. *Alta*, December 3, 27, 31, 1850.

4. Bancroft, *Popular Tribunals*, 1:122.

5. *Alta*, May 2, 1850, citing figures given in the *Watchman*, a contemporary religious newspaper. Court statistics, reflecting only arrests made, do not correspond exactly to actual crimes committed because crimes are not counted when no arrest is made. Arrest statistics have a further problem as an indicator of the amount of crime: they tend to be a better measure of changes in the level of arrest activity of the police rather than of fluctuations in the actual amount of crime. In this instance, we are merely using such statistics as they relate to criminal homicide for which court, arrest, and actual incidence would show the highest degree of correlation.

6. Grand jury report of August 1850, published in the *Alta*, August 22, 1850.

7. The phenomenon as it related to Gold Rush San Francisco was remarked upon by Mary Williams, *History*, p. 170: "Crowded lodging houses and vicious resorts of the city offered shelter, without inconvenient curiosity, and one might live at will beneath the scrub oak and underbrush of the outlying sand hills. The ever shifting stream of transient sojourners diverted attention from particular individuals, and the few guardians of public safety had no way of identifying old offenders, whether they came from the other side of the Bay of San Francisco or the other side of the Pacific Ocean."

8. One of the marks of a modern American city, already evident in cities of the eastern seaboard by the middle of the nineteenth century, is the diversity of the population mix, which by bringing a heterogeneous combination of cultures and value systems in contact with each other can result in conflict and criminal violence. In Philadelphia, New York, and

other American cities of the time, problems of communal violence were increased by the mingling of native Protestant urban dwellers, new arrivals from the rural areas, Catholic immigrants from Europe, and black freedmen. In Gold Rush San Francisco the phenomenon was even more pronounced. The editors of the *Annals* (p. 257) described the population on a fine day on Portsmouth Square in a passage that is also a compendium of just about every racial and ethnic insult available to our nineteenth-century predecessors: "All races were represented. There were hordes of long pig-tailed, blear-eyed, rank-smelling Chinese, with their yellow faces and blue garbs; single dandy black fellows, of nearly as bad an odor, who strutted as only the negro can strut, in holiday clothes and clean white shirt; a few diminutive fiery-eyed Maylays, from the western archipelago, and some handsome Kanakas from the Sandwich Islands; jet-black, straight featured, Abyssinians; hideously tattooed New Zealanders; Feejee sailors and even the secluded Japanese, short, thick, clumsy, ever-bowing, jacketed fellows; the people of many races of Hindoo land; Russians with furs and sables; a stray, turbaned, stately Turk or two, and occasionally a half naked shivering Indian; multitudes of the Spanish race from every country of the Americas, partly pure, partly crossed with red blood,— Chilians, Peruvians and Mexicans, all with different shades of the same swarth complexion, black eyed and well-featured, proud of their beards and moustaches, their grease, dirt, and eternal gaudy serapes or darker cloaks; Spaniards from the mother country, more dignified, polite and pompous than their old colonial brethren; 'greasers' too, like them; great numbers of tall, goat-chinned, smooth-cheeked, oily-locked, lank-visaged, tobacco-chewing, large-limbed and featured, rough, care-worn, careless Americans from every State of the Union, dressed independently in every variety of garb, not caring a fig what people thought of them . . . fat, conceited Englishmen, who pretended to compete in shrewdness with the subtle Yankee. . . . Then there were bands of gay, easy-principled, philosophical Germans, Italians and Frenchmen of every cut and figure, their faces covered with hair, and with strange habiliments on their persons, and among whom might be particularly remarked numbers of thick-lipped, hook-nosed, ox-eyed, cunning, oily Jews."

9. There were no doubt many injured Hispanics who turned to crime only after being driven from the mines by the patently discriminatory foreign miners tax. But there has recently been much arrant nonsense published as history that holds that these bandit gangs were freedom fighters battling the foreign interlopers as sort of a guerrilla extension of the Mexican War. There were gangs of Hispanic bandidos in California long before the coming of the first Americans.

10. Bancroft, *California Inter Pocula*, p. 235. In August, the council tried to push through an ordinance that would have prohibited Australians

from operating drays, rowing boats for hire, or selling spiritous liquors. The measure failed in the board of assistant aldermen.

11. The system was breaking down. In older, settled societies, townsmen might be reluctant to appear capriciously in court and swear out a complaint on a neighbor they had to live with every day. In the anonymity of Gold Rush San Francisco, such inhibitions began to weaken, adding to the congestion of court business. The *Alta* on November 3, 1850, complained that "it is a common occurrence . . . for individuals to lodge complaints against others for larceny and trouble themselves no more about it." Nine out of ten cases were discharged, the paper said, because witnesses failed to appear—and, it may be added, after the defendant spent a lengthy time in jail waiting for a court date.

12. In the end, the councilmen of 1850 were probably as crooked as the norm for municipal officials of the time, but they were no worse. They certainly were not as corrupt as the *ayuntamiento* government that preceded them, whose members led the extralegal body that found members of the 1851 council at such fault.

13. Soulé, Gihon, and Nisbet, *Annals*, pp. 718ff.

14. William Heintz, *San Francisco's Mayors*, p. 9, citing Bancroft, *History*, 6:220, at the end of a very long note.

15. Lotchin, *From Hamlet to City*, p. 152.

16. *Alta*, July 15, 1850; November 20, 1850; and Phineas Blunt, journal.

17. *Alta*, December 31, 1850.

CHAPTER 14: A PREVIEW

1. One of the possibilities we have been considering is that some of the merchant establishment may have been responsible for setting some of the fires that afflicted Gold Rush San Francisco. Even if true, such a theory would have been operative only during the city's earlier boomtown phase. After they decided to make the town their home—a process that did not occur overnight—such a practice would have been less likely.

2. Soulé, Gihon, and Nisbet, *Annals*, p. 357.

3. This ageless type was perhaps best described at a hearing a couple of decades later into Chinatown affairs: "A bummer is a man," testified one witness, "who pretends to want something to do and does not want anything to do. He never begs, but borrows with no intention of repaying. He hangs around saloons with the expectation of somebody inviting him to take a drink. These are his principal characteristics. If there is a building being erected, or a dog fight, or a man falls down in a fit, or a drunken man is carried off, it is necessary for him to be there to see that it is done right" (Dillon, *Hatchet Men*, p. 165).

4. *Alta*, February 15, 1851.

5. A slung shot is simply made of a piece of metal, usually lead, rolled up in a piece of cloth or placed in a stocking. When swung, it could easily crush a victim's skull.

6. *Alta*, February 20, 1851.

7. Ibid.

8. *Courier*, February 20, 1851.

9. Bancroft, *Popular Tribunals*, 1:185.

10. Privately organized military companies of young men were a common feature of nineteenth-century urban life. Usually drawn from the same neighborhood or ethnic group, as were volunteer fire companies, these associations provided leisure-time diversions for young men before the age of electronic entertainment and other modern distractions. The companies competed in drill and target shooting competitions and participated in public parades. Ostensibly part of the militia, with this notable exception, they played a small part in the disorders of the time.

11. Soulé, Gihon, and Nisbet, *Annals*, p. 317.

12. Coleman wrote in *Century* magazine in 1891. He went on to be the president of the Executive Committee of the second Vigilance Committee in 1856. See Nunis, *San Francisco Vigilance Committee*, pp. 27ff.

13. Blunt, journal. Uncharacteristically, he made no entries on February 20, 21, or 22. The police department must have been working long hours those days.

14. Windred was sent to the station-house jail, from which he escaped a month later and returned to Australia. Berdue was eventually released from custody when the real Stuart was caught and identified as the perpetrator of the Jansen robbery.

15. Williams, *History*, p. 170.

16. It has been pointed out that this would be a high rate of murder by current standards, which is correct. But (see note 5, chapter 4) we must make adjustments based on profound demographic differences between Gold Rush San Francisco and now before any meaningful comparisons can be made.

17. George R. Stewart, *Committee of Vigilance: Revolution in San Francisco, 1851*, pp. 7 and 327.

18. Williams, *History*, p. 171.

19. Stewart, *Committee of Vigilance*, p. 7.

CHAPTER 15: OFFICIALDOM UNDER FIRE

1. Bancroft, *Popular Tribunals*, 1:132.

2. Soulé, Gihon, and Nisbet, *Annals*, p. 278.

3. Ibid., p. 327.

4. Ibid., p. 328. Mayor Geary, who has received a generally compli-

mentary report card in the history books, seems to have been less than perfectly clean on this issue. After the *Alta* suggested that the scrip was being recirculated in violation of the law, Geary and four councilmen hastily burned a batch, as required, but without publishing the serial numbers, which was also a provision of the law.

5. For example, *Alta*, December 18, 20, 21, 24, 26, and 31, 1850.

6. Soulé, Gihon, and Nisbet, *Annals*, p. 324.

7. *Alta*, February 21, 1851.

8. It was not a problem unique to San Francisco. See Johnson, *Policing the Urban Underworld*, p. 59: "By the 1840s a class of bail bondsmen had appeared who spent their time obtaining the rapid release of captured criminals. Arrest had become a routine hazard for some felons, and 'straw bail' (a bond which the thief had no intention to honor) developed as a response to that problem. . . . They [thieves] usually gave a false name in court and quickly found a surety. The thief paid his bondsman a fee plus enough money to cover the forfeiture of bail and returned to work in a matter of hours."

9. *Alta*, April 8, 1851.

10. *Alta*, April 9, 24, 1851.

11. *Alta*, May 15, 1851.

12. Williams, *History*, p. 177.

13. *San Francisco Evening Picayune*, January 6, 1851.

14. *Alta*, February 14, 1851. Before concluding that Gold Rush police officers were particularly negligent of their duty, consider that one recent study (Jan M. Chaiken and Marcia R. Chaiken, "Crime, Trends and Targets," *Wilson Quarterly* [Spring 1983]: 120) reports that currently 12% of police make half of the arrests that result in convictions.

15. *Alta*, December 31, 1850.

16. See note 2 above.

17. Lotchin, *From Hamlet to City*, p. 152.

18. Soulé, Gihon, and Nisbet, *Annals*, p. 279.

19. Felix Argenti, prominent banker and member of the soon to be organized Committee of Vigilance, held the mortgage on the county jail property at usurious (though prevailing) rates of interest. Charles Gillespie, another prominent member of the committee, was involved with at least one member of the court of sessions in a scam to sell the county courthouse site at an extravagant price.

20. *Alta*, April 6, 1851.

21. *San Francisco Chronicle*, February 26, 1896.

22. *San Francisco Herald*, June 4, 1851. See also Bancroft, *Popular Tribunals*, 1:317, and W. H. Hutchinson, *California: The Golden Shore by the Sundown Sea*, p. 321. The courts now use plea bargaining to accomplish the same result. At the time Parsons was in office, there was a

general expectation (now reserved to conservative critics of the courts) that statutes imposing such and such a sentence for the commission of such and such an act meant what they said. As a practical matter, there are far too many offenses now to interpret the dictates of the law literally. If that were done, an unacceptable percentage of the population would be perpetually in jail (or perhaps people would stop committing so many crimes). Parsons was on the leading edge of experience with the phenomenon of more crime than the system could digest.

23. In the late 1970s in San Francisco, with a multimillion-dollar computer system designed in large part to track the dispositions of criminal cases, it was almost an impossibility to track 500 particular grand theft arrests. The criminal justice system is misnamed—it is not a system. It was the responsibility of various elements to introduce information about the status of the arrestees into the computer as they passed through the different agencies. Entry by some agencies was spotty at best. Also, some cases were continued so that no final dispositions were available. The results were thus not complete. So we should not be hasty in judging our precomputer predecessors so harshly for not being able to account for all the arrestees.

24. Silberman, *Criminal Violence*, p. 259.

CHAPTER 16: THE LAST STRAWS

1. *Alta*, April 29, 1851.

2. Theodore Hittell, *History*, 4:59.

3. Soulé, Gihon, and Nisbet, *Annals*, p. 366.

4. One factor contributing to the glut of goods is that by 1851 California had begun to produce more of its own needs. In the first Gold Rush years, most of what the immigrants used was imported (even lumber in an area containing vast stands of redwood timber). As more and more argonauts failed at finding gold, they began to look around and liked what they saw. They fell back on earlier farming skills and began to produce foodstuffs that had previously been imported. By 1851, this process had begun to affect the need for imported goods.

5. *Alta*, May 9, 1851.

6. *California Courier*, June 16, 1851.

7. Bancroft, *Popular Tribunals*, 1:162.

8. George Hampton, *Image*, January 25, 1987. The San Francisco press was willing to accept the arson theory, but when the suggestion was made by the city's commercial competitors that perhaps San Francisco might be too susceptible to devastating fires because of the prevailing topography and spring and summer winds, the *Alta* leaped to the city's defense: "Have they not heard of terrible fires of New Orleans, Baton

Rouge, Boston, Brooklyn, Pittsburgh, Philadelphia, New York? . . . Is there a city in the world where extension of civilization has not suffered from fire?" Just before the May 3 fire started, at the end of April, the paper offered another possibility, saying that "in the rear of Wilson's Exchange on Dupont and in many other places about town, burning coals of fire are disposed of carelessly. A single firebrand could burn down the city." Roger Lotchin accepts the news accounts that arson was rife on the grounds that they are the only source we have. I do not. Some of history lies between the lines. There was no doubt some arson, as there is in any age, but there is ample independent evidence that the newspapers inflated the amount occurring in Gold Rush San Francisco to serve their own interests. And if the arsons did occur, Rosales's idea that they were the work of businessmen themselves rings truer than the charge that they were caused by Sydney criminals.

9. James M. Parker, *The San Francisco Directory, 1852–1853*, p. 19.

10. *Alta*, May 23, 26, 1851, and *California Courier*, June 16, 1851.

11. Soulé, Gihon, and Nisbet, *Annals*, p. 567.

12. *Alta*, January 23, 29, 1851; March 16, 28, 1851.

13. *Alta*, April 13, 1851; May 4, 21, 1851; June 3, 23, 1851.

14. Perhaps this figure is not out of line for the whole of California. The apparently different rates of murder in urban and rural frontier California are discussed in note 6, chapter 26.

15. *Alta*, March 16, 1851.

16. *Alta*, May 29, 1851. In June, the *Euphemia* was towed to North Beach, where it was put into service as a lunatic asylum.

17. Calls were made for the establishment of a detective capability to follow up on crimes for which no one was arrested at the time of the offense. By now it must have been obvious that the ideal of prevention did not work perfectly. Eastern cities had retained their constables as a detective police. San Francisco was not to have a detective force until November 1853.

18. There is little else he could have done. According to the terms of the Judiciary Act passed by the state legislature that spring, the May term of the grand jury had been eliminated. The indictment against Lewis was returned by a grand jury convened by a visiting judge in May. If Parsons had continued with a trial brought about by the indictment of an illegally convened grand jury, he might have pleased his detractors, but he would most certainly have been overturned on appeal. As it was, Lewis was indicted by the July grand jury and eventually found guilty at a regular trial in July.

19. The above crime reports were extracted from daily editions of the *Alta*. Bancroft in his *Popular Tribunals* (1:203) lists the crimes he was able to find in June 1851. His compilation serves as a cross-check on the

completeness with which the newspapers reported on crime. Much closer to the events of 1851, when records were still readily available and with superb research resources at his disposal, Bancroft was able to come up with very few crimes not mentioned in the daily editions of the *Alta*. When all crimes are read together, it seems as though they were numerous. But really, there were not very many, at least by current standards.

20. *Herald*, June 4, 1851.

21. *Alta*, June 8, 1851.

22. *California Courier*, June 10, 1851.

CHAPTER 17: LEX TALONIS

1. Charles Rembar, *The Law of the Land*, pp. 92–96. Those who yearn for such simple justice should recall that the "hue and cry" was followed by the less often referred to "catch and kill," often without any inquiry into whether the accused had done anything wrong. Says Rembar: "The administration of most early Anglo-Saxon law was committed by two institutions: the blood feud and lynching. . . . Primitive societies typically use family-fighting to redress certain kinds of misbehavior, and mob execution for others. As society gets stronger, it devises better methods, and finally declares unlawful what were once the law's respected implements."

2. *San Francisco Chronicle*, July 8, 1987.

3. Brown, *Strain of Violence*, p. 67.

4. Ibid., pp. 21, 97.

5. Bancroft, *Popular Tribunals*, 1:62–67.

6. Ibid., 1:144.

7. Jackson, *Gold Dust*, pp. 304–5. In October, a drunken man who had killed his wife was hanged at Georgetown. The same month, "Irish Dick" was hanged at Placerville for stabbing a man who called him a cheat.

8. *Alta*, December 31, 1850.

9. *Alta*, January 5, 1851; February 7, 1851.

10. *Evening Picayune*, January 6, 1851.

11. *Alta*, February 9, 25, 1851.

12. *Alta*, March 5, 1851.

13. *Alta*, March 10, 1851; April 1, 1851. Forty years later, Coleman cast himself as the one who kept Berdue and Windred from summary justice. Late memories of such matters, particularly of those who have something to explain, should be viewed with some skepticism.

14. *Alta*, April 24, 1851; May 10, 1851.

CHAPTER 18: JOHN JENKINS

1. Bancroft and Coleman make much of the fact that Californians in 1849 felt so secure in their property that they did not even bother to lock

their doors (see notes 13 and 14, chapter 9). It seems that others felt the same way, even in the supposedly crime-ridden year of 1851.

2. Williams, *History*, p. 210.

3. Ibid., p. 212. See also Josiah Royce, *California, From the Conquest in 1846 to the Second Vigilance Committee in San Francisco*, p. 420 note. It was an unusually clear night for June in San Francisco, which means that the customary cooling summer fogs were absent, making it a good time for outside activity. Remember that the Hounds riot occurred on an "unseasonably warm" night in 1849 and the Berdue excitement started on a false spring day in February. Pleasant weather may not cause public disturbances, but it certainly creates an environment that facilitates their eruption.

4. Williams, *History*, p. 214.

5. Lewis, *This Was San Francisco*, p. 115, citing the journals of J. Goldsborough Bruff.

6. Brannan published a letter in the *Picayune* denying that he had claimed credit in the Union Hotel for hanging Jenkins. (He did not deny hanging Jenkins, just claiming credit for it.) Broderick, perhaps missing the distinction, promptly replied that Brannan had led the Jenkins matter from start to finish and was notorious for violence and contempt for the law, known as a turbulent man, ever ready to trample on the laws that opposed his private opinions and ends.

7. Attorneys, then and now, do not command a high public opinion. Clarke emerges as a truly principled and courageous man. It is one thing to disagree philosophically with the imposition of summary justice. It is another to stand up alone to the bloodlust of a crowd favoring hanging.

8. Stewart, *Committee of Vigilance*, p. 107: "he gave his name as John Jenkins, a palpable and almost arrogant *alias*, since that name would be for an Englishman practically John Doe."

9. Robert Hughes, *The Fatal Shore*, p. 235.

10. *Picayune*, June 12, 1851.

11. A review of every copy of the *Alta* up to the time of the establishment of the committee mentions the names of the other Australian criminals who came to the attention of the committee. That of Jenkins (or Simpton) is not among them. If he was as bad as we have been led to believe, it would seem that he would have been arrested for something, like all the others.

12. Helen Holdredge, *The House of the Strange Woman*, p. 39, mentions that, after the hanging, Marshal Crozier was present at the bar of the Union Hotel and is alleged to have exclaimed, "To hell with the courts."

13. Williams, *Papers*, p. 828.

CHAPTER 19: THE COMMITTEE TAKES CHARGE

1. Williams, *Papers*, p. 806.
2. Royce, *California*, p. 418.
3. Talbot H. Green, Brannan's associate on the *ayuntamiento*, would no doubt have been a member; but he had left the state, having been found out to be Paul Geddes, who had deserted his family and absconded with his company's funds in the East a decade before.
4. Williams, *Papers*, p. 806.
5. Charles Neider, ed., *The Autobiography of Mark Twain* pp. 300–301.
6. Mark Twain, *Roughing It*, p. 267.
7. Ibid., p. 270.
8. Wollenberg, *Golden Gate Metropolis*, p. 109.
9. Williams, *History*, p. 257.
10. Bancroft, *Popular Tribunals*, 1:240.
11. Ibid.
12. Williams, *History*, p. 223 note.
13. Royce, *California*, p. 324, discussing the unwillingness of California argonauts to fund criminal justice programs, says: "Whose gold, now hoarded by the pound in insecure tents, the prey to every vagabond, might have contributed to build a strong jail . . . ? Or, perhaps, was it not of a truth felt unnecessary to build a strong jail—unnecessary just because one chose in one's heart, meanwhile, to think ropes a little cheaper than bricks, and, for the purpose, just as strong?"
14. *Alta*, June 16, 1851.
15. Williams, *History*, p. 250.
16. *Alta*, June 19, 1851.
17. *Picayune*, July 18, 1851.
18. Asbury, *Barbary Coast*, p. 69.
19. Soulé, Gihon, and Nisbet, *Annals*, p. 612.
20. Marryat, *Mountains and Molehills*, p. 221.
21. Charles E. O'Hara, *Fundamentals of Criminal Investigation*, p. 214. The seeming difference between the statistics offered by O'Hara and those cited by *Firehouse* magazine (see chapter 10) can perhaps best be explained by the fact that O'Hara is viewing the issue from the perspective of a criminal investigator more interested in "serious" fires, whereas the earlier cited figures were put together by fire fighters whose day-to-day experience shows that many arson fires are set by pranksters who might set a debris box on fire for a little "innocent" excitement. O'Hara does not even consider fires set by vandals.
22. It seems that there were other examples of fires set by blacks for revenge in antebellum America; see Hollon, *Frontier Justice*, pp. 46–47, and Brown, *Strain of Violence*, p. 239.

23. In 1862 (*Alta*, June 3, 1862), Sacramento was plagued with a number of arson fires thought to be the work "of an organized band of desperadoes, either for gain or a spirit of malice." After an investigation, a number of young men were arrested, who, it was feared, had "been led into crime from rivalry as members of different fire companies. . . ." The editor was reminded of "similar instances . . . in Utica, New York, some twelve or fifteen years ago, in which a number of the scions of the most respectable resident families were detected setting fire to houses for the purpose of creating an alarm and bringing out the engines."

24. O'Hara, *Criminal Investigation*, p. 211.

25. *Picayune*, July 13, 1851.

26. *Herald*, *Alta*, and *Picayune*, June 13, 1851.

CHAPTER 20: THE REAL JAMES STUART

1. The committee immediately sent word that it had the wrong man to Marysville, where Berdue, sentenced to death as Stuart, was awaiting his execution. Authorities there were at first doubtful but finally sent the innocent Berdue to San Francisco to continue serving his sentence for the Jansen robbery. He was eventually released in August, when it became clear to everyone that he had not been involved in that crime either.

2. The man's true name was never determined with certainty. In addition to Stephens, he also used the names Carlisle and Campbell and others. Stephens may as well have been his true name as the others. In the document agreeing to reveal his confederates, he used that name, but his confession was given under the name Stuart. Perhaps that is the name the committee insisted upon.

3. He admitted that he was the one who hit Jansen with the slung shot and said that he and his colleagues had agreed to burn the town, if Berdue and Windred had hanged.

4. According to Stuart, he wanted to break into the First District station house and free his confederates, but others told him to let the lawyers do it; the next day, lawyer Parbut got one of them out.

5. There is some confusion about what this contract was. There is a signed document in the Vigilance Committee papers (signed by James Stephens and attested to by President Stephen Payran) in which Stuart agrees to implicate and convict at least ten of his criminal confederates and "make a full confession of all the details and of all knowledge of the various scoundrels now in this country. . . ." (Williams, *Papers*, p. 223). Williams thinks he was hanged because he did not admit the Moore murder. He more than lived up to the contract by naming twenty-six confederates, and there is nothing in the agreement that would require the admission of personal crimes. He certainly could not convict anyone if he was hanged, and that is exactly what happened. Some thus escaped the toils of the law.

6. Williams, *Papers*, p. 225 note.

7. Williams, *History*, p. 290. He escaped from San Quentin in 1854.

8. Ibid., p. 283.

9. San Francisco police officers were not required to wear distinctive uniforms until 1856. In England, police uniforms were part of the Peelian reform of the 1820s and 1830s, but in the atmosphere of individual freedom that pervaded postrevolutionary America, uniforms were looked upon as a badge of servitude. Officers in New York went on strike in 1844 to resist an order to wear uniforms. From 1849, officers in San Francisco were provided with badges, at first circular silver disks about the size of a $10 gold piece, later (by 1852) changed to a star. There were frequent press comments over the years that officers would sometimes avoid identifying themselves as police by wearing their stars in the folds of their clothing. By 1856, patrol officers in San Francisco were in uniform; by the time of the Civil War, when most young male Americans found themselves in some sort of uniform, the arguments citing servitude were put to rest. Even today, however, "plainclothes" work is looked upon as the most desirable among police officers.

10. Bancroft, *Popular Tribunals*, 1:370.

11. Eldredge, *Beginnings*, p. 564.

12. Davis, *Seventy-five Years*. p. 116. Santillán was the former curate of Mission Dolores before the conquest who claimed title to most of the lands later claimed and sold by San Francisco. See also Williams, *History*, p. 317; Bancroft, *Popular Tribunals*, 2:513; and Myers Myers, *Reign of Terror*, p. 190.

CHAPTER 21: A DOUBLE STANDARD

1. *Alta*, September 18, 1852.

2. *Alta*, June 22, 1852; August 12, 1852.

3. *Alta*, May 16, 23, 1851.

4. *Picayune*, January 6, 1851. Granted, the Bill of Rights only regulates the conduct of agents of the government, but if the regular authorities were held to that standard, they should also have been applied to the vigilantes.

5. *Alta*, June 18, 1851.

6. *Picayune*, June 18, 1851.

7. *Alta*, July 15, 1851.

8. Williams, *History*, p. 243.

9. *Alta*, July 10, 1851.

10. William B. Secrest, *Dangerous Men*, pp. 5–8. Lemon was prevented from killing Graham by the intervention of a bystander. In a return duel in Benicia a month or so later, Graham seriously wounded Lemon and the affair was ended.

11. Williams, *History*, p. 243.

12. Bancroft, *Popular Tribunals*, 1:214. The committee jealously guarded its records, containing unanswered slanders against many of its enemies, for decades. Finally, they were released to Bancroft so that he could write his sympathetic history.

13. Williams, *Papers*, p. 223.

14. Williams, *History*, p. 331 note. The contemptuous tone of the attorneys' reply calls into question the belief that people were generally terrified of the vigilantes.

15. Ibid., p. 231 Helen Holdredge in *The House of the Strange Woman*, pp. 160–61, without citing any sources, claims that James Arrington (or Hetherington; see index of Williams, *Papers*, p. 865) was from North Carolina. According to Holdredge, his brother William, a member of both the first and second committees, interceded for him and he was never in fact deported even though the committee claimed he had been to save face. Williams does not show William as a member of the first committee (*Papers*, p. 806) under either the spelling Arrington or Hetherington, but she does list him (*History*, p. 473) as a member of the Executive Committee of the second committee. It would have been helpful if Holdredge had documented some of the numerous charges she made against members of the vigilance committees. If she is correct, an even more pronounced reevaluation of their motives than is warranted by the existing record would be in order.

16. Blunt, journal. Contemporaries Barry and Patten, in their *San Francisco 1850*, p. 97, agree that he came from Boston. According to Whittaker (Williams, *History*, p. 284), Kay went first from Europe to the British penal colony at Tasmania and then to California. The committee would later complain that Kay had slipped through their fingers. Williams believes that this occurred because his departure on August 1 was prior to Whittaker's confession implicating him irretrievably in the crimes of the day. Yet the committee was in possession of Stuart's confession implicating Kay as early as July 9. Though it picked up several lesser criminals, it does not seem to have wanted Kay too badly. One is forced to wonder. The *Alta* of October 17, 1858, reported Kay's death in Boston from heart disease.

17. Williams, *Papers*, p. 230 note.

18. *Alta*, July 29, 1851.

19. Williams, *Papers*, p. 305.

20. He himself was later hanged by the 1856 incarnation of vigilance after killing a man in a shootout over disputed land in Marin County. (He killed another man in 1853, the same Baldwin who had been the victim in the theft from the Customhouse in Monterey—the case in which Stuart testified in the spring of 1851.)

21. *Alta*, August 14, 1851.

22. As pointed out by Bancroft (*Popular Tribunals* 1:242), the book of

minutes, maintained from the beginning, stopped at July 4 (when Payran replaced Brannan as president of the Executive Committee). In between, Bancroft says, were only loose papers, many of them half obliterated. One wonders what disappeared before Williams got to them. She says (*Papers*, p. viii) that important items available to Bancroft were missing when she came to do her work. It is likely that they were lost by the natural passage of time, but it is also possible that there was some judicious pruning done.

23. Theodore Hittell, *History*, 3:324.

CHAPTER 22: LAW AND ORDER

1. Williams, *History*, p. 271.
2. Ibid., p. 273.
3. Asbury, *Barbary Coast*, p. 78.
4. Williams, *Broderick*, p. 260.
5. *San Francisco Call*, May 15, 1887.
6. *Alta*, July 4, 1850; September 4, 1850.
7. *Alta*, December 19, 1850.
8. *Alta*, February 19, 1851.
9. *San Francisco Examiner*, January 16, 1881.
10. *Alta*, March 13, 1851.
11. *Alta*, May 28, 1851; July 22, 1851.
12. Williams, *History*, p. 321.
13. Duane was a thug and a bully, but he was not a coward. He was always in the forefront when there was fighting to be done. He was a member of the Empire Fire Company and frequently cited for bravery at the scene of fires. He was elected chief of the fire department in 1853 by members of the volunteer companies. On one occasion, he was charged with stomping and breaking the arm of a man who had turned in a false fire alarm. In 1855, a notorious dance hall he kept on Pacific Street was closed down by the authorities; the same year, he was involved in a fight with another police officer. He was banished from California by the 1856 committee but returned to San Francisco in 1860. Almost immediately (although weakened by food poisoning, which debilitated him for the rest of his life), Duane got in another fight in which he assaulted his adversary with his cane. In May 1866, he came up behind a man on Merchant Street with whom he had been disputing the ownership of a piece of land and shot him fatally in the back. He was acquitted in the trial that followed. Duane died in 1887, in bed.

14. Control of the venue where political discussions were conducted and decided was an important factor in political victory even into this century. George Dorsey, *Christofer of San Francisco*, pp. 11–12, reports that in the 1911 election for mayor of San Francisco in which "Sunny Jim"

Rolph bested incumbent P. H. McCarthy, "Fist fights broke out daily and, since McCarthy controlled the police, Rolph had to hire a phalanx of bodyguards to keep the peace at his street-corner rallies."

CHAPTER 23: WHITTAKER AND MCKENZIE

1. Judge Parsons asked Judge Campbell to remove the critical parts from the jury's report. Campbell refused, and Parsons resigned from the district court in October.

2. On August 12, Adams withdrew his not guilty plea in the Stevenson burglary; by the end of the month, after being adjudged guilty in that and another theft case, he was sentenced to twenty years' imprisonment.

3. *Alta*, August 14, 29, 1851.

4. It was generally believed that they were bad men, but there was really nothing to tie them to the crime. In common belief, murderers are supposed to return to the scene of their crime, but ten days later? Brannan was probably just being his impulsive self.

5. More gold by far was eventually to be produced by the Australian find than was taken out of California. On August 8, the departure of a ship loaded with returnees was reported in the *Alta*.

6. He had been arrested with James Hughes in late 1850 for robbery, but he was released for lack of evidence. He was also named by Stuart as one of his confederates.

7. As with some other prominent actors in our story, Whittaker was probably not his real name (Bancroft, *Popular Tribunals*, 1:335–49). A thirty-three-year-old Englishman, he had been transported to Australia at eighteen for housebreaking, been given a conditional pardon in 1849, and come to San Francisco in the Gold Rush. Stuart names him in his confession without giving him a prominent place. According to Hetherington, he was the smartest thief in the gang.

8. There is a reference in the *Alta* of November 16, 1850, that he had been sentenced to a $100 fine and ten days in the brig for stomping a man.

9. His statement about bribing Tilford's court squares with independent evidence in the press, but it would still be useful had there been some cross-examination. There are too many examples of persons under the control of their interrogators admitting anything their accusers wanted to hear. This is not to say that Whittaker was not a thief; but if the officials were as venal as he said, why did the Vigilance Committee not follow up?

10. Williams, *Papers*, p. 322.

11. *Alta*, August 25, 1851.

12. Williams, *Papers*, p. 462.

13. History has not been too generous with McDougal, but he was truly a brave man in this instance. A settler from before the Gold Rush, he was

nominated to run for lieutenant governor only because of his humorous quips at the constitutional convention, it was said. No one ever expected him to be governor; but when Burnett resigned in 1851, he was elevated to the office. He had not even been nominated by his own Democratic party in May to succeed himself in the September election. It was because the elections were approaching, thinks Bancroft (*Popular Tribunals*, 1:350), that McDougal injected himself into the affairs of San Francisco. "The existence of a popular organization for the suppression of crime," says Bancroft, "was a standing reproach on the honesty and efficiency of the authorities."

14. If the formerly supine mayor really intended to raid vigilante headquarters, unqualified support for the committee was falling apart.

15. On August 23, Van Bokkelen resigned as chief of police, saying he had been chided by members of the committee about the escape and that he did not want the committee to become less effective on his account. Oscar Smith, a member of the regular police force who had resigned to become a member of the Vigilance Committee, was appointed as his replacement.

16. In answer to this, the Vigilance Committee published a card (notice) that McDougal had promised to replace any judges they hanged.

17. Bancroft, *Popular Tribunals*, 1:357.

18. *Herald*, August 21, 1851.

19. Williams, *History*, p. 302.

20. Myers Myers, *Reign of Terror*, p. 65.

21. *Alta*, August 26, 1851.

22. *Herald*, August 26, 1851.

23. Williams, *Papers*, p. 468 note.

24. Myers Myers, *Reign of Terror*, p. 64. Myers Myers, who, it must be admitted, is not a particular fan of the committee, asserts, "As has been pointed out, arson is a felony from which burglars and robbers cannot profit—unless, of course, they are paid for it by those who do find blazes worth while. And that someone didn't wish McKenzie and Whittaker to talk can fairly be inferred from the extreme lengths to which the Vigilantes went, in order to whisk the two away from the sound waves audible to the living."

25. Stewart, *Committee of Vigilance*, p. 244.

26. Bancroft, *Popular Tribunals*, 1:360.

CHAPTER 24: VIGILANCE TRIUMPHANT

1. There are always a few respectable police buffs who are willing to serve as reserve officers, and there are those so enamored of ordering

others around that they would accept the job for nothing, but in general the only way to get adequate police service is to pay for it. One exception would seem to be the much-publicized Guardian Angels, a group of inner-city youths who purport to patrol high-crime areas. In fact, their patrol activities are more illusory than real, except when the cameras are rolling. Patrols are established in city after city; but after the television cameras retire, they soon fade away.

2. "We are worn out from our nightly watching" wrote "Justice" to the *Alta* on June 8, 1851.

3. In the midst of the Whittaker/McKenzie affair, on August 17, 1851, nine principal members of the Executive Committee offered to resign, citing jealousies within the group (Williams, *Papers*, p. 499).

4. Williams, *History*, p. 323.

5. Ibid., p. 326. There is some suggestion in party papers that the ticket was gotten up by land monopolists to realize their intention to acquire state lands. Brannan and Coleman were among those who initiated the slate.

6. Despite his earlier attempt to have the grand jury indict members of the committee for the murder of Stuart, they liked his strong law and order stand and endorsed his candidacy.

7. It would go down again before the end of the year; but at the start of the fall season in September, things looked good.

8. *Alta*, October 3, 15, 1851.

9. *Alta*, October 14, 19, 1851.

10. *Times and Transcript*, November 16, 1851.

11. *Alta*, October 10, 1851; November 10, 1851.

12. *Alta*, November 12, 1851; December 31, 1851.

13. Williams, *History*, p. 341.

14. Dillon, *Embarcadero*, p. 64. Long, sleek, and swift clipper ships had begun to replace slower fat-bottomed merchant vessels on important runs even before the Gold Rush, but the migration to California and the great profits promised by a speedy voyage gave impetus to the conversion. It can be said that the California trade gave birth to the golden age of sailing clippers. There was a definite economic advantage in having the best time.

15. *Alta*, November 1, 1851. Throughout, the *Alta* had counseled caution. On October 31, the paper counseled the public to suspend judgment until all the facts were in. The paper also cautioned, not unlike its predecessor in 1847, against any action that might convince shipmasters that the port of San Francisco was inhospitable, thus causing them to take their business elsewhere. (Let justice be done though the heavens fall.)

16. Williams, *History*, p. 343.

17. Lotchin, *From Hamlet to City*, p. 200.
18. Dillon, *Embarcadero*, p. 151.
19. Blunt, journal.

CHAPTER 25: THE YEAR AFTER

1. Asbury, *Barbary Coast*, p. 75: "During the two years that followed the hanging of Whittaker and McKenzie, San Francisco was as peaceful and law-abiding a city as could be found on the American continent. . . . Comparatively few murders were committed, no more devastating fires occurred, and hold-ups and robberies were the exception rather than the rule." More recently, Decker, in *Fortunes and Failures*, reports, "The 'necktie' justice of the 1851 Vigilance Committee did have an immediate effect. The number of murders, assaults, and robberies in San Francisco declined, the police force was enlarged [incorrect], and the courts prosecuted and convicted more vigorously those indicted on criminal charges."

2. Soulé, Gihon, and Nisbet, *Annals*, p. 421.

3. This was the sixth version of the Jenny Lind (the others had burned). It was erected of stone by impresario Tom Maguire at a cost of $160,000 and opened in October 1851. Since its opening, it had been a money-losing proposition.

4. There was probably as much corruption attached to its acquisition as was common at the time. According to the *Annals* (p. 396), after the Jenny Lind was remodeled into a city hall it turned out not to be such a bad deal after all. It certainly lasted a lot longer than the ramshackle wooden wreck bought by the *ayuntamiento* for only $50,000 less. After an earthquake in 1868, the third floor was removed from the Jenny Lind City Hall; but the basic structure held up until 1895, when the building was taken down to make way for the Hall of Justice erected that year at Kearny and Washington streets.

5. Eldredge, *Beginnings*, p. 607.

6. John Geary, one of the funded debt commissioners who discouraged the purchase of the lands, was among those, along with Broderick, it must be admitted, who bought properties for a song. Heydenfelt, the attorney who advised Geary and the other members of the commission that the sales would not hold up in court, became a member of the state supreme court that finally approved the sales.

7. Hot prowl burglaries are entries to steal from an inhabited dwelling while the inhabitants are present, as distinguished from those that take place in empty or uninhabited dwellings. As is obvious, it takes a great deal more courage or foolhardiness to commit a hot prowl burglary, with the chance the inhabitants will be aroused. As already mentioned, the fact

that many people slept on business premises during the night hours in Gold Rush San Francisco no doubt helped to keep the burglary rate down.

8. If it seems unusual that the thief could disappear so quickly, it should be recognized that the quality of urban darkness was different in the early 1850s than in later years. There were a few streetlights only in the most frequented streets of the city. The only light on the streets of the rest of the city came from the moon and stars and from windows. Late on moonless nights, muggers and other thieves could sit quietly in the darkness, unobserved even by police officers a few feet away, and wait for an unsuspecting victim to walk by. The darkness was like that now found in the country on starless, moonless nights: complete and impenetrable, except by artificial illumination.

9. The escapee's name was also Hawkins—William (he may have been related to the recently arrested black burglar of the same name who was at the time being held in jail on a burglary charge).

10. *Alta*, October 29, 1852.

11. Williams, *History*, p. 351.

12. Bancroft, *Popular Tribunals*, 2:18.

13. Williams, *History*, p. 351.

14. Edward D. Townsend, *The California Diary of General E. D. Townsend*, p. 70.

15. Bancroft, *Popular Tribunals*, 1:746.

16. T. H. Watkins and R. R. Olmsted, *Mirror of the Dream*, p. 47.

17. See note 14 above; see also *Alta*, October 15, 1852. One of the witnesses who had assisted in the arrest of Forni testified that before he was arrested Forni ran his knife blade in and out of the sand several times (to wipe off the blood?). The victim's knife was found securely in his own scabbard.

CHAPTER 26: SOME OBSERVATIONS

1. *San Francisco Examiner*, March 9, 1987.

2. *San Francisco Chronicle*, July 8, 1987.

3. *San Francisco Chronicle*, May 9, 12, 1987.

4. As discussed previously, the Gold Rush population of San Francisco was comprised almost exclusively of the highest crime profile group— young, single males. From such a population a much higher crime rate can be expected than from a city with a more usual population mix by sex and age. Estimates of the population of San Francisco (which grew from 2,000 at the beginning of 1849 to 50,000 by 1853) range from 25,000 to 40,000 in 1850. One recent source places it at 34,000. There were 16 reported criminal homicides in the city that year. Compared directly

with modern urban homicide figures, that translates into 48 homicides per 100,000 population, close to the current murder rate of 49.11 per 100,000 between 1982 and 1986 for Detroit, the city with the highest murder rate in the nation. The Gold Rush rate was then much higher than the current rate of 13.20 for San Francisco. But when the severely distorted demographic profile of Gold Rush San Francisco is taken into consideration, the rate could more reasonably compared to cities now in the middle range like New York (21.70) or Washington, D.C. (28.67), or with the national average for American cities (23.67). See note 5, chapter 4. In any event, at its worst the San Francisco experience was nothing like the figures in the legend, which would translate into 1,000 homicides per 100,000 in current terms.

5. Soulé, Gihon, and Nisbet, *Annals*, p. 567.

6. Perhaps such a high figure might have been a reality in the whole of California. As previously noted, there are indications that rural homicide rates in the frontier era far exceeded anything in San Francisco. We have seen that San Diego County had a homicide rate of 117 per 100,000 in the period between 1870 and 1875 (note 18, chapter 5). In 1855, a period closer to our own period of analysis, according to Patricia Bowie ("The Shifting Gold Rush Scenario, California to Australia to New Zealand," *Californians* [January/February 1988]: 23), there were 118 known murders in the mining counties of California. James King of William, editor of the *San Francisco Bulletin*, published a chart the same year (John Bruce, *Gaudy Century*, p. 42) claiming that there were 487 murders in California in one year, for which 6 were hanged by sheriffs and 46 by mobs. It would be interesting to see a study that comprehensively compares rural to urban murder rates in frontier California.

7. *California Chronicle*, December 15, 1853. In reporting on the trial of Charles R. Drew for the killing of Doctor Henry R. Gillis the preceding September, the paper said that "the District Attorney stated, in the course of his remarks, that twelve hundred murders had been committed in this city and county within the past four years, and there had been but one conviction before the courts."

8. Myers Myers, *Reign of Terror*, p. 50.

9. Williams, *History*, p. 390.

10. Ibid., p. 389 note.

11. *Herald*, April 14, 1852.

12. Williams, *History*, p. 390.

13. Bancroft, *Popular Tribunals*, 1:122.

14. Lotchin, *From Hamlet to City*, p. 374 note 41.

15. Brown, *Strain of Violence*, p. 124.

16. Ibid., p. 127.

17. Rembar, *Law of the Land*, p. 94.

18. Brown, *Strain of Violence*, p. 73.

19. Note 2 above.

20. Ibid.

21. See note 20, chapter 23. Also, Williams, in her *History*, p. 301 note, cites one writer who commented that "brutal levity characterized the execution, and so shocked public sentiment that the popular approval of the Committee was greatly weakened, and contributions were withdrawn."

22. Rembar, *Law of the Land*, p. 93.

Bibliography

BOOKS

Asbury, Herbert. *The Barbary Coast.* New York: Garden City Publishing Company, 1933.

Atherton, Gertrude. *Golden Gate Country.* New York: Duell, Sloan and Pearce, 1945.

Bailey, Paul. *Sam Brannan and the California Mormons.* Los Angeles: Westernlore Press, 1953.

Bancroft, Hubert Howe. *History of California.* 7 vols. San Francisco: History Company, 1886. Reprint; Santa Barbara: Wallace Hebbard, 1963.

————. *Popular Tribunals.* 2 vols. San Francisco: History Company, 1887. Reprint; New York: Arno Press, n. d.

————. *California Inter Pocula.* San Francisco: History Company, 1888. Reprint; New York: Arno Press, n. d.

Barry, T. A., and B. A. Patten. *San Francisco 1850.* Reprint; Oakland: Biobooks, 1947.

Beilharz, Edwin A., and Carlos U. López, eds. and trans. *We Were 49ers!* Pasadena: Ward Ritchie Press, 1976.

Benard de Russailh, Albert. *Last Adventure.* Translated by Clarkson Crane. San Francisco: Westgate, 1931.

Biggs, Donald. *Conquer and Colonize.* San Rafael: Presidio Press, 1977.

Boorstin, Daniel J. *The Americans: The National Experience.* New York: Random House, 1965.

Brown, John Henry. *Early Days in San Francisco.* Oakland: Biobooks, 1949.

Brown, Richard Maxwell. *Strain of Violence*. New York: Oxford University Press, 1975.

Bruce, John. *Gaudy Century*. New York: Random House, 1948.

Bryant, Edwin. *What I Saw in California*. Minneapolis: Ross Haines, 1967.

Buffum, E. Gould. *Six Months in the Gold Mines*. [Pasadena]: Ward Ritchie Press, 1959.

Burks, John. *Working Fire*. San Francisco: Chronicle Books, 1985.

Camp, William Martin. *San Francisco Port of Gold*. New York: Doubleday and Company, 1947.

Chandler, Arthur, ed. *Old Tales of San Francisco*. Dubuque: Kendall/Hunt Publishing Company, 1977.

Coblentz, Stanton A. *Villains and Vigilantes*. New York: Thomas Yoseloff, 1957.

Coit, Daniel Wadsworth. *Digging for Gold without a Shovel*. Edited by George P. Hammond. Denver: Old West Publishing Company, 1967.

Cole, Tom. *A Short History of San Francisco*. San Francisco: Lexicos.

Colton, Walter. *The California Diary*. Oakland: Biobooks, 1948.

Cooke, Alistair. *The Americans*. New York: Berkley Books, 1980.

Davis, William Heath. *Seventy-five Years in California*. San Francisco: John Howell Books, 1967.

Decker, Peter R. *Fortunes and Failures: White-Collar Mobility in Nineteenth-Century San Francisco*. Cambridge: Harvard University Press, 1978.

Dillon, Richard H. *Embarcadero*. New York: Ballantine Books, 1959.

————. *The Hatchet Men*. New York: Coward-McCann, 1962.

Dorsey, George. *Christofer of San Francisco*. New York: Macmillan Company, 1962.

Dwinnelle, John W. *The Colonial History of San Francisco*. San Francisco: Towne and Bacon, 1867. Reprint; [Albany, Cal.]: Ross Valley Book Company, 1978.

Eldredge, Zoeth Skinner. *The Beginnings of San Francisco*. San Francisco: Zoeth S. Eldredge, 1912.

Fogelson, Robert M. *Big City Police*. Cambridge, Mass.: Harvard University Press, 1977.

Gentry, Curt. *The Madames of San Francisco*. New York: Doubleday, 1964.

————, with Tom Horton. *The Dolphin Guide to San Francisco and the Bay Area*. New York: Doubleday and Company, 1982.

Graham, Hugh Davis, and Ted Robert Gurr, eds. *Violence in America, Historical and Comparative Perspectives*. Washington, D.C.: Government Printing Office, 1969.

Greer, James K. *Colonel Jack Hays: Texas Frontier Leader and California Builder*. College Station: Texas A&M University Press, 1987.

Grivas, Theodore. *Military Governments in California 1846–1850*. Glendale: Arthur H. Clark Company, 1963.

Hansen, Woodrow James. *The Search for Authority in California*. Oakland: Biobooks, 1960.

Harding, George L. *Don Agustin V. Zamarano*. New York: Arno Press, 1976.

Hart, James D. *A Companion to California*. New York: Oxford University Press, 1978.

Heig, Adair. *History of Petaluma*. Petaluma: Scottwall Associates, 1982.

Heintz, William. *San Francisco's Mayors.* Woodside: Gilbert Richards Publications, 1975.

Helper, Hinton. *Dreadful California.* Edited by Lucius Beebe and Charles Clegg. New York: Bobbs-Merrill, 1948.

Hittell, John. *The History of San Francisco and Incidentally of California.* San Francisco: A. L. Bancroft and Company, 1878.

Hittell, Theodore H. *History of California.* 4 vols. San Francisco: N. J. Stone and Company, 1898.

Holdredge, Helen. *The House of the Strange Woman.* San Carlos: Nourse Publishing Company, 1961.

Hollon, W. Eugene. *Frontier Violence, Another Look.* New York: Oxford University Press, 1974.

Hughes, Robert. *The Fatal Shore.* New York: Alfred A. Knopf, 1987.

Hutchinson, W. H. *California: The Golden Shore by the Sundown Sea.* Palo Alto: Star Publishing Company, 1980.

Jackson, Donald Dale. *Gold Dust.* New York: Alfred A. Knopf, 1980.

Jackson, Joseph Henry, ed. *San Francisco Murders.* New York: Duell, Sloan and Pearce, 1947.

Johnson, David R. *Policing the Urban Underworld.* Philadelphia: Temple University Press, 1979.

Keeler, Charles. *San Francisco and Thereabout.* San Francisco: California Promotion Committee, 1903.

Kemble, Edward. *A History of California Newspapers 1846–1858.* Edited by Helen Harding Bretnor. Los Gatos: Talisman Press, 1962.

———. *A Kemble Reader.* Edited by Fred Blackburn Rogers. San Francisco: California Historical Society, 1963.

Lewis, Oscar, ed. and comp. *This Was San Francisco.* New York: David McKay Company, 1962.

Lotchin, Roger. *San Francisco, 1846–1856, from Hamlet to City.* New York: Oxford University Press, 1974.

Marryat, Frank. *Mountains and Molehills.* London: Longman, Brown, Green, and Longmans, 1855. Reprint; [New York]: Time-Life Books, 1980.

McGloin, John Bernard. *San Francisco: The Story of a City.* San Rafael: Presidio Press, 1978.

Megquier, Mary Jane. *Apron Full of Gold.* San Marino: Huntington Library, 1949.

Miller, Wilbur R. *Cops and Bobbies.* Chicago: University of Chicago Press, 1977.

Monkkonen, Eric H. *The Dangerous Class: Crime and Poverty in Columbus, Ohio, 1860–1885.* Cambridge, Mass.: Harvard University Press, 1975.

Mumford, Lewis. *The City in History.* New York: Harcourt Brace Jovanovich, 1961.

Myers, Gustavus. *The History of Bigotry in the United States.* New York: Capricorn, 1960.

Myers, John Myers. *San Francisco's Reign of Terror.* New York: Doubleday and Company, 1966.

Neider, Charles, ed. *The Autobiography of Mark Twain.* New York: Harper Row, 1959.

Nunis, Doyce B., ed. *The San Francisco Vigilance Committee of 1856: Three Views.* Los Angeles: Westerners, 1971.

O'Brien, Robert. *This Is San Francisco.* New York: McGraw-Hill Book Company, 1948.

O'Hara, Charles E. *Fundamentals of Criminal Investigation.* Springfield: Charles C. Thomas, 1972.

Parker, James M. *The San Francisco Directory, 1852–1853.* San Francisco: James M. Parker, 1852.

Phillips, Herbert L. *Big Wayward Girl.* New York: Doubleday and Company, 1968.

Prassel, Frank R. *The Western Peace Officer: A Legacy of Law and Order.* Norman: University of Oklahoma Press, 1972.

Quaife, Milo Milton, ed. *Pictures of Gold Rush California.* New York: Citadel Press, 1967.

Rembar, Charles. *The Law of the Land.* New York: Simon and Schuster, 1980.

Richardson, James F. *Urban Police in the United States.* Port Washington: Kennikat Press, 1974.

Rolle, Andrew F. *California: A History.* New York: Thomas Y. Crowell Company, 1969.

Royce, Josiah. *California, From the Conquest in 1846 to the Second Vigilance Committee in San Francisco.* n. p. Reprint; New York: AMS Press, 1973.

Scherer, James A. B. *The Lion of the Vigilantes.* New York: Bobbs-Merrill Company, 1939.

Schneider, John C. *Detroit and the Problem of Order, 1830–1880.* Lincoln: University of Nebraska Press, 1980.

Secrest, William B. *Dangerous Men.* Fresno: Saga-West Publishing Company, 1976.

Senkewicz, Robert M. *Vigilantes in Gold Rush San Francisco.* Stanford: Stanford University Press, 1985.

Silberman, Charles E. *Criminal Violence, Criminal Justice.* New York: Random House, 1978.

Soulé, Frank, John H. Gihon, and James Nisbet. *The Annals of San Francisco.* New York: D. Appleton, 1855. Reprint, compiled by Dorothy H. Huggins; Palo Alto: Lewis Osborne, 1966.

Starr, Kevin. *Americans and the California Dream.* New York: Oxford University Press, 1973. Reprint; Santa Barbara: Peregrine Smith, 1981.

Steffens, Lincoln. *The Autobiography of Lincoln Steffens.* New York: Harcourt, Brace and Company, 1931.

Stewart, George R. *Committee of Vigilance: Revolution in San Francisco, 1851.* Boston: Houghton Mifflin, 1964.

Taylor, Bayard. *Eldorado.* New York: George P. Putnam, 1850. Reprint; Glorieta, N.M.: Rio Grande Press, 1967.

Townsend, Edward D. *The California Diary of General E. D. Townsend.* Edited by Malcolm Edwards. [Pasadena]: Ward Ritchie Press, 1970.

Twain, Mark. *Roughing It.* New York: Signet, 1962.

Valentine, Alan. *Vigilante Justice.* New York: Reynal and Company, 1956.

Watkins T. H., and R. R. Olmsted. *Mirror of the Dream*. San Francisco: Scrimshaw Press, 1976.

Williams, David A. *David C. Broderick, A Political Portrait*. San Marino: Huntington Library, 1969.

Williams, Mary Floyd, ed. *Papers of the San Francisco Vigilance Committee of 1851*. Berkeley: University of California Press, 1919.

————. *History of the San Francisco Committee of Vigilance of 1851*. New York: Da Capo Press, 1969.

Wirt, Frederick M. *Power in the City*. Berkeley: University of California Press, 1974.

Wollenberg, Charles. *Golden Gate Metropolis*. Berkeley: Institute of Governmental Studies, 1985.

Woodham-Smith, Cecil. *The Great Hunger*. New York: Harper and Row, 1962.

Young, John P. *Journalism in California*. San Francisco: Chronicle Publishing Company, 1915.

MANUSCRIPTS, PUBLIC RECORDS, AND REPORTS

Blunt, Phineas. Unpublished journal (Bancroft Library).

Criminal Victimization Surveys in San Francisco. National Crime Survey Report. Washington, D.C.: U.S. Department of Justice, Law Enforcement Assistance Administration, National Criminal Justice Information and Statistics Service, 1977.

Department State Papers, Benicia Military. (Bancroft Library).

The Laws of the Town of San Francisco, 1847. San Marino: Friends of the Huntington Library, 1947.

Minutes of the Proceedings of the Legislative Assembly of the District of San Francisco from March 12, 1849 to June 4, 1849. San Francisco: Towne and Bacon, 1860 (California Historical Society Library, San Francisco).

A Record of the Proceedings of the Ayuntamiento or Town Council of San Francisco from August 6, 1849 to May 3, 1850. San Francisco: Towne and Bacon, 1860 (California Historical Society Library, San Francisco).

San Francisco Town Journal 1847–1848, William Leidesdorff, Treasurer. San Francisco: H. S. Crocker, 1926.

NEWSPAPERS

Alta California (San Francisco)
California Courier (San Francisco)
Californian (San Francisco)
California Star (San Francisco)
San Francisco Chronicle
San Francisco Daily Herald
San Francisco Evening News and Picayune
San Francisco Examiner

Index